FAILURES IN ORGANIZATION DEVELOPMENT AND CHANGE

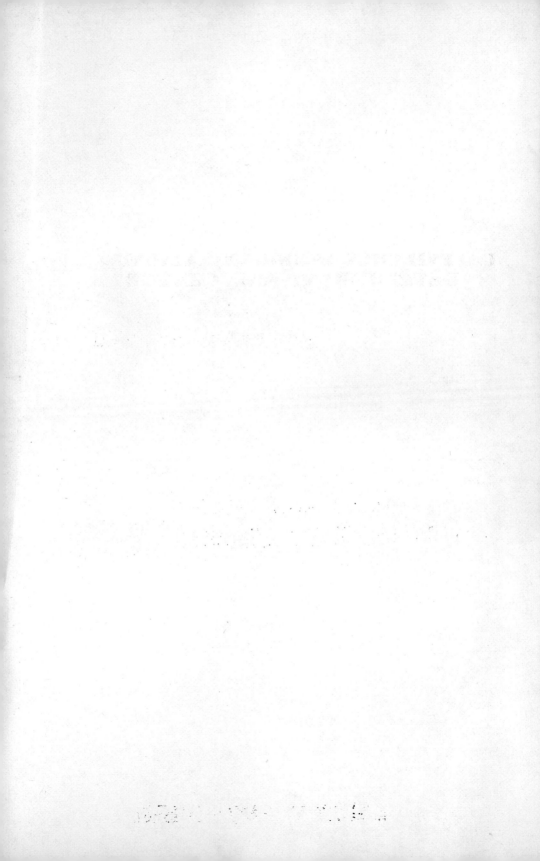

Failures in Organization Development and Change

CASES AND ESSAYS FOR LEARNING

PHILIP H. MIRVIS
DAVID N. BERG

A WILEY-INTERSCIENCE PUBLICATION

JOHN WILEY & SONS, New York • Chichester • Brisbane • Toronto

Library of Congress Cataloging in Publication Data:

Main entry under title:
Failures in organization development and change.

"A Wiley-Interscience publication."
Bibliography: p.
Includes index.
1. Organization. 2. Organizational change—Case studies. 3. Management—Case studies.

I. Mirvis, Philip H., 1951- II. Berg, David N., 1949-
HD31.F18 658.4'06 77-21625
ISBN 0-471-02405-8

Printed in the United States of America

10 9 8 7 6 5 4 3 2 1

CONTRIBUTORS

Clayton P. Alderfer, School of Organization and Management, Yale University, New Haven, Connecticut.

Warren G. Bennis, University of Cincinnati, Cincinnati, Ohio.

David N. Berg, School of Organization and Management, Yale University, New Haven, Connecticut.

Robert A. Cooke, Department of Psychology and Institute for Social Research, University of Michigan, Ann Arbor, Michigan.

William J. Crockett, Saga Corporation, Menlo Park, California.

Linda L. Frank, Exxon Corporation, New York, New York.

Robert B. Duncan, Graduate School of Management, Northwestern University, Evanston, Illinois.

J. Richard Hackman, School of Organization and Management and Department of Psychology, Yale University, New Haven, Connecticut.

Roy J. Lewicki, Graduate School of Business Administration, Duke University, Durham, North Carolina.

Donald N. Michael, Department of Psychology and School of Natural Resources, University of Michigan, Ann Arbor, Michigan.

Philip H. Mirvis, Department of Psychology and Institute for Social Research, University of Michigan, Ann Arbor, Michigan.

Allan M. Mohrman, Jr., College of Administrative Sciences, The Ohio State University, Columbus, Ohio.

Susan A. Mohrman, Graduate School of Management, Northwestern University, Evanston, Illinois.

Jay N. Nisberg, Jay Nisberg and Associates, Ridgefield, Connecticut.

Fritz I. Steele, Development Research Associates and Graduate School of Education, Harvard University, Boston, Massachusetts.

Richard E. Walton, Graduate School of Business Administration, Harvard University, Boston, Massachusetts.

PREFACE

Even now, reflecting back on the process of thinking, writing, contacting authors, and editing manuscripts, it is difficult to disentangle the many forces behind our decision to edit a book on failure in organization development and change. Undoubtedly there was the realization that a thoughtful and well conceived book would be a professional achievement important to both of us, yet as we review the entire experience, two other influences seem more profound. First, prior to editing this book, each of us had a very personal encounter with failure in organization change. This experience of failing had a sobering but instructive effect on both of us. As we struggled to understand the sources of our failures, including our own culpability, we sought out colleagues and friends to aid our understanding and to ease some of our pain. We found that we were not alone; similar experiences were a part of most of our colleagues' professional lives. We also found that most of these failures, while interesting and always rich with learnings, had never found their way into the professional books and journals of our field. Thus there was only the slimmest chance that these failures, and those of others in our field, had been of benefit to a concerned audience. And while we recognized some of the many reasons for this state of affairs, we were more interested in changing it—if possible.

The second influence on us was less concrete, but no less vivid. This book is to some extent a reaction against an ethos of success gone berserk. Around us we see a world and a profession that worship success without an appreciation that *success is often born of failure* and that to learn from our failures we must *nurture and support their examination*. This belief was and is a conscious motivation behind our work on this edition.

We have compiled a book that we hope will encourage organization members, professors, administrators, and students to both privately and publicly examine their failures in organization development and change efforts. The authors included in this volume, particularly those reviewing a failure in which they were intimately involved, have set a fine example. All were willing to examine their errors in the light of public scrutiny, and all were willing to have their names and reputations associated with a volume of this sort. In at least one case the authors' contributions were made in spite of the explicit advice of a colleague that it would be a mistake to risk the stigma of failure by linking their work with a book such as this. We thank our contributors for their courage and support.

We recognize that writing about one's failures is a difficult personal and professional undertaking. If in editing this book we have taken a step toward legitimizing both the thoughtful examination and regular publication of failures in our field, we feel we will have made a contribution.

We also believe that this book has some valuable and informative lessons for those of us engaged in the practice and understanding of organization change. The goal of examining failures is not an end in itself, but is rather, a means toward the future learnings and developments that follow. For those of us doing organization development, in whichever organizations we practice, with whatever approaches to change we use, this book offers some useful lessons.

In the spirit of development and change we intend this edition to be an intervention in our field. It is our modest goal to change publication practices so that a more systematic analysis of failure can reach interested practitioners, theorists, and researchers. In this way we believe the book can influence the learning process in our profession both by broadening the experience and knowledge base from which we all learn and by underscoring the importance of recognizing, confronting, and examining our failures. At present, it seems we are nearly alone in this endeavor. We hope to be part of a growing movement in this direction.

Finally, it is not accidental that this volume was edited by two young people, graduate students at the time it was written, who were given the freedom and license to concentrate on learning and learning how to learn! We could not have brought this book to fruition without the support of numerous people, most notably those who constitute our intellectual and educational heritage as well as those who have worked so hard with us during our most recent past. To all we offer our thanks for your encouragement, advice, energy, and assistance.

Additionally, we want to thank Jane Stanton, Susan Campbell, and Sherry Nelson for their help in preparing the manuscripts as well as Ron Brennan, Debbie Oppenheimer, and others at Wiley-Interscience for their guidance. A special thanks is reserved for our families and a close friend, Judith Meece, for their immeasurable contribution.

Without soil, water, and sunlight, not even the heartiest seeds can grow.

DAVID N. BERG
PHILIP H. MIRVIS

New Haven, Connecticut
Ann Arbor, Michigan
August 1977

CONTENTS

FAILURES IN ORGANIZATION DEVELOPMENT AND CHANGE

INTRODUCTION

Failures in Organization Development and Change

PHILIP H. MIRVIS
DAVID N. BERG

To be successful in our culture
one must learn to dream of failure.

Jules Henry
Culture Against Man

This section, like those that follow it, is about failure in organization development and change. One might react to an entire volume on this subject with surprise, perplexity, or even discomfort. But what is truly surprising is that we so seldom publicly acknowledge our failures and openly examine their implications. And what is perplexing is that we also accept that "to err is human" and counsel others to "learn from their mistakes." Thus what is discomforting is the incongruity between what we *practice* and what we *preach*. *This is failure in organization development and change*. This is what the contributors to this book begin to redress.

A book on failure is odd, but the oddity is that no such volume is available to the researchers, practitioners, organizations, and students who have erred (or will)! There have been many times when we could have used this help in learning from our failures. Consider the case of Albert Cranston, a private organization development (OD) consultant and a group of managers from Bulwark Laboratories. (The names of the consultant and the organization are fictitious—the events are not.)

Cranston and the managers were meeting to review the wreckage of a major organizational change effort recently aborted in one of the new facilities in the firm. Two years earlier he had persuaded the organization to implement a participative management system. He began the program with a series of presentations on the "Theory Y assumptions of management." When he lectured on the "principles of participation," however, the managers questioned the theory's relevance for their new responsibilities. Instead of acknowledging their misgivings Cranston scolded them for misinterpreting the material. During those same sessions he gave them a battery of psychological tests, hoping to use the data for individual counseling and review, but when he carelessly discussed some of the confidential material with superiors the counseling program deteriorated into a game of wits and deceit.

From the beginning of the program Cranston "sold" the managers on the advantages of participative management. He told them it would increase employee motivation and result in improved satisfaction and productivity. Yet he had not alerted them to the drawbacks of participation. Consequently, in the first months, countless hours were wasted in trivial group decisions. At the same time legitimate sources of expertise were ignored in the spirit of full participation.

Throughout the early months Cranston and the managers repeatedly discounted any signals that their program was adrift. Publicly they maintained that progress was slow but steady, though privately some of the managers worried that the rising turnover and production delays were due to *Cranston*'s new management system. But when the problems compounded, they neither voiced their apprehensions nor shared their suspicions. Instead they sought to "cover their tracks" by concealing project information from their corporate superiors. At their final meeting with Cranston their frustration and resentment surfaced openly.

As the tone of the meeting drifted from recrimination to gloom, Cranston suddenly brightened. "Sy," he called to one of his colleagues, "Don't you remember how it was at Aston Laboratories—how we turned things around?" Thinking a moment, Sy replied, "No." Cranston, his eyes bulging, pounded the table emphatically. "Don't you remember how much better things were?" Sy acquiesced blandly, "Oh, . . . yeah." It seems likely that with the passage of time Cranston will eulogize the Bulwark project in the same self-serving terms.

This is not an isolated incident. In universities, consulting firms, and organizations change agents repudiate their failures and propagate their successes. This leaves the public with an inflated, but distorted, perspective on organization development. It also deprives practitioners and their clients of the opportunity to benefit from their own and the mistakes of others.

A striking example of this trend is found in the Department of Health, Education, and Welfare's *Work in America* (1972). Among the 34 case studies of work "experiments" reviewed in this book, the human and financial results of most are characterized as unqualified improvements. Not surprisingly, a host of critics have challenged these results, calling into question the validity of the impressionistic and unreliable documentation. Their concern is legitimate: it is difficult to have much confidence in new techniques when their history is uncertain. Although much of the attention has focused on the need for better evaluation, a basic, and possibly more significant, concern is being ignored. In our present political and organizational environments, in which successful change programs result in enhanced reputations, enlarged budgets, and increased self-esteem, the conditions are rife for change practitioners, project directors, and organization members to devalue unpleasant information, to distort unsavory findings, and to deny responsibility when their change efforts fail.

It seems as though organization change is trapped in a self-defeating cycle in which a backlog of assumed successes has spawned a demand for future ones. To meet the expectations of clients and funding sources, then, change practitioners must ensure the success of their programs. Donald T. Campbell, in a recent interview, traced the immediate effect:

> To try something new you have to promise the moon. If you merely produce a few stars, everyone is disappointed. So we've created a conspiracy to avoid solid, honest results (Tavris, 1975, p. 52).

This cycle has other consequences as well. The costs and feasibility of replication, the checks and balances of the physical sciences, are prohibitive in organization change experiments. Thus it is often the positive results of a single pilot project that provide the impetus for broader implementation of the change technology. Those charged with this implementation, unaware of the unsuccessful endeavors of their predecessors, may make similar mistakes and produce similar results. The cycle of deception repeats itself; the lessons to be learned are lost.

INDIVIDUAL AND ORGANIZATIONAL LEARNING

Organizational behavior is learned behavior; it is shaped by the actions and experiences (both successful and unsuccessful) of organization members. The members of an organization formulate policies, plan activities, and produce goods and services, and although all of this represents the *behavior* of an organization it is reflective of what its members have *learned* to do. Indeed, there are parallels between the learning of individuals and the learning capacities of their organizations.

Individual learning, for example, is characterized by the development of *cognitive structures* (guides to interpreting the world) and the establishment of *habits of behavior* (guides to responding to the world). As individuals explore their environments and respond to them they experience the success of their actions and the limitations of their knowledge. This is the way children learn on the playground; the same is true of members of an organization. Learning is a process of developing new ways of interpreting the world and new ways of responding to that interpretation. Individual learning includes the acquisition of new knowledge and experimentation with new behaviors—both necessary for adapting to the increasingly complex and demanding environments that individuals encounter as they grow from childhood to maturity.

In an analogous manner organizational learning is characterized by the development of *information-processing capabilities* (guides to assembling and interpreting information) and the establishment of *standard operating procedures* (guides to responding to that information). Just as individuals learn by interacting with their environments, organizations learn by observing the results of their actions and by evaluating the consequences of those results. Organizational learning includes the acquisition of new information and experimentation with new forms of organization—both necessary for adapting to the evermore complex and demanding environments that organizations face over time.

Whereas individuals in an organization are the learners because their cognitive structures define and limit the organization's information-processing capacities and because their behaviors determine and bound the organization's response capabilities, an organization might properly be called a *learning system*. Indeed, there is the familiar input-output cycle inherent in this learning process. When designing its actions, the organization draws on the thinking and experiences of its leaders and members, processing and combining them with information gathered from its environment and external knowledge producers. After taking action an organization gathers information on the impact of this action on investors and consumers, evaluating the results and relating them to its mission and goals. Over a period of time, then, this information flow forms a *feedback loop* that maintains the organization's understanding of its environment and, if necessary, stimulates a change in the organization's response to it.

Positive feedback serves to maintain the system. By signaling the successful accomplishment of objectives it reinforces current thinking in the organization and ensures the continuity of policies, practices, and production. It enables the organization to maintain its standard operating procedures and preserves its energies for performance rather than reorganization. Negative feedback, in contrast, is an inducement to change (Katz and Kahn, 1966). By highlighting the failure of the organization to meet its goals and objectives it invites the infusion of new ideas and encourages the modification of work activities. It forces the organization to unlearn the old "routines" and to invent new alternatives.

For the most part this feedback loop has been sufficient for organizational learning and adaptation. This has been particularly true of industrial organizations that have been successful not so much in adapting to their environments but rather in neutralizing them (Galbraith, 1973). At the same time it is becoming increasingly evident that this feedback loop will be insufficient for coping with the environments of the future. Indeed, with the growth of government agencies, the proliferation of service organizations, and the increasing competition for scarce resources among all kinds of organizations, it is becoming apparent that many organizations must improve their learning capabilities to respond to the environments of today! To appreciate this point consider how they are learning.

The fast pace of change in an organization's environment—the opening of new markets, the change in consumer expectations, and the growing calls for social responsibility—has signaled the need for improved information-processing capabilities. Organizations can no longer be content with monitoring their environments; instead they must search them. They can no longer be content with identifying problems; instead they must anticipate them. Thus organizations are preparing long-range plans and broadening their communication networks, both of which are representative of improved information-processing capabilities.

At the same time organizations are responding to changes in their internal environments. The rapid pace of internal change—the demands for new skills, the changes in the composition of the work force, and the clamor for more meaningful work—has signaled the need for experimenting with new forms of organization. Organizations can no longer be successful if they regard their employees as "cogs-in-a-wheel"; instead they must treat them as their most precious (and costly) resource. They can no longer be successful if they monitor and control their employees; instead they must utilize their skills and experience in the management of the organization. Thus organizations are restructuring their work environments and opening up new lines of communication with their members.

Finally, in this complex and changing world there is a growing recognition that organizations depend on *both* internal and external sources of information and expertise. Developments in areas as diverse as technology, social values, and educational practices all have implications for organizational growth and survival. So organizations are discovering that they have to rely on one another for the information they need to prepare for the future. Modern society is too complex and changing too quickly for any single organization, even a huge conglomerate, to be an island unto itself. Consequently many organizations find themselves part of a larger feedback process, in which they draw on ideas from many segments of society, experiment with the application of these ideas, and take some responsibility for reporting on the results. In light of this expanding exchange of information, organizations can be viewed as learning systems embedded in the context of a learning society, learning not only from their own experiences but from those of other parts of society as well.

LEARNING FROM ORGANIZATION DEVELOPMENT AND CHANGE

Organization development is representative of this exchange of knowledge; it is

> a complex educational strategy intended to change the beliefs, attitudes, values, and structures of organizations so that they can better adapt to new technologies, markets, challenges, and the dizzying rate of change itself (Bennis, 1969, p. 2).

The knowledge exchange begins when organization change theory, developed primarily in universities, is transmitted to the change practitioners. It is subsequently blended with a change technology and applied to an organization. Once a change program is under way knowledge of the program's results provides the feedback required by the organization to monitor and refine the change effort. Beyond this purpose, however, *both* positive and negative feedback are needed by the learning system to evaluate the utility of the change technology and the validity of its theoretical foundations. Thus this feedback provides learning not only for the experimenting organization but also for practitioners, social scientists, and the interested public. To maintain a purposeful exchange organizations must have valid data to guide their change programs and produce valid data to improve their learning and the learning of others.

The critical links in this exchange are the change agents, the internal organization development specialists, and the external consultants who assess the change program and document the change results. They gather the information needed to test the theories and technologies and they assist the organization in evaluating and interpreting the program's results. Further, they are responsible for transmitting the findings to an interested public. Thus change agents serve a broad client system—not simply their own clients—but other practitioners, social scientists, and the public as well. Without open and forthright exchange between and among these parties the purposeful learning system will deteriorate.

The scientific tradition attests to the importance of this exchange; its norms and values promote learning from both successful and unsuccessful experiences. Vickers (1970) writes:

> Scientists are as prone as anyone else to human frailty or even to intellectual error. They owe their reputation for responsibility and for accuracy to the tradition which exposes their thought, step-by-step, to the criticism of their colleagues (p. 33).

Indeed, in the physical and medical sciences countless treatments and theories have been discarded when research on their failings pointed the way to the eventual breakthrough. Watson's discovery of the double helix is an exemplary account of the series of failures in DNA research that led to a successful solution.

Similarly, some failures have led to advancements in organization change. Fleishman's (1953) unsuccessful implementation of a management training program heightened our awareness of the problems in transforming "off-line" training to an "on-line" situation. Lawler, Hackman, and Kaufman's (1973) failure to involve supervisors in the development of a job redesign program increased our appreciation of the need for supervisory participation in the enrichment of jobs for hourly employees. Bennis (1966) and Argyris (1970) also comment on some unsuccessful experiences when characterizing effective methods of organization change. There are, however, few other documented failures in the organization change literature.

There is a growing awareness of this imbalance in the field. An editor of a leading periodical in this area writes: "Published reports of such failure are all too rare" (Goodstein, 1975, p. 411). He attributes this to the consultants (their concern for their images and incomes) and to the journal editors (their reluctance to publish any kind of negative statistical or professional results). Yet other forces are at work here.

Organizations and their members are equally averse to acknowledging their errors and confronting their mistakes. Many organizations subscribe to the belief that errors reflect an absence of motivation or proficiency, and their members equate erring with a loss of personal or professional control. Thus organizations are unaccepting of errors and unsympathetic toward erring personnel. Their members are anxious about their mistakes and fearful of the consequences of having made them. They place a premium on survival and, when failing, "assert that no error has occurred, or that if it did it was unimportant, or that if it was important, it was somebody else's fault" (Michael, 1973, p. 133). The roots of their behavior lie in our culture's criterion for success and the consequences for those who fail.

FAILING IN AMERICA

The criteria of success and failure are endemic to a particular culture (Williams, 1960). The American culture places a premium on accomplishment in the form of educational achievement, occupational advancement, and personal attainment. Opportunity and advancement are favorite cultural slogans, for the majority of American parents hope for a better life for their children. To foster and sustain these values our culture associates success with hard work and competence. At the same time it equates failure with indolence and inability. These values are not inherent in our children; they must be learned from parents, teachers, and institutions.

Society initially charges parents with this socializing function. Children begin life with a vast repertoire of potential skills and interests. As parents establish their children's standards of conduct and selectively reward compliance, children learn what is expected and what is approved. They internalize their parents' expectations and strive to fulfill them in their actions and behavior. Children who meet parental expectations have succeeded; children who err and disappoint have failed.

Parents and children alike share in the fruits of this socialization. Parents' standards and restrictions strongly influence their children's achievements (Winterbottom, 1958); thus it is not uncommon for parents to revel in the accomplishments of their sons and daughters. At the same time they share in the disappointment of failure. Arthur Miller's classic American play *Death of a Salesman* poignantly captures the trauma of failure in the success-driven family. As Willy Loman despairs over his son's failure, he sees part of his own. Yet his suicide does not challenge the value of success; it merely asserts its pervasive effect on those who do not succeed.

Just as parents are concerned that their children succeed in school, schools are concerned that children succeed in their occupations. Schools take over where parents leave off: they teach children to cope with a competitive environment. In this way the teacher's role is analogous to that of the parents. Teachers also establish standards and provide rewards for desired behaviors. Their standards are internalized by the children as well. Sometimes this can become a self-fulfilling prophesy in which the teachers' expectations are mirrored in the children's performance (Rosenthal and Jacobsen, 1968). Consequently modern educators have encouraged teachers to avoid labeling failure, a grade that has disappeared from the report cards in many school systems.

Still, many children do not succeed in school. The educational process frustrates many students and a sizable minority who begin high school ultimately drop out. Holt (1964) contends that it is because "they are afraid, above all else of failing, of disappointing the many anxious adults around them" (p. xiii). This fear produces worrisome students—those who cope with their academic failure by fleeing from school. It also penetrates the children who stay in school. They learn that errors are bad, and the imputation of incompetence discourages them from forming a bold relationship with learning. At the same time they discover a variety of strategies for coping with the academic competition. Children learn that bluffing and guessing are accepted methods of succeeding. As they mature they see that crib notes and cheating serve the same purpose. Indeed, by college age they even have a guide to making the "small compromises" necessary for surviving *The Undergraduate Jungle* (Crafts and Hauther, 1976). Although all this may temporarily stave off their failures, it also counterfeits their learning.

When students leave school and enter the professional community, they face comparable conditions. At Harvard, for example, a young graduate student was recently dismissed for falsifying his research data. At the same time, a prominent physician reported that he had misrepresented years of cancer research. This bears witness to the personal and professional pressures for promotion and publication confronting members of the scientific and professional community today.

Corresponding pressures face those who join business organizations, government agencies, and school systems. They, too, are expected to produce successful results. Success is the key to income and advancement; failure opens the door to disappointment and dismissal; but just as they learned to cope with this situation in school, in their organizational lives these coping strategies are well rehearsed.

On the one hand, organization members may be stricken with a pervasive need to avoid failure. This can result in depressed aspiration levels, avoidance of achievement situations, and staid, unimaginative behavior (Birney et al., 1969). On the other, when failing in their endeavors, these same individuals can be at their imaginative best by distorting errors or denying that they ever occurred. Reconsider the situation at Bulwark Laboratories, the organization in which the participative management project failed.

At the start of the project Cranston, the change agent, confidently predicted its success. He subsequently devoted considerable energy toward that end. When the project soured, he would not accept the results. Independent evaluators found, for example, that measures of employee satisfaction, motivation, and cooperation showed no improvement after the first months. Cranston discounted these data, calling them "shallow paper-and-pencil measurement." What shortcomings in the program he did acknowledge, he blamed on the site. He challenged their commitment to participation and their comprehension of participative management.

Managers and workers at the site, however, offered a different perspective. They blamed Cranston and his whole approach to the change. When some were asked what they did to make the project successful, they claimed that their other responsibilities precluded their full commitment to the program. Beneath this morass of rationalizations and recriminations lay the change effort that failed. Why can they not learn from experience? It appears that Cranston and the managers are denying the prerequisites for learning from failure. They are neither acknowledging their failures nor accepting responsibility for their occurrence.

In part, their reaction to the failure may be related to their desire to protect their self-images. Individuals with high self-esteem often ascribe success to themselves while blaming failure on outside factors or others (cf. Weiner et al., 1971). In the Bulwark case personal acceptance of the failure by Cranston and the managers would have raised questions about their competence and impugned their self-esteem. Public acknowledgment of the errors would only have heightened their defensiveness and vulnerability. Thus they distorted events, discounted information, and disassociated themselves from the failings, all as a means of protecting their self-images.

When their individual predilictions are coupled with an environment that demands accountability and rewards success, we can understand why they ignored or suppressed the unfavorable data and blamed one another for the failings that were exposed. This is not to suggest that individuals cannot recognize their own errors nor that they cannot accept the consequences of their mistakes. Indeed, when the benefits of accepting negative information outweigh those associated with denial, individuals will acknowledge their errors and adjust their behavior (Janis, 1968). Rather it is to suggest that in the case of an organization development and change effort an entire network of persons and groups is involved and each has its separate sources of accountability. Under these circumstances, it is the combination of coping strategies, and in some cases the outright collusion between the parties to the change, that prevents change agents, organizations, and society from learning from the failures.

SUPPRESSING FAILURES IN CHANGE

Although all parties to the change—the change agent, the organization, and the funding source—experience its failings, the responses and coping strategies of each are distinct and bear examination.

The Change Agent

The change agent's reputation is a precious benchmark. The primary source of financial support for change programs comes from client organizations or the Federal Government. To the uninitiated or unsuspecting client the practitioner's reputation means high visibility and likely success. To the beleaguered and budget-conscious federal agency the academic's reputation is often as important as the nature of the proposed research. As a result, failure is an unwelcome intruder into the practitioner's portfolio and the academic's vita.

The reputations of private consultants also establish them in a cadre of professionals at the forefront of knowledge utilization. They are perched between the university and the organizational community, and their mission is to translate theory into practice and temper it with a hard-nosed appreciation of the problems in application. In short, they are expected to have mastered the *art* of organization change.

Some practitioners, however, seem to master only a single art of change. Their diagnosis of the organization is aimed toward finding problems suited to their particular expertise. Sometimes they neglect a diagnosis completely and prescribe their favored treatments irrespective of the client's ailment. In those instances failure threatens their practice and livelihood, for when they discover that their change programs were inappropriate or simply salved the wounds while they festered, the generalizability of their methods is threatened and their professional reputations are besmirched. Although they might acknowledge the applications and limitations of their change technologies, instead they often disregard the experience, thereby protecting their methods from suspicion. By adopting this strategy they may fool themselves and the public, but their change technologies become nothing more than placebos.

For those who diagnose an organization's problems the cost of an unsuccessful treatment is also menacing. Private consultants are accountable solely to their clients, and their continued support is contingent on results. When their change programs fail to produce acceptable social and economic goals, their diagnostic skills are assailed and their termination is sometimes imminent. It is not surprising, then, to note that some consultants shroud their diagnoses in the cloak of expertise and limit their evaluations largely to impressionistic criteria (Kahn, 1974).

Unfounded promises, selective and secretive diagnoses, and nominal evaluations are the symptoms of future failure suppression. Private consultants are caught in the web of clients' expectations and the limitations of the ability of their technologies to deliver. Rather than nurture the technology and discover and share its failings, consultants are reduced to marketing an inflated but underdeveloped product.

The academic change-agent role is designed to avoid that pitfall—ostensibly protecting its occupant with the umbrella of tenure and limited client accountability—but academics are not simply the artisans of change. They are also responsible for the development of the theory. First, they are expected to formulate it, then to predict its effects. This prediction implies a knowledge of cause-effect relations; thus skillful academics are expected to control the effects. In short, they are expected to have mastered the *science* of organizational change.

When a change project fails, it implies that the academic developed a faulty theory or formulated imprecise predictions. Academic journals are loath to publish articles fraught with this implication. Academics are equally averse to reporting their failures lest this be the interpretation. As a result journals report a collection of successful change programs. Failures go unpublished and gather dust as technical reports.

The academic community has recognized the role conflicts associated with the activist change agent and impartial evaluation functions. Many organizational change periodicals include critiques of a change agent's field work and research results by outside reviewers. These retrospective critiques are necessarily incomplete, for they are limited to the information reported about the change activities. To provide for a more complete and unbiased accounting of a change program some researchers have called for independent, third-party evaluation (Barnes, 1966; Weiss, 1972). Indeed, Title X of the U.S. Department of Health, Education, and Welfare requires an impartial assessment of certain government-sponsored change efforts.

There is some evidence that the conclusions of external evaluators are likely to differ from those of the change consultants. Gordon and Morse (1975), in a review of evaluation efforts published in sociological journals, found, for example, that evaluators who were not affiliated with a change program or its funding agency were significantly less likely than affiliated evaluators to find positive results. Specifically, they determined that under varying research designs the ratio of positive findings by affiliated versus unaffiliated evaluators was 1:7.

Although each of these approaches has its merits, they do not confront the conditions that prohibit a solid, honest evaluation of the program by the change agent and the organization and the subsequent acceptance and airing of negative results. The academic change agents, like the private ones, face a profession in which success is rewarded and failure is taboo. But even if they were inclined to study their failures, they would have to contend with their funding agencies, which also contest the legitimacy of learning from failure.

The Funding Agency

It seems to be evident that a project's funding source, particularly a government agency, would demand a full accounting of the program's results, yet in many change efforts the bulk of the funding goes toward the action and applied side of the budget and evaluation is given only secondary consideration. Recently, however, the trend has been toward more vigorous support of evaluation. Although this advances the cause of evaluation, unbiased assessments and full disclosure of the project's results do not necessarily ensue.

The research budget and reputation of a funding agency are linked to governmental priorities and the agency's reputation for successful results. This places a strain on the agency and can lead to a schizoid response. On the one hand, the agency will tighten its controls and demand project accountability. On the other, it will fund promises and reward success. As a result change agents prepare effusive proposals filled with hopeful hypotheses and grandiose goals. Once the change project is underway, however, and the hypotheses are unconfirmed and the goals unfulfilled, the agency faces a dilemma. Sometimes they will cease funding. This signals not only the end of the project, but an end to any learning from it. In addition, the organization, school system, or community group will have lost its money, and the project officer, staff, and change agent will be out of work. At other times the agency will wink at the project's goals, bow to political pressure, and let the program continue. At this point the agency will accept any successful results and may even encourage the change agent and evaluators to "dig" for them. As everyone searches for the silver lining, the funding agency, the organization, and the change agent are satisfied. Only those who wanted to learn from the program are disappointed.

The Organization

The price of failure is magnified for organization members. The reputations of project directors and internal change consultants are often at stake; monetary and moral support are the recompense for success. Moreover, for organizations in the early stages of experimentation the success of a pilot project may prove a fruitful seed for future change activity. This translates into larger staffs and budgets and more visibility and prestige. Therefore the pressures for positive results may blind the participants to their misdirections or encourage them to plow ahead in hopes that their errors will not be unearthed.

These pressures for success are reinforced by the consequences of having failed. Many organizations take pride in their change efforts; they call them *demonstration projects*, which often means that they are supposed to demonstrate success! Indeed, *The New York Times*, the national magazines, and television's *60 Minutes* have publicized successful change activities; but the breadth of the public ballyhoo is related to the project's real or imagined results. So organizations cannot fail to succeed; neither can their members. They share a common fate in which success demonstrates proficiency in the management of change and failure suggests change is managing the organization. Hence failure raises the specter of an intractable organization staffed by incapable personnel. Once again the conditions are rife for everybody to distort whatever changes did or did not occur.

Combined, the pressures facing change agents, funding agencies, and organizations weave a taut knot around failure (see Table I.1). The change project that fails is disavowed or suppressed. As a result so is the legitimacy of learning. This chart reads like fiction—it brings to mind the land of *Through the Looking Glass*, where little Alice sought to learn only from her successes. Carroll's book is fantasy; failure in organization development and change is not.

FINDING NEW DIRECTIONS

Society has always tacitly acknowledged the benefits of failure, and colloquialisms that urge us to learn from our mistakes abound. Sometimes this yields unexpected discoveries. In 1950, Dr. John Rock began the development of a pill to facilitate pregnancy. Instead, he was one of the early founders of the oral contraceptive. More often, though, failure instructs those who err and points them in new directions.

Much can be learned from studying failures in organizations. Research on the inefficiencies of various organizational designs, leadership practices, and decision-making styles has spawned the development of contingency theories that specify the appropriate organizational form or practice for a range of conditions (e.g., Fiedler, 1971; Lawrence and Lorsch, 1967; Vroom and Yetton, 1973). But, as Kurt Lewin once counseled, "In order to gain insight into a process, one must create change and then observe its variable effects on the new dynamics" (Marrow, 1969, p. 235). It is those who change organizations and those who participate in the change who have the most to learn from reviewing their own mistakes.

Society is recognizing what we have lost from not learning. Some writers decry our fixation on academic and occupational success and note its fallout in physical maladies, institutional apathy, and personal estrangement (Milner, 1968). Others challenge our concern for certainty, predictability, and control which make us anxious when we find that events are uncertain, unpredictable, and beyond control (Maslow, 1969). Still others have taken social scientists and practitioners to

Table I-1. Actions that Prevent Learning from Failure

	At the Start	At the End
Change practitioners	At the beginning of the organizational development effort the change practitioners leave the objectives of the project unspecified. Accordingly, they proceed with a selective evaluation, focusing on the successful aspects of the project. Alternatively, no evaluation is undertaken, and the client is left to conduct an impressionistic assessment.	To protect their reputations the change agents who conduct evaluations deny that failure occurred. They distort the data or suppress the negative results. To cope with objective failings, the consultants disassociate themselves from those aspects of the project or blame members of the client organization. To preserve their professional standing change agents report only the project's successes or fail to publish the results at all.
Client organizations	At the beginning of the organizational development effort the client organization forms its own amorphous expectations. Some of these expectations are unrealistic, ensuring failure; others are trivial, ensuring success. Yet no objective criteria are established for evaluation, and assessment is limited to a few unreliable indicators.	In response to failure the organization can distort the findings and focus on the project's successful results. The organization minimizes internal discussion of the project and limits public dissemination. The client organization blames the consultant and various external factors for the project's failings. Over the long term the organization comes to devalue or dismiss organizational development techniques.

Table I-1. (Continued)

	At the Start	At the End
External funding sources	In allocating monies for organizational development, the sponsoring agency funds on the basis of the consultants' record of success rather than on the merits of the proposed work. The project's hypothesized results are vague and the eventual analyses are not expected to address them. The funding agency provides limited financial support for evaluation, and assessment becomes a secondary priority.	To counter failures the funding agency discontinues project evaluation. They may stigmatize the failing consultants and prevent them from receiving future funding from their agency.

task, noting that their cozy relationship with corporate and governmental interests can compromise their integrity and prevent a full disclosure of their unsuccessful activities. This introduction is only a footnote in this trend—it discusses why we have not learned from our errors. The book offers an alternative.

It is written because organization development and change programs do fail. They fail because of incomplete theories, inaccurate diagnoses, inappropriate change technologies, intractable organization members, incapable change agents, and inflexible organizations. By ignoring these failures, or by covering them up, the common problems are labeled unique and the generalizability of the methods and results is assumed. Dominant practices are not questioned and the shared beliefs about organization change remain sacrosanct. Exploration of the failures can challenge these beliefs—has this no place in the field? This book asserts that it has.

The organization of the book parallels an organization change: the first section describes the entry into and diagnosis of the client organization; the second discusses the application of change technologies; the third characterizes the termination and diffusion of the project. Each section is introduced and previewed by the editors.

The chapters illustrate ways of learning from failure in organization development and change. They recount change efforts in manufacturing organizations, service industries, government agencies, community groups, and schools. They describe job enrichment efforts, T-group experiences, survey-feedback projects, OD and community development efforts, work restructuring projects, and a host of other organizational change techniques. The majority are case studies which describe change efforts that failed. Most of them report the change agent's account of events, though two represent a third party's assessment. They differ in their focus and depth and in their tone and emphasis. This is to be expected, for some are from academics and others are from project directors and organization members. Yet each case represents the author's sincere efforts to acknowledge errors and to derive the lessons for both practice and research.

The cases are flanked by a series of essays which discuss the conditions that breed failure in the beginning, during, and at the end of a change effort. These essays consider the cultural factors that inhibit change, the professional characteristics of change agents that enhance or reduce its effectiveness, and the problems involved in diffusing change throughout an organization.

The cases and essays are buttressed by introductory and concluding chapters. This introduction has examined the societal pressures that have prevented us from learning from our failures. The conclusion considers the emergence of a new belief system that will encourage us to learn from them. This introduction has detailed the ways in which we have dealt with our failures in the past. The conclusion describes how we may learn from our failures in the future.

Many books have described what we have learned from organizational change; others have detailed the tasks ahead. Davis and Cherns (1975), who represent the latter group, prescribe that, among other challenges, "researchers and practitioners must learn . . . how to identify and measure a successful outcome . . ." (p. 8). This book inserts a caveat into their charge: researchers and practitioners must learn how to identify, acknowledge, and examine their failures and must assist their clients and guide their students in learning to do so.

I

ENTRY

The primary goals of an organization development (OD) practitioner entering a social system are to gain access to its members—to their attitudes, behaviors, and experiences—and, once inside their world, to participate with them in bringing about meaningful change. Thus David Berg describes the entry process as the "beginning of this mutual involvement, including choosing to undertake the [project], agreeing on the ground rules, drawing up a contract, and building a working relationship. . . ." Yet Fritz Steele counters, "Mention behavioral scientists in many organizations and people immediately begin complaining about manipulation, invasion of privacy, interpretation, and the like." Their statements characterize the dilemma facing practitioners as they begin the process of change.

There are many horns to this dilemma and many ways to negotiate them. A practitioner, for example, can enter a social system covertly or overtly, at the top or from the bottom, for purposes of social change or purposes of action research. At one level these are strategic differences; at another, they are questions of values. Although we can debate the strategic issues, the values of OD are straightforward and clear: organization development requires the involvement, commitment, and support of all those individuals who are touched by the change (Argyris, 1970).

These values, in turn, delimit strategies. OD practitioners who espouse them strive to enter an organization in an open and forthright manner, cultivating mutual trust with their clients, promoting openness and a willingness to confront both personal and performance issues in organizational life—issues sometimes hidden from overt observation but equally removed from covert participation. There is both closeness and detachment in this entry process—the closeness that enables us to serve the interests of all members of social systems, as well as our own, and the detachment that lends credibility to our profession and objectivity to our scholarship. Entry provides an opportunity to establish norms of openness, honesty, objectivity, and mutual involvement. It is the time when clients and practitioners begin to examine one another's values and assumptions and test one another's integrity and commitment. It is the time when the change process begins, or, alternatively, as the cases in this section report, when the change process ends.

It is appropriate, then, that Fritz Steele begins by discussing the impact of cultural values on the practice and conduct of OD. Drawing on his experiences in the United Kingdom, he portrays a cultural environment inhospitable to social scientists, change, data, and the principles of organization development. As Steele poses the question, "Is OD possible under certain conditions?" he also asks whether change efforts are doomed from the start because of the irreconcilable differences between professional and cultural values. Chapter 1 concludes with some suggestions for analyzing and confronting value differences between OD proponents and their clients during the entry phase of change projects in the United States.

David Berg's case, the next chapter in the section, describes an organizational diagnosis project that never moved beyond its beginnings. It reports the events and emotions surrounding the project's termination, and there were varieties of both. Berg was intrigued by an organization whose ideological commitment to the feminist movement led it to experiment with alternative forms of organization. As he began the study, however, he became entangled in an internal power conflict. The loose structure of the company acted like a fishnet: the more Berg struggled to free himself, the more entangled he became. Some members of the organization saw him as a disruptive force; others identified him with the "ruling elite." In the second half of the chapter Berg tries to distinguish the personal and organizational contributions to the failure and concludes with some thoughts on avoiding similar entanglements in the future.

The final case in this section is already well known but worthy of continued examination. Roy Lewicki and Clayton Alderfer describe their attempt to study, and intervene in, a labor-management dispute. In reviewing their troubles, these authors take a hard look at a number of key issues in the entry process, including trust building, neutrality, and commitment. Of particular interest is their discussion of the intergroup problems in entry and intervention. As they "conceptualize the events," Lewicki and Alderfer describe the complex interactions of multiple *groups* (including the consultants), a situation common to many change efforts but one that is often ignored. They conclude with a discussion of the theoretical, methodological, and practical implications of entering an organization of "warring groups."

After reading this section one is left with a healthy respect for the complexities and dilemmas of the entry process. David Berg writes, "When a consultation or research project ends in its infancy, there is a special feeling of regret." The experiences of the authors in these chapters shed some light on the complexities of entry and provide practical recommendations for OD practitioners for surmounting some of the dilemmas of *successful* entry.

1

Is the Culture Hostile to Organization Development?

The U.K. Example

FRITZ STEELE

In reviewing my intermittent professional activities over several years of visits to the United Kingdom, I have identified a failure that shows up in the pattern of my experiences rather than in the failure of a specific project. Quite simply, I have never been able to negotiate an effective organization development (OD)* contract with any firm in the U.K. I have had a large number of lunchtime "exploratory discussions," but none has ever gone past the gastronomic stage.

As I reflected on this rather sorry record, it occurred to me that it might not have been due entirely to my abrasive American manner—that English consultants whom I knew also seemed to have an uphill struggle in establishing a systematic OD process in U.K. organizations.

Adapted from Fritz Steele, "Is Organisation Development Possible in the U. K. Culture?" *Journal of European Training,* **5**, No. 3, Copyright 1976.

* When I refer to organization development, I mean any systematic behavioral science intervention that is aimed at improving the system's ability to be self-correcting. The specific targets of change may be the structure of the system, the social climate, or the day-to-day behaviors of specific members.

All OD and other attempts to change the structure and processes of an organization are influenced by a number of factors: the felt need or "pinch" of the clients, their readiness to consider new alternatives, the quality of the entry, diagnostic planning, implementation, and evaluation processes that are developed by change agent and clients, and so on. But there is another factor that can be a strong yet somewhat invisible determinant of the success or failure of an OD effort: the cultural context of the country in which the organization is located. By "culture" I mean the societal norms and values that influence members of the organization, societal pressures and formal regulations, technology and artifacts, traditions, and basic shared assumptions about the world and life in it.

The OD process grew mainly (but by no means exclusively) out of consultant experiences in the United States. As such, it is rooted in a particular cultural context, and one cannot assume that the chances of success of this process are high in another country, even though OD assumptions make sense in terms of a system's long-term needs.

For instance, my own work and contacts in the United Kingdom have caused me to have some strong doubts about the extent to which OD work will be supported there. In an attempt to explore this question, I asked participants in several London seminars on "New Developments in OD" to help me identify those factors and assumptions in the culture of the United Kingdom that would tend to block the effective application of OD principles.

The following discussion is one outcome of those seminars. It identifies seven assumptions that I consider fundamental and necessary for providing a context for OD activities. If people do not hold (or at least recognize) these assumptions, they will have considerable difficulty understanding *why* anyone would want to engage in such irrelevant or potentially "dangerous" OD activities as, for example, intensive team self-analysis or intergroup conflict resolutions. Each assumption is followed by those relevant features of the U.K. culture that may be blocks to effective OD intervention.

The descriptions are distillations of my own experience and of comments at the seminars. They are certainly not "proofs" of anything nor are they intended to be. They are quite suggestive, however, of the specific restraining forces that an OD specialist must confront when doing work in a U.K. organization. In addition, I believe that they illustrate how the cultural context can influence OD efforts in general, not just in the United Kingdom.

SEVEN UNSHARED ASSUMPTIONS

Assumption 1. Doing better is a good thing.

It is worth the effort and possible temporary discomfort for a person, group, or organization to try to improve methods, policies, or action patterns in order to become more effective or productive.

Cultural Factors

The concept of striving to do better is in conflict with a strong U.K. value associated with *style*: that *how* one lives, works, and plays is as important as the effectiveness of one's actions. In addition, there is a strong current of *valuing security and stability* versus the unknown risks of rocking the boat in an effort to do better, especially when a case can be made that "we must be doing all right now or we wouldn't still be here." (Obviously not necessarily true—one's mistakes may not yet have added up to a critical mass.) The gentlemanly emphasis on *how one plays the game* can also be used as an apology for not playing it effectively or productively.

Assumption 2. The facts are friendly.

This assumption says that in the long run one is generally better off dealing with the *reality* of one's situation versus how one would wish it to be. One outcome of this assumption is the placement of high value on having an information flow in the organization that is both accurate and widely shared.

Cultural Factors

The most obvious block is a *strong set of traditional norms about the avoidance of embarrassing and unsuitable topics*. Even those organizational members who know that blind, uninfluenceable social processes are created by these norms still tend to feel guilty or under risk when attempting to promote more open data sharing. It is unfortunate but true that a system's problems and influences do not necessarily adhere neatly to those categories of factors that are considered acceptable for polite, courteous interaction.

Adherence to tradition also tends to subvert dealing with the facts of a situation because it encourages a regression to past solutions and behaviors in times of crisis even when the current dilemma requires very different behavior.

Assumption 3. People should have a personal ownership of their own life space.

A strong ethic underlying OD is the value that people have a right, in relation to the organization, to influence those decisions that have an immediate impact on their life experiences; for example, some American companies are beginning to treat personnel records as the joint property of the person (subject) and the company and to obtain the subject's permission before disclosing this information to a third party.

Cultural Factors

An obvious block in the U.K. to the ethic of personal ownership or influence over one's existence is the whole deeply rooted *class structure*, with its assumption of fundamental differences between different classes. Some people are assumed to be capable of managing their own affairs and those of others, whereas other (lower) types are assumed to require the benevolent (but firm) hand of the former in order to survive.

A deep sense of the *legitimacy of hierarchical authority* is a companion value to the class structure. Although many people say that class distinctions are not what they once were in England, others have remarked to me that the *players* may have changed somewhat but the *game* remains more or less the same. It is fostered by the notion that it is morally wrong to question the legitimacy of control by someone who claims to have formal authority to decide one's fate.

The desire for security and stability is another factor here, with those in the upper echelons feeling that their own struggle to get to a comfortable position should not have been in vain—that they *deserve* more personal influence and control over their own lives and the lives of others than those who have neither inherited it nor worked their way up to it.

Assumption 4. A challenging environment requires the system to be adaptive in terms of its structure and process.

As the rate of change of so many environmental variables increases, it is no longer likely that the "perfect" organization can be created to do a particular set of tasks indefinitely. Tasks change, newly hired workers are different in their attitudes and motivations, and so on. Structures and policies that were excellent when created can quickly become outdated and harmful to the long-term survival of the system. The organization needs to have conscious procedures for adapting and reshaping itself.

Cultural Factors

A number of factors in the U.K. culture tend to work against this adaptive approach. One is the strong emphasis on the values of *tradition and continuity*—that it is a good thing (in its own right, regardless of the impact on effectiveness) to do things the way they have been done in the past.

Historically, *the U.K.'s geographic (island) isolation* may have contributed to the assumption that "we don't have to adapt to the outside world, since it will always remain outside." Even though this is obviously no longer true, many people seem to feel and act as if it were.

Symbolic reference to and maintenance of *the monarchy* may also encourage a strong emphasis on continuity of form in social systems, independent of the functionality of that form. The monarchy is at least an indicator of this attitude, if not a contributor to it.

The general attitude of valuing the past shows up in many aspects of British life, from entertainment to styles of dress to ceremonies. This is, of course, not necessarily bad, but it can have some costly consequences when it spills over into work organizations in which members need to deal with things as they are, not as they used to be.

Assumption 5. Change does not have to be haphazard.

Every person, group, or organization has some choice about (a) which changes will occur, (b) how prepared they are for the changes, and (c) how well or badly the changes are managed. The emphasis is on *proactive planning for possible futures* versus reactive acceptance of whatever stimuli come in from the environment or whatever internal forces operate inside the system.

Cultural Factors

I believe that there is a *strong strain of fatalism* in the culture of the United Kingdom, which tends to orient people toward adapting to what fate brings them rather than toward trying to influence what the future will be. The tradition of the "stiff upper lip" is symbolic, as is the prodigious ability of the British public to buckle down and muddle through crises that are often caused by influenceable decisions taken by fellow members of their society. There is a strength and gutsiness that is both admirable and possibly overvalued: more attempts at conscious change would require less making-do because there would be fewer crunches. Although rational, this view can falter in the face of an apparent strain in U.K. culture best exemplified by the cold bath: *if it hurts, it must be good for me.*

Assumption 6. The results of change actions are not always 100 percent predictable and controllable.

This is the complement of Assumption 5: although it is possible to initiate change rather than wait for it to happen, it is not always possible to have perfect information, in advance, about the consequences of the change. People must be willing to take action and then deal sequentially with new issues that are created by that action. Also, unpredicted consequences are not necessarily *bad* consequences: they may be new opportunities.

Cultural Factors

The *intellectual tradition of rationality* that leads managers to reject the concept of taking actions whose consequences are not predictable is a long one. Even though this unpredictability is actually true for many of the actions they take every day, if these actions fit into some accepted pattern of "how we do things here" they can be rationalized without ever having to deal with the question of whether their effects are predictable.

In addition, there is a strong bent toward the attitude "prove it will be practical" rather than an acceptance of the fact that less than perfect foreknowledge of the future is part of mankind's fate; nor is there much proof of practicality for many of the traditional practices that are holding the system back.

In general, the concept of taking action without certainty in order to obtain more data about a situation or problem is in direct conflict with *felt needs for security and certainty as a basis for action.* This resistance is possibly most visible in the civil service but by no means limited to it.

Assumption 7. Behavioral science knowledge can contribute to organizational health.

We are now in a position to apply behavioral science concepts in an effective manner to the problems of organizational and personal development. This knowledge can be used both in the design of effective systems and the change methods that help us to achieve these systems with minimum human costs.

Cultural Factors

A number of interesting factors operate in conflict with this assumption. First is *the very strong value placed on privacy and the inviolability of one's person and one's home.* Mention behavioral scientists in many organizations and people immediately begin complaining about manipulation, invasion of privacy, interpretation, and the like. No matter that the behavioral scientist is often trying to get the members to *stop* doing these things to one another (which they do with great frequency and expenditure of effort) and to deal with one another more openly and directly.

Second, there seems to be a general *mistrust of a professional's* input into the day-to-day life of organizational members. Presumably these members feel that their own experiences must have made them experts in organization development (when it usually does nothing of the kind). This mistrust may be related to the British tradition of the *gifted amateur*—the person who knows a great deal about a number of areas but who does not do too much of any one thing. This concept relates back to social class notions about "well-roundedness" and the stigma attached to those who apply themselves in an ungraceful manner to one narrow field.

IMPLICATIONS

From this discussion one might deduce that I do not think it is possible to do systematic organization development work in U.K. organizations. In fact, I do feel pessimistic about the likelihood of self-renewal in many of them, but a number of qualifications do afford a more positive outlook.

First, of course, is the fact that my picture of the culture is greatly overgeneralized, and it is an open question how accurately it describes the underlying assumptions of British society today. Many would say that the features I describe have disappeared, whereas others would maintain that under the surface there has been little real change in basic values and assumptions.

Second, not all organizations tend to be mirrors of the culture in which they function. Some are even more like the mode, others deviate from it. Similarly, people vary in the extent to which they continue to hold traditional societal values. It should be possible for consultants to work with pockets of deviants or subsystems of larger organizations in which the subsystem's culture tends to support self-examination and self-renewal activities.

Third, many U.K. companies now function in a much broader context than the island isolation described earlier. They are truly multinational and their cultures must change accordingly. I know of several cases in which the climate of the parent British company has been under pressure as a result of influences from foreign subsidiaries. Common Market operations, if continued over a long enough period, will also exert pressures to improve effectiveness in order that the organization can survive in competition with foreign organizations that are not so securely bound by tradition.

This suggests the more general point that work organizations have other environmental factors besides their country's culture: their market characteristics or the rate of change in such factors as suppliers and labor supply, to mention only two. These factors can be sources of a felt need for change in the system, and consultants can use this need as the starting point to the development of a more proactive stance toward problems. The general strategy would be to work on concrete problems in which there is a real, visible cost associated with their not being solved. Then work can begin on generalizing the intervention to the system's problem-solving processes themselves.

As far as applying this discussion to OD activities in U.S. organizations, I think there are several specific parallels. One is that the cultural context is a factor in every change effort—it may be working for you or against you, but it pays for the consultant to do a "cultural diagnosis" as a part of scouting out a new project so that he or she will not take too much for granted in the early stages of the project. It is all too easy to be unaware of the assumptions we are making when we try to influence clients in new directions that may seem less than useless to them. As one antidote to this unconscious conflict, I have lately used the seven assumptions described here—sharing them with clients and trying to test the extent to which the assumptions make sense. When they do not, we have another step to cover in the entry process.

A second U.S. generalization is that there does not seem to be a single cultural context. It varies greatly in different regions of the country; for example, the OD assumptions seem to me to be relatively prevalent in the Southern California region and relatively less accepted in the New England area (which unfortunately is my home; no wonder I travel a lot in my work).

Finally, there is, of course, the implication that anyone with limited time and energy (which is all of us) should be selective about where he or she attempts to do OD work. Companies vary in their climate's support for self-renewal activities, as do units within a company. Countries vary in the same way, and the main point here has been that the United Kingdom would seem, on the average, to have a low probability of payoff for effort expended. Because the same can be said of many companies and regional cultures in the United States as well, the issue is really our own consciousness in diagnosing possible work settings and choosing those that have some degree of cultural support of OD. We should be as proactive in this as we tell our clients they should be.

2

Failure at Entry

DAVID N. BERG

This is an account of an attempt at an organizational diagnosis of an interesting and, in many ways, unique company. AMW is a public relations firm staffed almost exclusively by women and strongly committed to the values of the feminist movement. This commitment has led the organization to experiment with a variety of nontraditional management practices with the goal of applying the precepts of feminist ideology to the task of developing and maintaining a complex organization. Late in 1973 I approached the firm with a proposal to study this "living experiment." Unfortunately the proposed diagnostic study never got beyond what is often called the "entry" phase.

When a consultation or research project ends in its infancy, as this one did, there is a special feeling of regret. Unlike the disappointment that follows the realization that a particular plan or solution did not work, a project's early termination is an occasion for profound sadness. Not only all the work and preparation but, perhaps more importantly, the potential are suddenly lost—not ruined or undone—but simply and sadly lost. What lingers is the haunting illusion of what might have been.

I wish to thank Elizabeth Douvan for the financial support that made this project possible and Clayton Alderfer, Joseph Berg, and Philip Mirvis for their helpful comments on an earlier draft of this chapter.

Perhaps that is why it is particularly difficult to examine failures and setbacks which occur during the start-up phase. Most of us would rather move on to a new project and the promise of success rather than dwell on these painful questions: What could I have done differently? What signals did I miss or choose to ignore? What characteristics of the organization made this project hazardous? What have I learned about myself, OD, and organizational behavior that might help me avoid the same mistakes next time around? With these questions in mind, here is the story of a fascinating project that never quite happened.

THE ENTRY PROCESS

Most organization development projects, regardless of their focus, begin with a diagnostic process of one kind or another, for this diagnosis provides the information necessary to understand the strengths, weaknesses, and salient problems of the organization (Levinson, 1972). Although there are many approaches to "diagnosing" a human system, in conducting the project described here it was defined as *an overt process of gathering valid information which the client system chooses to participate in and which is aimed at developing a shared understanding among the members of the organization about the common problems they face* (Alderfer, 1976). For this approach, as for many others, successful diagnosis requires the involvement of the members of the organization. The accuracy, depth, and potential usefulness of the outcome depend on the trust that is developed between client and consultant. The process of beginning this mutual involvement, including choosing to undertake the diagnosis, agreeing on the ground rules, drawing up a contract, and building a working relationship, is called *entry*.

The entry process is a complex and critically important phase for both client and consultant. Both parties must make important decisions based on initial and perhaps superficial impressions and relatively little concrete information about each other. The client must decide whether to participate in the OD effort and the consultant must begin to design and plan the diagnosis. In addition, both client and consultant bring experiences and expectations to their initial contacts that may influence and intensify their "first impressions" of each other. Finally, much of the information that could help both parties in making their decisions is understandably "hidden" in these first few meetings and discussions. All of these factors make the entry process particularly susceptible to misunderstandings and mistakes.

In the AMW case the entry process failed to establish a research relationship (diagnosis) because the numerous hazards encountered were not successfully managed. The case is written as a first person account and includes notes from a journal kept during the course of the project. The concluding section presents my analysis of the circumstances that led to the termination of the diagnostic relationship and some Monday morning suggestions for avoiding similar entry hazards in the future.

THE CASE

Background

The AMW company is a nationally prominent public relations firm located in a major West Coast city. The company was founded in 1972 by eight women whose goal was to provide quality public relations services to professional women and to businesses and organizations owned and/or managed by women. The eight women shared a strong commitment to the ideology of the feminist movement and AMW was created to support and promote women's undertakings in the areas of business, entertainment, and literature. The founders all had experience in public relations, but at the center of the group was a woman who had been in the forefront of the early attempts to publicize and legitimize the activities of the feminist movement. Diane's reputation was the foundation on which the firm was built. Her charisma attracted not only clients but media coverage as well. By the end of its second year the AMW staff had grown to 50 and the firm had established itself as a viable and financially self-sufficient operation, a particularly remarkable accomplishment in light of the highly competitive field in which it operated. Success and growth seemed to be principally the result of two factors.

First, the timing of the company's incorporation was nearly perfect. Women were entering the professional world in increasingly large numbers, many explicitly voicing their support for the goals of the feminist movement. In addition to contracts from women like these, many of whom were initially unable to pay for the company's services, AMW also began to receive accounts from individuals and organizations that wanted to make a contribution to the company's avowed goals by retaining its professional services. The entire process was enhanced by the wide publicity that surrounded the firm's beginnings.

Second, Diane succeeded in recruiting a highly competent public relations executive, Jan, to manage the company's financial and organizational affairs. Jan had extensive experience (20 years) as a senior partner in one of the city's established public relations firms, and she ran AMW with a sure hand. Together, Diane and Jan were the prime movers in the company's growth and success.

The company was organized into five departments: the market research and statistics (computer) departments (18 people); the graphics department (6 people); the publicity department (6 people); and the staff of account executives (12 people, including most of the original founders). In addition, there were people who did the billing, secretaries, and a few volunteers. The financial success of the company was due primarily to the market research and statistics departments which provided paying clients with competent service. The account executives occasionally took on unprofitable accounts for ideological reasons, and these "obligations" often involved the graphics and publicity departments.

It is important to note that the ideological values of the firm played a major role in its internal life as well as in its relations with clients, other professionals, and the general public. It was common knowledge, for example, that salaries were allocated on the basis of experience *and* need, that everyone was invited to provide input on the selection of major clients, and that distinctions among individuals were made on the basis of departmental function in the organization rather than position in an organizational hierarchy.

Initial Contact: November–December

I first approached the firm with a proposal for an organizational diagnostic study. A number of the firm's characteristics interested me as a doctoral student in organizational behavior. First, the membership of the organization was 90 percent women and all leadership positions were held by women. Second, the organization was strongly committed to the feminist movement and to the social values congruent with the ideals of that movement. This commitment had some direct and explicit implications for the structure and behavior of the organization. Third, the organization was apparently surviving in a highly competitive environment. Of particular interest to me was the influence of a social ideology on organizational structure and processes and the operational nature of certain social values in particular; for example, nonhierarchy and maximum equity.

My first contact was made in mid-November. On the strength of the firm's reputation for openness, I simply walked into the offices "cold" and presented some of my ideas to a member of the publicity department (Carol). As I walked to the door for that first meeting, I expected to find a carpeted office with a receptionist and an expansive waiting waiting room. Instead, there were no carpets that could be described as lush and the general feeling was one of being crowded. The walls were unpainted and littered with posters, bulletin boards, and all kinds of announcements. Dress ranged from jeans to fashionable dresses and all seemed to be applying themselves to their work with great energy.

After some discussion, Carol seemed enthusiastic about my ideas for a diagnostic study and its potential rewards for the organization. She informed me that there was a policy group at the firm that met weekly to discuss policy and to plan the firm's activities. I asked her to inquire about the feasibility of a study and the possibility of presenting the idea to the policy group. We agreed to talk again in a few weeks.

At Carol's suggestion, I sent a letter to Jan that included (a) a brief personal introduction, (b) my interest in studying and understanding the role of social values in determining organizational functioning, (c) the potential contribution of such a study to the literature on organizational behavior and to the growth of the company itself, and (d) a suggestion for a personal meeting as a next step in the process.

In the letter I stressed four points about the research:

1. A study of AMW might help other organizations to understand and possibly emulate AMW on a behavioral level.
2. The study presented an opportunity to find out what the firm practices as well as what it "preaches."
3. My values about research and organization appeared to be similar to AMW's values about organization.
4. The research would provide the firm with an opportunity for self-scrutiny, participation, and openness, values we both seemed to hold.

Two more weeks passed before I phoned Jan to follow up on the letter. Then, after five unsuccessful attempts, a meeting was arranged to discuss the proposal. During our conversation Jan expressed an interest in the idea and a desire to talk about the goals and requirements of the project.

The meeting with Jan was a confused one. During the 40-minute appointment there were two or three phone calls and three or four personal interruptions. I attempted to present a brief outline for the study that stressed the value of an organizational diagnosis to the field of organizational behavior and to the firm. I expressed my belief that an understanding of AMW would help other organizations to begin to experiment with alternative organizational styles and suggested that the self-scrutiny implied by a diagnostic study would help the organization to understand the current and future problems inherent in maintaining its values in the face of continued growth.

Jan expressed continued interest in the study but had two reservations. She felt that the study had little to teach the firm about itself because they were already spending a great deal of time on the "human side of the business" and she also warned that members of the firm might not like someone taking up their time to "study" them. I asked for the opportunity to present the project to the policy group in order to be able to answer questions about the demands of the study and the research methods to be used. Jan agreed. My notes reflect my thoughts and feelings at the end of our talk:

> The discussion with Jan was up and down, never really began and was constantly interrupted. It is clear to me at this point that my project is a low-priority issue.
>
> The belief that a systematic look at the organization won't produce some learning is discouraging for two reasons. First, the tone as well as the content of such a statement conveys a little of the opposite message and, second, it means that what I believe is a contribution to the organization for its participation in the research is not perceived as a contribution at all!
>
> I was impressed with the openness and sensitivity of all the people I met. Jan impressed me as the mother of the "family" (her words) who is concerned with everything that goes on in the firm. While I was there she made decisions about a complicated legal matter and the need to find someone to help clean up after the preceding night's Christmas Party.

As I prepared for my meeting with the policy group, I was aware of the unexpected once again. My meeting with Jan gave me the impression of a centralized decision-making process, yet here I was scheduled to meet with the policy group. The policy group consisted of the

12 account executives and was charged with planning the activities of the company. They met for approximately three hours each week in an open forum to which all members of the organization were invited. When the firm was small, all members had attended. Now the attendance averaged 20 to 25 and the "hard" side of the business as well as the support staff were not usually present.

The room in which I made my presentation measured about 20 by 30 feet with pastel-colored desks (about eight of them) placed around it. Like the rest of the physical layout, everything was open—no doors, no partitions, no apparent distinctions, and as with most of the rooms at AMW it felt warmly cluttered, spilling over, chock-full but not slovenly, like a pair of comfortable old jeans, informal yet functional. There were about 25 people in the room, sitting on chairs or on the floor or lying in the doorway. I spoke from the spot where I entered, unable to move.

My presentation followed the outline of my letter. I gave a brief personal history and described my interest in AMW. I also outlined the general methodological approach as consisting of interviews, observations, and a mutually designed questionnaire and described the commitment the project would require and the feedback that the firm could expect. I then proposed a preliminary "get acquainted" stage during which I would spend two or three days a month at AMW to conduct a sample of interviews and to introduce the project to the staff. At the end of this time I proposed to present a research "contract" to the firm that would outline the three-month, on-site diagnostic period and would serve as a basis for a joint decision about continuing the research.

The discussion that followed raised these points:

1. How much time would be expected from the individuals and the organization?
2. Was the intent of the study to *evaluate* the social ideology or to *understand* how the ideology was translated into practice?
3. Would the researcher's presence interfere with the sense of intimacy that was so central to the office's work?

Near the end of the meeting someone asked whether the people "upstairs" were to be included in the project. I replied that I was not aware of the existence of this group. I was also informed that all the other "departments" should be included. I readily agreed and made a mental note about the existence of the people "upstairs."

The meeting ended with a commitment from the policy group to make a decision on the first stage of the project within three weeks. Their decision was to proceed.

In contrast to my meeting with Jan, I felt comfortable, relaxed and prepared during my presentation and the discussion that followed. The interaction seemed to include a flow that the first meeting had lacked. I attributed the difference in the atmosphere to the staff—in particular to its ability to manage interpersonal relations.

I viewed my presentation as an experiential setting for observing how a large, central group in the firm deals with something or somebody coming from "outside" (its environment). If relationships across the organizational boundary reflect relationships between internal parts, then I believed I had some pretty powerful data about AMW; for example, my experience with presentations of this kind suggests that during discussion time the nature of the interaction is usually a dialogue between the group members and the outside presenter. This dialogue is characterized by critical questions from the group that force the presenter to defend his or her ideas, reasons, methods, motives, and so on. The session at AMW did not fit this pattern. As questions were posed on crucial points the discussion (positive/negative, supportive/critical) developed almost wholly within the group rather than being directed at me. There was no need to defend my proposal, for I was not being attacked. The members of the group were using one another to generate and discuss relevant issues raised by my presentation, and when I was asked a question it seemed aimed at getting more information instead of putting me on the spot.

At the end of the meeting I was satisfied that, whatever the outcome, the meeting had not been just a quick once-over.

The First Visits: January–March

My first formal visit occurred approximately 10 days after the decision. I talked first with individual members of the policy group. My goal for the two-day trip was to introduce myself and the study to as many people as I could. The lack of an explicit hierarchy made it virtually impossible to carry on a traditional entry program (top down), and so I set out with the minimal objective of talking to someone in each of the departments of the firm.

It should be noted that the lack of an "organization chart" made the initial contact mutually stressful and ambiguous. There was no letter of introduction and no memo from the president. The situation was stressful for the organization members because many of them knew nothing about my history or intentions nor the extent of the policy group's support (primarily Jan and Diane). The stress for me came from constantly feeling adrift without the guidance or support provided by organizational authority. This feeling was further reinforced by the fact that I had no room, desk, or chair to use and the atmosphere of "forced openness" meant I was always in the middle of something.

During the next two days I spoke with a number of people. In addition to getting an introduction to the work-flow side of the business, the interviews made me aware of an unexpected phenomenon: there seemed to be a serious ingroup/outgroup distinction in the firm. This information was not only of interest for the diagnosis, it also raised the question of effectively managing the entry process. An unwitting identification with one or the other group could seriously affect the quality and quantity of the information collected and even influence the future of the study. Thus I was told by members of the outgroup to be careful not to be "co-opted" by the ingroup (policy group). There was a clear need to touch all the keys simultaneously, that is, enter through all members at the same time, but it was also clear that this was physically impossible.

At this point my notes described my feelings about the ingroup/outgroup problem which was just beginning to surface:

One difficult issue is my personal attraction to many of the people here. I will have to be very careful to manage these feelings in order not to project an "ingroup" identification or, worse, distort data on the basis of the real identification that I feel.

The seductive quality of the ingroup is immense and it is the ingroup that invited me into the organization in the first place.

For the organization, on the other hand, the first trip seemed to be summed up in a note written on a "comments" sheet circulated among the staff:

What's in it for us? My hunch is possibly a lot IF we are willing to level with him and not stick entirely to the ideological, the-movement-is-us trip but get into the how/if/why/when this tends to break down.

Before my second visit I took a number of steps to deal with the problems of communication I had encountered on the first trip: specifically, the informal nature of *all* communication and the apparent lack of communication between subgroups ("ingroup/outgroup," "upstairs/downstairs"). I sent a letter to Jan explaining the purpose of the next visit and included a *separate* letter for the staff members on the same subject. I asked Jan to distribute the second letter. It articulated two goals for the visit: (a) the solicitation of suggestions on what the study might accomplish for the firm and how it might be designed to attain these ends, and (b) a discussion of the role of the researcher during the on-site time in the summer and possible strategies for a better understanding of the workings of the organization.

I also decided to begin discussing the concept of a "liaison group" with Jan and other members of the firm and therefore included a description of the proposed group and the ideas behind it in both letters. I wanted to create a formal pro-tem group that would include organizational members who represented a cross section of the firm; departments, different tenures, ingroup/outgroup, and so on. This group could serve as liaison between the company and the research, thus providing a much needed communication link and ensuring that the research activities and outcomes would be influenced by the concerns and needs of the organization.

As I look back on the notes I made at the end of that first visit they seem prophetic:

ISSUE: How was I okayed? Who was included in the decision (who was excluded) and what are people's feelings about that process?

I have discovered that the written work that I submitted was circulated together with a "comments" sheet and that the main theme of the comments was: let's do it but let's not give him much time, i.e., let's do it but let's not do it.

March. On arrival I asked for the use of a small room and was led to a vacant office. Thus established, I spent the next few days conducting 13 interviews with people from all but one of the departments in the company. Included in this sample was Diane. This was my first contact with her since the initial policy group meeting. In addition to these interviews, I spent about half of my time walking around and talking informally with people about the study.

The second visit not only continued the entry process but began in earnest the diagnostic process that I hoped to continue through the summer. The notes I made at the time illustrate the beginning of that diagnostic process:

Made an interesting discovery today while I was sitting at a desk in one of the communal offices making a phone call. I saw a memo from Jan to the staff about vacations and holidays. It was interesting because (a) the firm rarely uses memos as a means of communicating and (b) the last time I was here everyone raved about the flexibility around vacations and sick leave. The memo spelled out the holidays and the number of sick days allowed. It also mentioned the different vacation periods for people with different tenure and closed with a sentence about the fact that the Committee would review everyone's salary in June and December. It was not clear who the Committee is and on the copy I was reading the words were blocked in by whoever was reading it.

The memo began with the statement that its contents were the result of five or six "quorum" meetings, whatever that means.

I finally spent a half hour with Diane, who, along with Jan, heads up the firm. I was excited about the interview and it was a pleasure. She was warm, friendly, and supportive and said she guessed that the firm was looking to me to learn some things (a first!). When I probed, she said she felt a little like I was a consultant. I said that at this time I felt like my role was diagnostic not consultative but that such information often filled that role depending on the organization.

Learnings in brief today:

1. Jan is the chief in this organization. It is virtually common knowledge that her know-how, experience, energy, and vision are the driving forces behind the success of the firm. She makes all the critical (and noncritical) decisions, hires, fires, raises, demotes, okays, and so on.

2. There definitely is a hierarchy. Not only a functional one but a nominal one as well. These people are referred to by their titles internally (I witnessed the introduction of the business manager to group of employees' nieces) and they are the ones who provide input to Jan on promotions and evaluations.

3. There is a constant struggle between the ideologues and the professionals. Some clients who were taken on six months ago would never be taken on now (unprofitable and risky).

4. AMW is genuinely perceived as a flexible, open, free, and unstructured place where mobility is possible and an air of "family" persists. It's not like it used to be, however; no rap sessions, no more total attendance at policy group meetings, no communal decision making (although there doesn't appear to be unilateral decision making either), more difficult communication and feedback.

The Final Visit: April

After the second visit I sent a copy of the research contract to the company care of Jan. The third visit was to be the final "precontract" one and I intended to devote my time to discussing the contract: project goals, time requirements, feedback models, publication rules, and confidentiality. I arrived at the firm and presented the written contract to the policy group and individually to every other member of the organization. At the end of the day I had heard from only three or four people and they were "regulars"; that is, people who regularly talked to me.

After consultation with a colleague that evening about what to do next I spoke to Jan the next day about the lack of response, which I interpreted to mean that the organization members were not taking the project seriously. I expressed my doubts about undertaking a project of this nature in such a climate. Jan took out a piece of paper and wrote the following memo to all employees:

> You should have received a note from David Berg dated April 15 which describes what will be involved in the study of our organizational behavior. If you have any questions or comments please speak to him or call him at extension 06. Speak now or forever expect to cooperate.

In response to the memo several people expressed their support for the project and three others submitted written statements of their refusal to participate. Later that day Rene, a self-proclaimed member of the outgroup, came and told me that she would not be participating in the study. She seemed conflicted and told me that she had decided on this course of action as a means of demonstrating support for the people "upstairs" who had never been included in the decision to undertake the research. It became apparent that the 10 "upstairs" people would not participate in the study. Rene wished me luck as she left. My notes convey a dawning realization:

> After lunch, while talking with Jan's assistant, I discovered the meaning of the word "quorum" which I had seen on a memo. Small five-person groups make most of the decisions and people often are not told that a decision has been made.
>
> Rene withdrew from the study today as a matter of principle. She was aligning herself with some people upstairs who had not been consulted about the project. She made it clear that her refusal to participate had nothing to do with the study per se. The people upstairs can register their frustration and anger against *me* and not against the firm or its hierarchy because the study is voluntary. I'm caught in the middle.
>
> There may be no way to go back to Step 1 and get these people on board, in which case the going will get rougher.

I get the impression that what makes the communication and decision-making problems worse here is that everyone expects to be included and to have some influence because of the values the firm stands for.

After a meeting with Jan and Diane I decided to meet with the upstairs group later that day. During that meeting the resistance to the study was clearly articulated: (a) it was felt that the study would hurt the firm, cause disruptions and personality conflicts; (b) the people did not trust the researcher's pledge of confidentiality (both internal and external); and (c) they resented not having been included in the original decision about the project.

Someone in the group remarked that this meeting was the first time they had all been together and suggested that they ask Jan for a new vote on the project that would include them. I affirmed that this would be consistent with my pledge to reevaluate the project at this time.

That evening, after the upstairs people had met with Jan, and long after most people had gone home, a small group of senior account executives met until 9:00 PM discussing the project and the advisability of a vote, given the current climate in the organization. Immediately before that meeting Jan and I had talked about the project. Following are my notes of that conversation:

Jan is concerned about the possible defection of the upstairs group and asked if I would consider a third-floor-only study. We sat and talked, warmly and quite frankly, about the risks of the study, the interfloor conflicts, and the approach-avoidance nature of the firm's commitment to the project. She seemed to take it all in—calling it fascinating. I told her I felt that the process of dealing with the study was a good mirror of the process that existed at the firm from day to day. She knew it was true.

The next morning I discovered that there had been a decision to have an organization-wide ballot on the project. Jan, still very supportive, presented a voting format that the preceding evening's group had drawn up. I then distributed the following ballot to 45 firm members:

1. I am ____ am not ____ in favor of going ahead with the David Berg project.

2. Regardless of how I voted above, I feel the following percentage of the staff should be in favor for us to proceed:
   ____ 51%
   ____ 60%

_____ 70%
_____ 80%
_____ 90%

The final vote was 33 in favor, 17 against. There were few people who did not have an opinion. The "no's" had submitted a list of their names (10 of them) the day before the vote and the "yea's" had gone so far as to call staff members who were out of town to record their positive votes. The second part of the ballot resolved nothing. When the votes were averaged, the size of the plurality necessary to continue was 67 percent, virtually indistinguishable from the actual tally (33–17).

Whereas Jan interpreted the numbers as a signal to proceed, Diane was concerned about the 17 dissenters. Although she made it plain that the choice was mine, she thought it would be impossible to do a study with such a large number refusing to participate. Jan's opinion, too, began to change during the next 24 hours to agree more with Diane's. I was also concerned about the vote, for it seriously jeopardized the potential validity of the case study. The critical issue seemed to be whether the leadership would actively support the project and contribute to the researcher's efforts to bring some or all of the "no" votes into the project.

From my initial observations I believed that people were not so much against the study as against the process by which the project had gained a foothold in the firm. In many ways the project had merely served to focus an already existing resentment against the decision-making process (power distribution) in the organization. Ironically, the only way the dissident faction could exercise some influence in the firm was to reject the project that had given them influence in the first place.

Meetings and phone calls with Diane revealed that neither she nor Jan felt it would be possible to broaden the base of support for the project. Diane told the researcher that although she had voted "yes," she had also marked 90 percent as the plurality necessary for continuing the project. She did not feel that the firm was ready to undertake a project that raised substantial divisiveness within the organization. My final notes on the project concerned that meeting with Diane:

> When I left the meeting with Diane, I was convinced there was no study. But something still bothered me and I realized that I had underestimated Diane's influence in the firm and particularly with Jan.

It's been hard. I'm now on a plane back home, two days late. I have to decide and I feel torn. Some people are strongly in favor. Diane could pull the rug out any time. Fifteen people are against the project. How many would become involved with time? I have focused an intergroup conflict around the issue of the study, and although some people are getting very involved others are getting very tired of the hassle.

After considering all the information I decided to terminate the project and sent a letter to Jan and Diane and a shorter, less detailed letter to the entire staff expressing my disappointment that the study would not take place. In the first letter I expressed my belief that the study had been caught in an internal conflict. Finally, I thanked them for their time and effort.

ORDER OUT OF CHAOS

What Happened?

Now I would like to return to the questions posed at the beginning of this chapter. What could I have done differently? What signals did I miss or choose to ignore? What characteristics of the organization made this project hazardous? In trying to understand what happened, a number of events stood out as particularly significant in the life and death of the project.

My personal and professional identity and needs had a substantial impact on the entry process in ways that I was not aware of at the time.

The fact that I initiated the contact with AMW, a nationally famous public relations firm, led me to be very cautious during the initial stages of the entry. Because there was no "felt need" at the company for an organizational diagnosis, I thought of myself and the project as an imposition on the time and energy of the people in the company. In spite of the policy group's decision to undertake the study, the low priority of the project was reinforced by numerous written and verbal comments. As a result I was more than careful not to offend or antagonize anyone because I imagined that any unpleasant experience could cause the project to be terminated. In addition, and probably more important, I did not want to lose the opportunity to study a unique and highly visible organization and so was reluctant to engage in activities that I feared would jeopardize the future of the project (e.g., confrontation or conflict), even when those activities were appropriate and necessary.

These attitudes and activities served to reinforce the existing belief that the study was not a serious *organizational* undertaking. Few people took the project seriously until the days immediately preceding the final vote when the potentially disruptive impact of a diagnosis became evident. The leadership in particular had not been prepared for this situation, and the failure to alert them to the possible unsettling effects of the project was caused in part by my reluctance.

The fact that I am male undoubtedly influenced the course of the project. I use the word "undoubtedly" because the impact of this "demographic" characteristic is still hard for me to understand. The policy group's decision to participate in the study, for example, had been influenced by the fact that it was a man who was proposing the project. Many people felt that the "positive findings" of a man would carry more weight than those of a woman because most people in the outside world would probably dismiss a woman's findings as strongly biased in favor of the organization. I was also told that some members who simply did not like men would probably not support or participate in the study.

On a different level the relationship between a male researcher and a "female" organization created another set of sexual dynamics. The unconscious and often subtle influence of sexuality on the research relationship makes it difficult to trace the impact of these forces on the outcome of the project, yet the words I used to describe the women at the firm ("warm," "supportive"), my feelings about them ("personal attraction"), and their impact on me ("seductive") suggest that this influence was not a trivial one. My attraction to the women in the company, for example, may have contributed to my reluctance to confront or alienate them. It is interesting to note that I was consistently unable or unwilling to see the sexual aspects of the research relationship until after the project was over. One possible explanation is that this "blindness" was a defense against what I believed were inappropriate sexual feelings. Whatever the explanation, my lack of awareness made it more difficult to confront sexuality as an influential factor in the entry process.

My unwitting identification with the "ingroup" caused me to become embroiled in an intergroup conflict that led to rejection by the "outgroup."

As a number of authors have pointed out, and this case confirms, the practitioner's point of entry into a system is extremely important (cf. Kahn & Mann, 1953). The entry point can produce a lasting first impression, which, although meaning little to the practitioner at the time, is extremely significant to the organization members. Particularly in situations in which two or more groups are in conflict, the practitioner risks being labeled a member of the group through which he or she entered, and along with this label come the suspicions, mistrust, and negative affect that usually accompany intergroup conflict (Blake and Mouton, 1962; LeVine and Campbell, 1974; Sherif and Sherif, 1969). As in the AMW case, this perceived identification often leads to serious problems with the "outgroup," including restrictions on access ("We will not participate in the study"), distortion of information ("Jan wouldn't want you to do that"), or open hostility.

My identification with the ingroup (policy group) occurred at the moment of initial contact with the firm. Unknown to me, the partial attendance at this meeting symbolized an ongoing conflict around the decision-making process and around the questions of equality and participation. Although I was soon aware of the need to "touch all the keys simultaneously," my initial activities and the unstructured nature of the organization made that process extremely difficult. The lack of formal structure and the existence of strong norms against making the informal structure explicit meant that I was forced to uncover the operational structure as part of the entry before I could use it to help confront the issue of intergroup conflict. In the end the ingroup-outgroup conflict focused on the project itself. By voting against the study the outgroup was also voting against the policies and practices of the ingroup which had sanctioned the diagnostic project in the first place.

It is important to realize that in traditional organizations the formal structure often provides the practitioner with the "protection" necessary to complete the entry process. The authority structure sanctions the entry and the hierarchical design provides navigational guidance through the system. In such an organization the practitioner has the advantage of being able to expect and look for certain intergroup conflicts. Armed with this awareness, he or she can take steps to confirm or dispel (whichever the case) impressions about the motivation for the project, its source and support within the organization, and the practitioner's relations with the people at the top (or in a certain division). In an organization like AMW, which has no formal structure, there may be absence of official sanctioning and no clear guidelines about whom to see and what the relevant trust/neutrality issues might be during the entry process.

Even in traditionally structured organizations it is difficult to anticipate all the major intergroup conflicts. As at AMW, the awareness often comes after the entry has begun. This is the paradox of organizational entry: an awareness of intergroup issues comes *as the result* of some initial contact and diagnosis, but in order to manage these tensions the practitioner must understand them *before* the entry process gets underway!

This paradox attests to what most practitioners know—that the existence of intergroup conflict in an organization presents serious problems during entry. In spite of reliable information about a system and in spite of appropriate precautions around multiple or simultaneous entry, there is high probability that the ambiguities of initial contact with a human system will cause a practitioner to become enmeshed in a variety of intergroup tensions. At AMW these problems were compounded by the loosely structured nature of the company.

The "loose" structure of the AMW company made a traditional entry process virtually impossible and resulted in apparently insurmountable communication problems.

As Alderfer (1976) describes them, underbounded or loosely structured systems do not differentiate well among their internal parts (groups, departments, individuals). In the extreme the underbounded system is one in which people are not sure who is a member and who is not or what activities anyone is required to perform. As a result of the lack of boundary definition these systems are characterized by unclear authority structures, uncertain role definitions, and a general lack of integration.

At AMW the looseness was apparent everywhere one looked. In part, this was an explicit attempt to avoid developing a rigid, formal, and hierarchical bureaucracy which would foster the kind of insensitivity and depersonalization that AMW was trying hard not to perpetuate. Consequently the "family" approach to running an organization was designed to encourage broad participation in decision making, shared responsibility and commitment, and greater equality among the firm's employees. The result was an underbounded system of purposeful design.

The entry phase of the project was derived from my experience and the literature on entry and it was designed for a more bounded system. When the virtually inevitable intergroup issues developed, I was conceptually unprepared because of the unfamiliar "loosely structured" nature of the firm. This lack of formal structure made it difficult to take the traditional steps for confronting an intergroup crisis because it was not clear to me who should be approached in order to gain access to and credibility with the firm's various groups. By the time this knowledge had been acquired the damage to the research relationship had been done.

One difficulty in particular serves to underscore the fact that the traditional entry model was poorly equipped for an underbounded system. The absence of a formal communication network made all communication (purposely) cumbersome. Memos were rarely used and I was forced to deliver all communications individually or ask that letters or announcements be posted or circulated.

With hindsight it also becomes apparent that the confusion and resentment around decision making would inevitably focus on the entry process, for it provided the first concrete, firm-wide decision-making opportunity. The firm's antipathy toward any formal authority structure created the "quorum" system for making decisions, and the development of this system became extremely ironic. Faced with a growing organization, the leadership realized the need for quick decision making by people with relevant information; yet it was reluctant to make explicit a suitable authority structure for fear of destroying the legitimacy of the open decision-making process. The quorum system that evolved eventually subverted the intent of their ideals while attempting and appearing to perpetuate it. For many people the frustration was heightened by the implicit ideological promise that each person would exercise influence over the firm's decisions.

Monday Morning

The unique features of the AMW company ought not to obscure the broadly applicable learnings that emerged from this case. The dilemmas encountered by the researcher during the entry process at AMW are common to OD practitioners across a wide range of organizational settings. It is my hope that the AMW experience may help other OD practitioners and social scientists manage the entry phase more successfully and thereby open the door to further organization development and research activities.

Practitioner Needs and Goals. In beginning an OD project the practitioner's awareness of his or her own needs and goals is as important as an understanding of the expectations of the organization. The simplicity of this statement belies the real and difficult personal struggle it implies. As this case illustrates, the practitioner's own needs for success, social and professional esteem, and status or profesional visibility can strongly influence the choices to be made during entry. Often these choices serve the practitioner's "personal" needs rather than the professional demands of the situation. Although an awareness of one's own needs does not guarantee a successful entry, it does help ensure that the practitioner's examination of both personal and professional motivations behind the countless decisions that must be made during this phase of organization development will be a serious part of this process.

OD Teams Versus Individual Practitioners. The identity characteristics of the OD practitioner can exert a strong, but unrecognized, influence on the entry process. Such characteristics as the practitioner's sex, race, age, and background may be sufficiently disturbing to the client system to preclude any relationship at all. On the other hand, the practitioner's personal characteristics may limit or exaggerate his or her own sensitivities, creating blind spots or biases that can have a serious impact on the entry process. Perhaps even more important, certain practitioner identity characteristics may elicit varying reactions from organization members. Thus the entry experience for one practitioner (young and black) is likely to vary considerably from that of another practitioner (older and white), doing the same things in the same organization. In this situation different views of the organization are a result of different but equally *real* experiences, not practitioner bias.

OD teams that attempt to match their own composition to those of major organizational "identity groups" can increase the likelihood that the practitioners will be able to identify and respond to issues of race, sex, age, and background. OD teams composed to fit the identity characteristics of the organizations in which they are working can help the practitioners to recognize these problems and explore ways to resolve them constructively. As in all others the value of an OD (or research) team depends on the ability of its members to work together and on each member's willingness to examine the relevant team dynamics as well as organizational dynamics. The presence of different perspectives is of little value if team members are unable or unwilling to accept and discuss these differences.

Entry Under Conditions of Intergroup Conflict or Competition. The presence of intergroup conflict or competition makes entry (and subsequent change) hazardous for the practitioner or researcher. As the AMW case illustrates, the practitioner's point of entry can lead to inadvertent identification with one "side" of a conflict. This identification can, in turn, lead to serious problems in communication, access, participation, and involvement. Because conflict between hierarchical groups (e.g., union–management), functional groups (e.g., sales–production), and identity groups (e.g., black–white) exists to some extent in all organizations, one should anticipate that it will influence the entry process. Unless the OD team can reach all the relevant groups simultaneously, it risks becoming entrapped by intergroup conflict, even when forewarned. As a practical matter, however, simultaneous contact with multiple groups, especially when the intergroup dynamics of an organization are unfamiliar, is nearly impossible. Is there an alternative?

One promising approach is the use of a "liaison group" (Alderfer, 1977) early in the entry phase. As a first step the OD team attempts to identify the major groups in the organization and invites them to select representatives who will serve as a link between the consulting or research team and the organization. In its initial meetings this group may identify significant groups that are not represented but should be. After its formation this microcosm of the organization can (a) provide access to the various groups in the organization, (b) help to establish a mutual trust between organization members and OD team members as a result of ongoing personal relationships with both groups, (c) facilitate communication between the organization and the OD team, (d) provide a structure that will allow members of the organization to participate in and influence the decision-making process during entry and thereafter, and (e) allow the OD team to make almost simultaneous contact with major subgroups during the life of the project.

Entry, Intervention, and Choice. Although entry is the first step in an organizational diagnosis or OD project, it is also a time of choice. One of the goals of the entry process is to provide people with the information they will need to make a decision about organizational or personal involvement in the proposed project. This information comes in many forms, both intellectual and experiential, but all of it should be designed to give the client system some idea of the costs and benefits of the project, its risks and its ground rules, the organizational and personal "stakes" involved, and the time and energy required. To accomplish these goals the OD team must often intervene or make important changes in the normal activities of the organization and its members. This active intervention during entry is not always comfortable for the practitioner or the organization but it is sometimes crucial. In the AMW case, for example, the loose structure of the company made it difficult to approach people, to get feedback from them on proposals, answer questions, or systematically involve them in the choice process. Instead of alleviating some of these problems the researcher opted not to "disrupt" the organization any more than he had to. This decision not to intervene turned out to be a serious mistake.

It is impossible to prescribe a set of interventions that will invariably facilitate the entry process, for it may differ from organization to organization. The organizational structure, however, is of particular importance. In settings in which there is little formal structure it may be necessary to create some. At AMW this might have included calling a meeting of the whole staff, creating a liaison group, or even developing an ad hoc formal structure to serve the purposes of entry. Conversely, in a highly structured, traditional organization the OD team may have to "loosen things up" in order to effect entry. Regardless of the situation, active intervention by the practitioners may be necessary to success.

A further note on entry as a choice point. In change projects that are initiated, supported, and conducted by people inside the organization it often appears that the issue of choice is a moot one. Whereas external consultants sometimes present the OD project as a choice, internal change agents are often directed to work with a group or division in the organization. In the latter situation it would seem that the preceding discussion of choice would have little relevance. The issue of psychological choice for individuals remains an important one, however, even in situations in which it appears that organization members have no choice but to participate. Even under such conditions the individual *chooses* to be open or closed, active or passive, supportive or hostile, honest or deceptive. The process of entry provides people with the information and experience they will use to make these choices.

The Value of Outside Help. If the profession of organization development teaches us anything about ourselves, it is the value of requesting and receiving help when it is needed. Once again the simplicity of this statement is perhaps deceptive, for although it is difficult to give help wisely and competently it is sometimes much more difficult to ask for and accept it. Any OD effort or research project benefits immeasurably when the professionals involved are skilled at both.

CONCLUSION

Every OD activity or research project has a beginning. It is a difficult time with its own special challenges, demands, and hazards. For the OD practitioner this entry phase is like walking into a darkened room and searching for the light switch. At the same time, the client is trying to discover who just walked into the room. By the time your eyes have adjusted to the dark or you have succeeded in finding the light, your host may have fled, called the police, or mistakenly clobbered you from behind. The analysis of the AMW case is an attempt to provide some light during that initial darkness.

One must be cautious, however, with the recommendations described, for although the examination of individual cases can be a valuable undertaking the principles of science warn us against inferring widely applicable propositions from a single event. Nevertheless, although some of the learnings spawned by the "failure at entry" in the AMW experience are personal, many more are professional and can add to the knowledge and skill of those of us engaged in bringing about organizational change.

3

The Tensions Between Research and Intervention in Intergroup Conflict

ROY J. LEWICKI
CLAYTON P. ALDERFER

There is a growing tradition among applied social scientists of examining failures in social intervention (Bennis, 1966; Doob, 1970; Walton, 1970; Klein, Thomas, and Bellis, 1971); not only do we support this norm but we also wish to contribute to it, for we believe that others, as well as ourselves, can learn from our experiences.

This chapter reports an unsuccessful attempt to study and ameliorate a labor-management relationship. The labor and management groups described in this investigation had a 20-year history of bitter and mistrustful relations. One senior behavioral scientist with whom we consulted (and who had extensive experience with the situation) said that he thought nothing could be done to bring the parties to-

---

Reproduced by special permission from *The Journal of Applied Behavioral Science*, "The Tensions between Research and Intervention in Intergroup Conflict," by R. J. Lewicki and C. P. Alderfer, **9**, No. 4, 423–468.

We should like to thank Chris Argyris, J. Richard Hackman, Douglas Hall, Leonard Solomon, and Edward Klein for their comments on an earlier version of this chapter.

gether. We made an attempt to change the character of this relationship; retrospectively, we feel that the outcome might have been altered if we had known earlier what we know now.

Two general questions in the area of research and action on intergroup relations are at issue. First is the use of social science analysis and intervention appropriate for labor-management disputes? Walton (1969), in his book on interpersonal peacemaking, speculates whether power-bargaining and legal-justice mechanisms might not be more suitable for labor-management conflicts than applied behavioral science techniques. To what degree and in what ways are the theories and principles that are useful for understanding and changing interpersonal relationships also relevant for intergroup relationships? Although much recent work on social intervention has focused on the resolution of interpersonal disputes, the dynamics of intergroup conflict may suggest that a considerably more complex model needs to be developed.

Second, how does an applied behavioral scientist effectively pursue the point goals of research and intervention in a highly polarized situation? Can either goal be achieved without the other? Is it better to alternate efforts aimed at one goal with those directed to the other? One of the longest strikes in the history of the two parties occurred about a year before our attempted study began. If it is true that both parties lose in a prolonged strike, then it would seem that both would have suffered enough to search for new alternatives. Our approach offered a new alternative; in the final analysis one party refused to accept it. We shall attempt to determine why.

HISTORICAL DEVELOPMENT OF EVENTS

In the following section we (the researchers) attempt to trace the sequence of events that constituted the life and death of this project. Our analysis of significant events, the strategies used by the various parties and researchers, and some prescriptions for the future follow this historical account.

The Time and Place

The events that are reported here describe the researchers' year-long relationship with the labor and management groups of a company in "Oak City," a community of moderate size in New England.

The Cast of Characters

The following pseudonyms designate the major personalities involved in our abortive intervention:

The Company

Speer, Vice President for Administration
Graham, Group Head of Labor Relations
Willow, Local Head of Labor Relations

The Union

Brown, International President
Sanders, International Vice President
Ponzi, President of the Local Lodge
Kirby, Staff Representative from the International who worked closely with the Local during and after the strike.

Mid-January 1970

Speer met with a group of Yale faculty to discuss opportunities for research and consultation at his company. He indicated that the company was interested in investigating the reasons for a long strike that had crippled it the year before. He attributed the strike to several factors: (a) "the changing character of work motivation"; that is, the work force at this particular plant had changed to include more blacks, younger and better educated men, who were no longer satisfied with their jobs or the incentives normally offered by the company; (b) particular dynamics in the relationship between the local and the international union; and (c) conflict between local union leadership and its rank-and-file membership.

February 26, 1970

Lewicki and Alderfer, interested in the request for research, met with company heads Speer, Graham, and Willow. The focus of the research discussed at the January meeting was reviewed. Lewicki and Alderfer expressed a desire to study current and future relations with the union. as well as the causes of the strike. They also indicated that the union should be actively involved in this study so that valid data could be obtained and the union might profit from their findings. Speer agreed to consider the best way to approach the union and to interest it in participating.

March 19, 1970

Speer informed Lewicki that he had discussed the study with Sanders, Vice President of the International Union. They had had a "good discussion" and Speer had "sold" Sanders on the idea of doing the research. Although Sanders wanted to discuss the study with Brown (President of the International Union), he was willing to talk to the researchers first.

April 1, 1970

Having scheduled a meeting with Sanders for April 13, the researchers discussed a possible format for the study and developed an agenda for the meeting.

They agreed to propose a behavioral science examination of the interpersonal and intergroup relations in management and the union and between union and management during the period of the strike *and* at that time. Data thereby acquired would serve two purposes: (a) it would allow the researchers to test hypotheses on the interrelation of intragroup and intergroup dynamics in conflict settings, and (b) it would provide the company and the union with useful feedback about their internal and intergroup relations.

The research proposal called for several steps. Once the union and management groups had consented to the study, a joint union-management Liaison Committee composed of the researchers and several representatives from each group would be formed to advise the researchers on problems to be studied, to plan and implement the research, and to determine ways in which its findings could be disseminated. The researchers would collect most of the data, first by interviews and then in questionnaires distributed to a broader sample. The data would be summarized and a feedback report prepared in approximately one year. Further steps would then be discussed. The cost of this research was also estimated in the hope that both groups would share the expenses (although no explicit sharing program was proposed at that time).

April 13, 1970

Lewicki and Sanders discussed the study. Sanders felt that the proposed study would be important and interesting but indicated that he must secure the approval of Brown; once Brown's approval had been obtained Sanders would call on Speer to discuss ways of involving the local union.

April 22, 1970

Lewicki wrote a letter to Sanders in which he formally stated the outcome of the April 13 meeting and outlined the proposed study. A copy was sent to Speer at the company offices.

April 28, 1970

Speer indicated in a call to Lewicki that the research objectives, as stated in the April 22 letter to Sanders underemphasized the causes of the strike and overstressed current relations. The strike was the main reason for initiating the study, and the company felt a strong investment in discovering the flow and significance of events at that time. Particularly mentioned were events relating to the behavior of the bargainers, the bargaining issues, the role of mediators, and the aspects of group dynamics in the company and the union organizations (including race relations, representativeness of the union leadership, and others).

April 30, 1970

Lewicki called Sanders to check on his understanding of the proposed focus of the research. Sanders stated that the letter accurately reflected his own understanding of the April 13 meeting and restated his desire that the study emphasize current and future, rather than past, relations between the union and management. He indicated parenthetically that in his view management was "caught off base" by the strike and still did not understand why it happened. In his opinion the company was more interested in learning where management went wrong than in discovering new and better ways for the two groups to work together.

May 4, 1970

Lewicki and Alderfer prepared a memorandum that suggested some modifications in their original proposal to incorporate management's wishes for greater emphasis on historical events related to the strike. The new proposal offered to shorten the cycle between data collection and feedback phases. (We felt that one of the company's fears was the loss of control of the project.) Although we felt strongly that a valid historical account depended on trustful relations, we wanted to be responsive to management's need to influence the nature of the product it would be receiving.

May 6, 1970

Speer called Lewicki and responded favorably to the revised proposal.

May 14, 1970

Sanders called Lewicki to say that the International had agreed to pay half the cost of the study. He promised to inform Ponzi and Kirby that the money was available, but emphasized that the decision to proceed would be made by the Local.

May 27, 1970

Speer called Lewicki to ask what was happening and was told of the events with the International. He asked to have the memorandum of May 4 "formalized" and sent to him on Yale stationary. Lewicki agreed.

June 2, 1970

Alderfer and Lewicki discussed how to respond to Speer's request. Lewicki had drafted a letter which failed to mention that the initiative to "formalize" the April 22 proposal had come from management. Alderfer felt strongly that, "for the record" and in the spirit of being open and above board, this fact should be stated. Alderfer was generally more doubtful about management's trustworthiness than Lewicki, but the latter agreed to the change even though his feelings about the matter were not so strong.

June 15, 1970

Lewicki received a letter from Speer which contained two intercompany memoranda that referred to the study as the "1969 Oak City Negotiations-Post Negotiations Audit." This reference seemed to substantiate the historical emphasis favored by management. The memos also raised the possibility of "an incidental inquiry into . . . strikers' sources of funds while on strike" and suggested that it might be "desirable to use the Yale people in this as well." Though Lewicki did not like the implications of that suggestion, he decided not to confront it until the actual planning of the study occurred. (This was the only written communication we received from *either* party at any time during our negotiations with them.)

July 13, 1970

Sanders called Lewicki and Alderfer to say that the local union had turned down the proposed study. He said that the Local officers were highly suspicious of the company and that they predicted that management would use the results against them. After talking with Sanders, Ponzi and Kirby had taken the proposal directly to the Local's Executive Committee and they had collectively rejected it.

At this point the researchers took the first of a series of steps to salvage the project. On hearing that the Executive Committee had turned down the study without ever meeting the researchers, we felt that their choice was strongly emotional and they could not have been fully informed. We therefore asked Sanders if he would arrange a meeting for us with Ponzi and Kirby so that they might see who (and what) they were rejecting. It occurred to us that these leaders might be "passing the buck" to their Executive Committee rather than telling Sanders outright that they did not favor the study. Sanders told us, however, that they had seemed favorably disposed to the undertaking when he talked to them.

July 24, 1970

On Ponzi's invitation Alderfer went to the local union's Executive Committee meeting. Alderfer began by giving a brief history of the project, indicating that management had taken the initiative, and that the researchers wanted to involve the union from the start. At the conclusion of the talk one member asked why "you always start with the big guy." The researcher responded that management had taken the initiative and that we had then called on the union. The member repeated his comment, and the researcher replied that someone had to begin negotiations. The member posed his question a third time, whereupon the researcher said that he felt that he wasn't being listened to. Another member remarked that "you have to start somewhere."

Union members asked what the researcher hoped to get out of the project. Alderfer answered that the goals were better understanding for all parties and improved relations between labor and management. The researcher added that he was not naïve about the possibility of either side using the data to subvert the other. It would be unethical behavior on his part to help either side undermine the other. The research proposal to establish a joint union-company-researcher committee, he explained, was to ensure that each party would have the opportunity to keep the other honest.

Asked about the anticipated influence patterns of the committee for the study, the researcher responded that he wanted three-party influence. The researchers expected to be influenced by both labor and management, but also expected to exert influence on them in return. The researchers had some ideas about factors in the study that were necessary if it were to be worth doing; at the same time they needed union and management help in deciding on a number of important topics: who should be interviewed, what key questions should be asked, and how the data would be fed back to the parties.

One member asked what the researcher thought management wanted. He replied that they seemed to want better relations and saw the study as a possible way of improving them. At this point one man voiced his doubts, based on some current management practices in the plants, about the veracity of management's claim: "How could they say that to you and do some of the other things they are doing?" he asked.

As the discussion proceeded a number of Committee members began to say such things as: "I think we can learn something from this kind of study." "We don't have anything to hide."

Ponzi said that the Executive Committee would decide whether to attend a Liaison Committee meeting after Alderfer had left.

July 27, 1970

Alderfer called Ponzi and learned that the Committee had decided to go the next step in exploring the study.

August 3, 1970

The researchers met subsequently with Speer, Graham, and Willow at the company offices. Alderfer and Lewicki wanted to begin selecting management representatives for the Liaison Committee. The researchers specified that a number of candidates who would be acceptable to both the union and the company be suggested and a number of names were listed.

Prodded by the researchers, Speer discussed the other consulting groups who were already working in the plants. A description of those programs—one was the elimination and redefinition of jobs through an inventory control program, a second was the reevaluation of the wages attached to particular jobs—led the researchers to understand the distress expressed by the union at the meeting with Alderfer. However, the company indicated that these programs were near termination.

The researchers left after suggesting that a meeting be held with the candidates, that the researchers attend this meeting to discuss the study, and that the representatives be chosen by a group decision. Our overriding feeling was one of acting as a third force in the relationship: we were trying to suppress the company's tendency to overdetermine the format and goals of the study while encouraging the union to consider entry into the research setting. We felt good about the company's desire to minimize win-lose bargaining tactics at the Liaison Committee, their willingness to devise a study beneficial to both parties, and their candor in describing current consulting programs, but when we suggested that the Liaison Committee meeting be held in the union hall Speer said, "We have to keep this thing balanced."

August 20, 1970

A meeting held at the company was attended by the researchers, Speer, Willow, and eight company men suggested at the August 3rd meeting. Speer reviewed the strike and its impact on the company; Lewicki and Alderfer described the history of the study, its possible rewards and costs for each group, and the potential functioning of the Liaison Committee. Participation among group members was high; a number of people actively questioned the researchers and discussed the study. Concern that the study could backfire and "open up old wounds" was expressed, and the researchers were asked how they could maintain credibility to both sides. Guidelines for selecting the company representatives on the Liaison Committee and topics for intensive focus in the study were suggested. After considerable discussion the researchers left with a commitment that the group would select representatives.

We felt considerably better about the company after this meeting, particularly with respect to Speer's behavior. His description of the history of the project had been accurate and complete. Our fears that he would attempt to dominate the meeting were not confirmed; the other group members (his subordinates) appeared to be willing to talk and to disagree with him. Moreover, this was the first time that we had obtained a variety of company views on the causes and problems of the strike. Though many men at the meeting indicated that they had not been close to the actual negotiations and had gained most of their information from company newsletters and mass media, different perspectives and ideas were voiced. Finally, Speer publicly expressed his confidence in the competence of the researchers. This was the first explicit indication that he was willing to trust our judgment in the design and execution of the research.

August 21, 1970

Willow called to say that the company group was in favor of the study and had selected four representatives: Graham and three other men who were at the meeting (all of whom held middle-level management positions at the company).

Early September 1970

Through contacts with the union and the company groups we settled on September 22, 1970, for the first Liaison Committee meeting.

September 16, 1970

A telephone call to the union Local about the upcoming meeting suggested that the union might be substantially less democratic than we had thought. In contradiction to our assumption that the Executive Committee had selected representatives at its July 24 meeting after Alderfer had left, Ponzi indicated that the Local had not yet chosen its representatives and that he and Kirby would make the decision. Because Ponzi had been told which representatives the company had selected, it was possible that union representatives were chosen to match them.

THE LIAISON COMMITTEE MEETING

September 22, 1970

The Liaison Committee meeting was held in a large conference room in a building near the company's major plant and commonly used by both union and management people. Lewicki and Alderfer, arriving first, took seats in the middle of the length of the table, on opposite sides. As the members appeared (three company people first, then four union people, and last the fourth company person), they took seats with other members of their group. When everyone was seated, Lewicki and Alderfer were situated at opposite ends of an imaginary net through the center of the table, the two groups lined up on either side. No other seating arrangement could have more dramatically reflected the competitiveness between them or the third-party role of the researchers.

We had prepared an agenda, which was distributed to each person. It proposed to review the history of the project, the possible research foci, and the role of the Liaison Committee; for example, influencing research topics, interview samples, dissemination of the research findings, and determining how the study would begin and end. Copies of the April 22 letter to Sanders and the June 2 letter to Speer were also made available.

The researchers began the meeting by asking if a tape recorder could be used. Kirby objected, but others indicated agreement if the tape were kept confidential.

After the tape began, Lewicki and Alderfer reviewed the history of the project. Kirby stated that the union had decided to attend this meeting to gather more data and to make a decision about its participation. When asked by Graham how the union was going to collect these "data," Kirby replied that the people would "formulate some opinions as to whether or not we recommend to the rest of the Executive Board going ahead with this program as a result of this meeting."

Kirby questioned the proposed interview sample for the first study. He seemed strongly concerned that the company would not permit top management or stockholders to be interviewed. Lewicki explained that the Liaison Committee would determine both the size of the sample and its representative character. Alderfer stipulated that one of the main functions of the Committee was to keep all parties "honest."

Kirby asked for the company's reasons for initiating the study. Graham answered that, following the strike, "We readily admitted that maybe the company is making mistakes in its approach to labor relations and collective bargaining." The company people were interested in discovering the factors that caused the strike and labor relations problems in the local plant and other plants throughout the country. They were willing to work on the "two-pronged approach" suggested by the researchers—to study the strike *and* current relations.

Kirby responded that he wondered why the company had taken this route. Why, he asked Graham, couldn't the company people approach the union and begin a dialogue on those very issues? Graham answered that the company people didn't feel ready to begin the dialogue without the research as a vehicle. Kirby agreed that the union probably wasn't ready for it either. "The union would have some natural fears. A study such as this is not as simple as the way it was just laid out." "But," said Kirby, "there is one big fear [among the union]—that you just might want to have this study to improve on your technique next time."

At this point another company representative said that he believed the two issues were central to the meeting—avoidance of a "management only" study and the provision of data useful to both sides. The researchers agreed that this was the stated aim and both Kirby and Ponzi acknowledged it as the research goal.

Kirby then offered another major objection on the union's part: the study did not mesh with the current job design and wage evaluation programs, which were perceived by the union as major threats to job security and current wage scales.

> I can tell you what I told [a company manager] just the other day, said Kirby. I have a feeling that every time I leave a meeting that we're just farther apart—you know—all of our meetings with the company personnel people. . . . Our own people are wrestling with this right now, he continued, and acceptance of this type of thing [the study] is awfully hard for them to digest in the place of their everyday practical experience.

Graham responded that, regardless of the conditions in the local plants which polarized the two sides in the past,

> they shouldn't cast any kind of shadow over the success of the research job that we want to do. . . . I don't believe that some of these things are going to go away immediately. . . .I don't look at [the study] as a short-range panacea for all labor problems, but we hope to be in business for a long time—if we are, *you* will be.

Kirby asked to have that last statement in writing and the meeting erupted in laughter.

Kirby took this as an indication of management's commitment and turned to the composition of the interview sample. A rather lengthy discussion followed. The union clearly wanted to ensure that top management people, perceived as key to the strike activities, were included. Kirby returned to this issue later in the meeting.

After discussing dissemination of the research findings, Alderfer laid down several ground rules for the research: the researchers would not identify individuals by name; the findings would be used by the participants; confidentiality would be maintained, because only generalized findings would be submitted to academic journals, and although the company and union people could review them before publication any interpretation of the data made by the researchers would be unalterable by the parties. This led Kirby to question whether the researchers were unbiased and to ask their opinions of strikes and unions.

Alderfer and Lewicki gave detailed descriptions of their biases and predispositions. Both indicated that they were not biased toward unions or management, were unopposed to strikes, and thought that management should also have the right to strike. Both indicated that they were often under pressure because of their work with both sides, particularly from many students who felt that their efforts were directed at helping a system that should be more radically changed. Both were committed to improving the organizational effectiveness and conflict resolution of union and company groups. Although neither had direct experience in labor-management relations, both felt that their work with other organizations was directly relevant and applicable. A description of some of those experiences seemed to satisfy both groups. (There were no verbal confirmations, however.) We felt that this was a key interchange in developing union and management trust in us, though it was clearly not an item on our own agenda.

A company representative asked the union when it could make a decision. Ponzi replied:

> We should come up with something soon. We have already talked about it with the [Executive] Board, so it is not too much for them. There is a Board meeting tonight, so we should have some clear-cut decision by the end of the week or early next week.

The company indicated that it was already committed and needed no further time.

Ponzi asked if the researchers planned to use the findings to write a textbook case on labor relations. The researchers responded that the initial plan was to collect data to help both union and management; although the data might be used to write scholarly articles, they would not take the form of "do's and don'ts" for labor relations. Many voiced the opinion that how-to-do-it textbooks on negotiations were worthless and the researchers emphasized that this was not their intention.

Kirby indicated that he had no further questions. Ponzi then made a statement (almost inaudible on the tape) that the union would have to take the study to the membership as a general policy procedure to make sure that the members knew what was going on and to give them an opportunity to voice objections if they did not want to participate in the interviews or questionnaires. Lewicki does not remember hearing this statement at all; Alderfer, although acknowledging that he heard it, did not confront Ponzi with these new data about the union's method of decision making. In view of the union's clearly stressing several times during the meeting that the Executive Committee would make the decision, the researcher may have perceived this membership review as a perfunctory rubber stamp to the Executive Committee's approval.

Repeating an unanswered question that Alderfer had raised earlier and assuming that the union would approve the study, Lewicki asked if a tentative date could be set for another meeting. Kirby replied that he believed it would be "pretty presumptuous" and stated that it would be easy to set up another meeting if the union decided affirmatively. The meeting then ended.

September 29, 1970

Ponzi called Alderfer to inform him that the general membership of the Local had voted "no." Ponzi said that a strong level of mistrust prevailed among the membership because of the job-design and wage-evaluation programs being conducted by the company. We were surprised, particularly because we did not remember Ponzi's statement that the entire membership had to approve the study. It had become apparent to us that each time we thought the local union was committed Ponzi and Kirby submitted decisions to a larger decision-making body.

September 29, 1970

Alderfer called Graham to report the union's decision. Graham expressed disappointment and said that he would check into it in an attempt to gain more information.

October 7, 1970

Lewicki discussed the union's decision with Graham who felt that it was the result of the job-design and wage-evaluation programs, a large decrease in the company's business, which was causing massive lay-offs, plant closings and poor morale among the workers, and an internal split in the union Executive Committee over leadership personalities and style. He noted that a union election would be held early in 1971 and suggested that a change in leadership might lead to more favorable conditions for the study.

He also stated that the Executive Committee of the Lodge had presented the study at a membership meeting on September 27, the first union meeting in several months with a quorum. There were many items on the agenda. The study was outlined briefly by the Executive Committee, received casual and limited discussion, and was voted down.

October 15, 1970

At their request, the researchers met with Ponzi and Kirby to discuss errors that might have caused the project's demise. Before this meeting the researchers had prepared a number of possible "strategic errors" to test out.

After beginning with some open-ended questions, the investigators attempted to explore several specific issues. In response to the general questions about why the study didn't happen, Kirby and Ponzi replied that management had been the primary cause: the company's job design and wage evaluation programs, layoffs and perceived violations of the latest contract settlement.

To a degree, the union seemed (perhaps unconsciously) to class us with the other outsiders who had been brought in by management and who had worked against union objectives. When actually asked whether they trusted us, however, the union people replied that they had looked for signs that we couldn't be trusted but had not found them. Particularly significant were the answers to questions about how we felt about strikes and the labor movement. Although they trusted us not to be harmful, they did not see us as likely to be helpful either. Kirby indicated that if we really could contribute something the union leaders could do their jobs better. He did not believe that.

Both leaders said that they fully expected management to use the findings against the union and against members of management, who would be "purged" as a result of the company's losses in the strike.

Kirby acknowledged that not taking us to meet the membership was a deliberate strategy, employed to reduce the likelihood that the membership would support the research. He revealed that he and Ponzi could probably have "sold" the study if they had wished to, but for all the foregoing reasons they were not in favor of endorsing the research until there was some evidence that management was more trustworthy.

They also indicated that we might have been more successful if we had spent more time with union people. Kirby said that it had been a severe mistake to acknowledge that management had initiated the study, but both stated that nothing at the Liaison meeting, such as the tapes or the data proposal, had hurt the study's chances. In the final analysis it came down to their relations with the company; they were not about to give in to anything management wanted until some of their own initiatives had been met. They acknowledged that a study might be possible at some future date if management became more responsive.

December 11, 1970

The researchers also held a meeting with Speer, Graham, and Willow to discuss steps that the researchers could have taken to save the project, asking the same questions they had raised with the union. Management felt that spending more time with the union would probably have ameliorated the "management" stigma on the researchers. They also maintained that approaching the union through Sanders was still more acceptable (to them) than any attempt to reach Local officers. They did not feel, in spite of Kirby's statement to the contrary, that involvement by any of Speer's superiors, such as the group vice president or the president of the company, would have influenced the union's position.

The management group remained actively interested in doing a research study and planned to communicate with the new Executive Committee after the elections. They also felt that after months of plant closings and layoffs business would soon begin to prosper again. Finally, they were now less interested in reasons for the strike (and attempting to recapture data at least two years old) and much more committed to exploring current and future relations between the union and management groups. They also suggested a management-only study to provide answers for the management group.

CONCEPTUALIZING THE EVENTS

What is to be learned from this case? The researcher of intergroup behavior can examine the research negotiations as an intergroup event to capture in microcosm the long-term relations between the parties. The action-interventionist can raise a series of normative questions about the strategy and tactics of the third party in this setting. Could we have brought the two parties together or was the tension between them too great to permit our entry? Each of these questions is explored in detail.

Research Negotiations as a Microcosm

The difficulties we faced on entry seemed to indicate a suicidal struggle between two warring groups. To a certain degree our difficulties serve as a mirror of the social system's functioning, a microcosm of the relations between the groups; for example, restricted communication, distorted perceptions of one another, different leadership practices, and some special characteristics of the union.

Restricted Communication with the Researchers. Although the union leaders told us that we could have helped our case by spending more time with them, they did little to make this possible. The one time in which the Local leadership took the initiative in calling us was to say that the membership had voted down the study.

There was no written communication from labor or management to the researchers except the one brief note from Speer to Lewicki. That document, it will be recalled, gave some indication of the company's orientation toward the strike and suggested that its view of the study was a narrower and more tactical one than the investigators'. Probably neither labor nor management was willing to commit itself in writing for fear of being held to something it would later regret. Meanwhile the researchers drafted several letters and proposals which were shared with both sides.

Both the union and management held back certain strategic information from the investigators. Management informed us about the wage evaluation and job design activities from the company only when we asked why the union was so upset about current events. Although they did not describe it in quite those terms, the union team seemed to see management's strategy as combining both "carrot and stick"; they made it plain that they were not about to bite the carrot until the stick was laid down.

In one tactic persistently used by the union immediate decisions were avoided by consulting with a larger group of members *without* informing the investigators or inviting them to be present. The Local leadership discussed matters with their Executive Committee before ever seeing the researchers. After the Liaison meeting the union group conferred with the active membership without inviting the investigators.

Distorted Perceptions of Each Party by the Other. Consistent with what is known about intergroup relations (Blake, Shepard, and Mouton, 1964; Sherif, 1966), our conversations with either party alone tended to evoke negative stereotypes of the other. The managers found it easy to impugn the motives (seeking political power) and competence (weak leadership) of the union. Similarly, the union tended to see management as untrustworthy and out to take advantage of "the little man." Neither seemed willing to examine the ways in which it had behaved to worsen relations, but both groups did tentatively offer some openness. The union leadership claimed to be willing to talk with management at any time about *current* problems. Management, in the researchers' presence and at the Liaison meeting, acknowledged that it had made mistakes *in the strike* and wanted to learn from them. It would not be too farfetched to suggest that the union leaders believed they had "won" the strike and had no desire to examine that perception, whereas management felt that it was "gaining" by employing work-design consultants and felt no urgency to open that matter for discussion.

In hope of finding some way to bring the two parties together, the researchers may have too quickly seized on any signs of openness from either party. We never fully determined whether those signs were mutually compatible and thus conducive to building a productive relationship.

Different Leadership Practices. In all our contacts with the union we faced a dual leadership team: Kirby, the International representative, and Ponzi, the Local president. Those two men were quite different in style and mode of interaction. Kirby was younger, more talkative, and took a more challenging stance in our discussions. His comments were more confrontative of the researchers than supportive of the interests of the Local membership. He seemed to enjoy conflict and showed great confidence in his approach. Ponzi, on the other hand, was more reserved and less active. He never really directly challenged the researchers, but he did occasionally comment on how the Executive Committee felt or how the members reacted. Unlike Kirby, he seemed to enjoy and to suffer the various grievances and problems he had to handle as president. For Kirby the company management seemed to be a respected, though mistrusted, adversary: it was "the competition." Ponzi's image of management seemed to be that of a feudal lord who exploited his serfs. He seemed the angrier of the two, though more oblique in expressing his feelings. Kirby was tall, trim, and athletic looking; Ponzi was shorter and heavier. We came to believe that Kirby was the more dominant of the two. Although there were never directly observable data, we began to believe that the imbalanced interaction pattern between the two might be a source of discomfort for Ponzi. Was Kirby so active because Ponzi had asked for help or because the International was doubtful about the latter's performance?

The leadership pattern in the managerial team was quite different: three clear levels were apparent. Speer was the highest ranking, the most active, and the most confronting member. The other members spoke less often, less forcefully, and more tentatively. Graham was present more often and spoke more frequently than Willow. The hierarchy among the three contained little ambiguity; whatever this interaction pattern may have lost in terms of flexibility, it gained in effective coordination and sustained pursuit of purpose.

We were never sure whether the union was more democratic than management. Their rhetoric contained more democratic language, but their leaders' behavior produced mixed messages—sometimes increasing members' involvement and sometimes decreasing it. Management, on the other hand, did not speak the language of democracy: their job was to manage the company as well as they could. When prodded by the researchers, they cooperated in broadening the range of participants in the research project discussion and in actively encouraging that it be open. We had no way of knowing what practices they used when the researchers were not present, except when they told us, and it was apparent that they told us less than everything relevant to the research negotiations. They never asked us what they might do, on a day-to-day basis, to increase the probability of the study. They told us about the job design activities only when we asked.

Special Union Characteristics. Throughout the research negotiations the union was reluctant to engage us, despite our efforts to make the study's potential risks and benefits approximately the same for both labor and management. One could argue that the union (or union officers) had some interest in maintaining the perception that it was a "management study." On leaving the final meeting with Kirby and Ponzi, we asked them if they would be willing to reopen discussions if management made some changes. Kirby responded positively. Perhaps the desire to use acceptance of the study as a bargaining point was related to a sense of powerlessness among the union leadership.

A number of examples in the research literature suggest that it is not uncommon for the union to be the more reluctant party in efforts to bring labor and management together. As the low power group in the formal organization, a strike, or the threat of a strike, is its most powerful weapon. To begin to cooperate with management they must not only accept its trustworthiness but also their own competence to conduct an open and informal interaction. Ponzi and Kirby told us that they could not afford to believe that we could offer a new approach because that would mean that they could be doing their jobs better, thereby implying that they had doubts about their own competence. More importantly, they were reluctant to face the possibility that they had something to learn. It may be that the level of self-esteem among many union leaders is chronically so low that they are not ready to face the turbulance of new ventures without considerable reassurance from those with whom they are cooperating. Solomon (1971) has reported experiences that support this point.

Behavior of Researchers as Third Party

From the outset of our work on this project it was apparent that the reason why the study was potentially useful to all parties might also be the reason why it could not be done: relations between union and management was so conflictual that any effort to become a legitimate third party would be impossible. Once we decided to develop a relationship with the parties our task became that of building for ourselves the attributes of a useful third party (Walton, 1969). Critical issues in this effort involved establishing ourselves as neutral in the labor-management conflict, building trust among the parties, establishing our competence, and (for our own well-being) deciding when these tasks were impossible.

Problems with Neutrality. Ample data indicate that the researchers' entry into the union-management relationship was strongly linked with the management position. In spite of our continuous attempts to portray ourselves as the neutral third party, the union persisted in seeing us as company spies. Alderfer was confronted with this at the meeting with the Executive Committee and it surfaced again at the Liaison and post-Liaison meetings with Ponzi and Kirby.

We readily admitted that the initiative for the study came from management. Although this could have been considered an indication of management's willingness to begin a more trusting relationship, the union's interpretation was quite different. The union believed that we were one more group of consultants, who under the guise of "research" were going to attempt to gather data to bolster management's posture for the next round of contract talks. Because the union felt they had "won" the last round and because they were angry with the job-design and wage-evaluation consultants, they felt no strong justification to trust us.

The implications for the third-party behavior are not clear. On the one hand, we could have sacrificed honesty for expediency and told the union that the study was the researchers' idea. One would quickly argue, however, that this is scarcely appropriate as part of an intervention strategy to promote openness and trust.

Building Trust and Establishing Competence. We struggled with devising ways to increase the level of trust between the parties. We tried to make our objectives explicit, yet not force either party toward steps it was not prepared to take. Trust is easier to destroy than to build, and it was not clear that either party had ever experienced it with the other. We sometimes wonder whether the parties would recognize a change if one occurred or whether they wanted to change at all.

We attempted to increase the level of trust between ourselves and the parties several times. Our request to meet with the union Executive Committee was one attempt. This gesture seemed to produce the intended effect of persuading the union to consider the project more carefully. Our proposed criterion for the selection of representatives to the Liaison meeting was a second effort: they should be trusted by both groups and influential in their own. As the foregoing data suggest, we were able to influence management more than the union.

The Liaison meeting was another opportunity for trust building. The tape recorder was openly discussed before it was used. Although Kirby objected initially, using the occasion as an opportunity to accuse everyone else of being mistrustful, everyone present did agree to record the session if confidentiality were protected. The quality of the interaction at the Liaison meeting suggested to us the possibility of building a joint relationship. Most of the issues raised privately by the union were repeated publicly and management seemed genuinely responsive to them. The liaison meeting, as a testing ground for further trust development, seemed to work—but it didn't. Why not?

One reason may have been that neither the researchers nor management adequately pressed the union for a commitment to the next steps. The union leaders had asked so many questions—and had received responsive answers—that it was difficult to believe that they were not convinced. Yet no one asked much of them in the immediate situation; the suggestion to set a date for another Liaison meeting was rejected by Kirby and was pursued neither by management nor the researchers. The researchers said that they needed commitment eventually but asked for none in the short run. Perhaps the researchers should have asked for an immediate evaluation of the Liaison meeting and a definition from the union leaders of their next steps (to see whether the researchers should ask again to attend a meeting of a wider range of union members). An immediate evaluation would have revealed invalid perceptions of the climate of the meeting and would also put the two groups on record in front of each other. A definition of next steps would have enabled us to initiate interaction with a broader cross section of the union, if that were a prerequisite to moving ahead.

One of the many paradoxes in this study is the recognition that self-perceived competence may not be a universal blessing. We obtained some clear indication from the management group that Speer had confidence in our ability. Stated directly at the meeting to select management's committee members, this view was first shown indirectly when management-group members willingly accepted our suggestions for structuring the project. The union never said anything about their perception of our competence until we asked them, and they then remarked that they could not really afford to see us as competent because that would mean that they could do their own jobs better. This suggests that a party must at some level recognize the need for help before he can see a third party as able to help. Certainly we did not exhaust all possibilities in demonstrating competence to the union, but neither did it provide us with many opportunities.

Perseverance in the Union-Management Relationship. If the first question to be asked is, "how do you enter?" the second is, "how do you know when to leave?" Many readers of this case study will argue that the researchers would never have been brash enough to assume that they could work effectively in this situation. Others might have attempted the intervention but would then have read the handwriting on the wall when the Executive Committee first rejected the study.

Argyris (1970) suggests that a client who initiates a relationship with a consultant should be committed to accept the interventionist's strategy and techniques for working through the problems. Obviously the client-consultant relationship requires that both sides negotiate the working conditions and agree to terms that will not ignore the needs, desires, or standards of either group. If this commitment is absent, the interventionist has the choice of leaving or trying to obtain it.

In this case the union was clearly uncommitted from the outset, and the company's commitment was renegotiated as the relationship with the researchers developed. The researchers assumed that the union viewed the strike as a losing situation, that they would be interested in gaining information about their own dynamics during the strike, and that building better relations with management was a desirable goal. Whether the union actually suffered from the strike was difficult to establish; the union never admitted it, and Sanders' analysis was that the union was "one-up" on management. Although cooperation with management was desirable, the union perceived it as a long-range goal that demanded a number of preliminary concessions from management. Thus the union was locked into the competitive bargaining process, intent on maintaining a hard-line position until the company demonstrated an overwhelming sincerity in trust building.

DIFFERENCES BETWEEN INTERPERSONAL AND INTERGROUP NEGOTIATIONS

Much of what we have discussed so far seems as relevant to interpersonal peacemaking as it does to intergroup conflict resolution. One of the major outcomes of this adventure is a greater understanding of how intergroup negotiations differ from interpersonal confrontation. Most issues relevant to interpersonal relations also supply to intergroup relations, but there is a host of additional considerations: group dynamics are not the same as individual dynamics.

Negotiators Are Group Representatives

The individuals we dealt with during the year in which we attempted entry were group leaders as well; thus their roles as individuals were always in some jeopardy. The managers we dealt with all knew that the chief management negotiator during the strike had been fired because he had performed so poorly. The union leaders also knew it and it sometimes led them to question whether the managers who volunteered for the committee were aware of the risk they were taking. From management, whose perceptions on such matters were obviously open to question, we heard that the union was internally split over who should be Local president. Some people felt that Kirby's primary role might be to replace Ponzi with a "stronger" leader; we did learn after the project had died that the union had chosen a new leader at the next election.

Another facet of the group role is the barrier that it creates for developing a trustful relationship with an outsider. The group leader knows that the third party is interested in him initially because of his position and secondarily because of his individuality. Thus it will probably take longer, require more energy, and demand more proof for genuine trust to develop.

Hierarchical Concerns Among the Parties

Because groups were involved in the negotiations, the issues of relative authority, status, and resources did not pertain only to the people we encountered but also reflected their groups. We wanted to do as much as we could to equalize their situational power (Walton, 1969), but this turned out to be a more complex undertaking than it usually is for interpersonal conflict resolution. On the surface management seemed to be far more able to afford the study than the union, but although Sanders put money at the Local's disposal to pay for the study the union never acknowledged it to the researchers.

Our affiliation with a nearby university may have increased the hazards of our relations with both parties, but probably more so with the union. The usual town-gown tensions were present, and it was not uncommon for Oak City politicians to remind the city that the university was tax exempt and therefore benefited from, without paying for, its municipal location. Ponzi held a local political office.

The union and management were complex organizations with multiple levels of authority. We therefore faced the dilemma of choice of level to initiate contact. Argyris (1970, p. 271) suggests that

> if the interventionist is to have the best possible opportunity to help the client system generate valid information, make free and informed choices, and develop internal commitment, he should strive to begin at the highest levels in the organization necessary to accomplish these tasks.

Two major strategic mistakes may have been made. First, although the researchers did secure the approval of the union's top management (Sanders and Brown), we did not use their enthusiasm for the project to help influence Kirby and Ponzi. Sanders' lack of pressure on the Local was reflective of his managerial style—to permit a large degree of autonomy in its operations and decision making—but we might have asked him to join a meeting to discuss the matter. Not having involved Speer and his superiors more actively may have been a second omission. Such involvement would have assuaged Kirby's fears, expressed at the Liaison meeting, that the company's top management was uncommitted and unwilling to supply data. We assumed that Speer had secured top management approval and did not realize that

Kirby would view it as a problem, although he had not mentioned it as a major factor for ultimately rejecting the study.

We might also have insisted on a joint meeting between Sanders and Brown and top company management. The relations between those parties appeared somewhat less conflictual than the interrelations between Graham-Willow and Kirby-Ponzi. That Speer initially approached Sanders and not Kirby or Ponzi to test the idea of the research was no accident. We felt that he was more comfortable talking to Sanders.

The Researchers as a Group

The research interventionists also had both internal and external group dynamics to manage. Some, such as those mentioned above, pertained to our university affiliation and left us little choice (except the option to conceal it), but others allowed for more active choices.

Both researchers were behavioral scientists in the same academic department. Alderfer was more experienced in executing the format of research that we originally proposed to the groups. Lewicki was therefore willing to defer to his judgment at several critical points.

Perhaps their clearest stylistic difference was that Alderfer was more specific in his conception of the interventionist role and more demanding in the relative commitments required from union and management. Lewicki, on the other hand, was more willing to trust the intentions of the two groups and to proceed with the study, even if the researchers had to compromise certain goals and standards. Lewicki was afraid that Alderfer would be too hardnosed in his demands that the union and management conform to the researchers' specifications for the study and that it would therefore not be done. Alderfer was afraid that Lewicki would be so conciliatory that the researchers would eventually collude with one or both groups in a destructive manner.

Although these differences were present, the general strategy included frequent discussion and division of labor. Lewicki went to visit Sanders; Alderfer attended the union Executive Committee meeting. Alderfer thereafter tended to maintain the interface with the union, whereas Lewicki was the primary contact with management. Both spent a great deal of time together discussing impressions, sharing feelings, planning agenda, and reviewing their own commitments to the research.

We were also committed to a program of research that sought to collect data for our own benefit as well as for theirs. It is difficult to say how much our research role directly conflicted with our third-party role. In developing the research, we spent little time with the union early in the negotiations; we assumed that those interactions would take place when the study was approved. Had we acted more as third-party consultants concerned only with the relations between the parties and not with our research as well, we might have met with the union immediately and behaved quite differently. We might have approached Sanders or Ponzi ourselves rather than letting Speer do it. We might then have spent time informally sounding out Ponzi, Kirby, and the Executive Committee. On the other hand, we were continually confronted by the union with questions such as "what is in the project for us?" Dropping the research objective would have left us with no obvious motivation except "to help." Would this have been believed even if it were true? Could we have taken this stance?

CONCLUSIONS

This retrospective analysis helps us to understand our mistakes, but it does not solve the dilemma for the third party who might be interested in responding to the pleas of one side in a conflict. It is convenient to state that the two sides should collaboratively call in a third party, but there are many conflict settings in which this type of mutuality is absent, particularly those conflicts that are the most complicated, most intense, and require a third party's skills. It is also convenient to say that the researcher may have to work as a mediator or process consultant before the research can begin; but then how can we capture data on this critical phase of reversing the competitive cycle between the two parties?

We can offer two suggestions to help avoid these difficulties. The first, in response to entry into the setting, states that if a third party is approached by one of the groups in conflict he should make contact as quickly as possible with the other party. The third party should make the contact and should do so even before exposing himself to any history of or data on the difficulties between the two sides. Although this is still not ideal (in that the third party does not approach the groups simultaneously without previous communication), it offers the immediate opportunity to test and establish the third party's neutrality. The third party should explore and confront any perceptions of his bias and extend an offer to both sides to engage in an initial contact with the researcher.

The second suggestion is that the combined researcher-interventionist may have to sacrifice his research goals for short-run gain. While establishing a relationship between the two sides he may have to spend his time meeting with the parties and establishing their trust in him: his competence to work in this setting, his willingness to listen, to be impartial, to protect the interests of both sides, and to work toward mutually beneficial confrontations between the parties. Data generated during those sessions can be observed and recorded for later incorporation into a more formal (Walton, 1969) research model.

II

CHANGE

"Almost no one save for some cynics and cranks, would argue with the goal of humanizing bureaucracy," begins Warren Bennis. But William Crockett writes, "I know that bringing change to such an institution—to its processes, organization, attitudes, objectives, and way of life—is neither casual nor automatic nor easy." Between these views lies the optimism that initiates many change efforts and the sharp realities that change agents and organizations must contend with along the way. Both Bennis and Crockett share this common recognition, as do the other authors in this section. Their optimism is apparent in the change technologies they describe; their appreciation of the problems is evident in the errors they report.

Planned change in America has a long and complicated history dating to the early planners and social architects that formed and shaped our institutions. Social science involvement in the processes of planned change has a much shorter history, though seemingly as complex. The roots of their involvement, as Benne, Bennis, and Chin (1961) note, lay in the ideological controversies at the turn of the century. At that time social scientists, notably Ward and Sumner, considered whether they should attempt to shape history or let history take its course. That they debated this matter affirmed their rejection of predestination. With that rejection, and the passage of time, social scientists soon immersed themselves in the "planning of change."

Kurt Lewin (1945), in his first description of the purposes of the Research Center for Group Dynamics, gave birth to the "applied science of change." He wrote:

> In the field of social management, we are just awakening to the fact that a better knowledge is needed than the day-by-day experience tradition and memory of an individual or a social group can provide. . . . We need understanding on a scientific level. . . . There are increasing symptoms that leading practitioners in government, in agriculture, in industry, in education, in community life are becoming aware that the statement "nothing is as practical as a good theory" holds also in the field of social management (p. 129).

These were bold words, yet they were tempered by a cautious and experimental approach to change. At that time planned change was a fledgling science, borne in an orthodox scientific community. Thus the early change efforts were carefully monitored and thoughtfully evaluated. The early successes (Coch and French, 1948) gave the field vision and virility; the early failures (French, Israel, and Ås, 1960) lent it temperance and stability.

These early change efforts were paralleled by both successful and unsuccessful endeavors. In 1947 Bradford, Benne, and Lippit, guided by Lewin, developed the T-group laboratory approach to change. One year later Floyd Mann began experimenting with the survey feedback technology, administering surveys to employees and feeding back the data through an "interlocking chain of conferences." Shortly thereafter Eric Trist and Kenneth Bamforth began their study of autonomous work groups in the coal-mining industry. In this section we continue this early tradition, carefully monitoring and thoughtfully evaluating the strengths and limitations of these change technologies as they are being applied today.

This section begins with an essay in which Clayton Alderfer and David Berg cast a critical eye on the organization development profession and the various "types" of OD practitioner. Following an analysis of its history and current state, the authors present a conceptual scheme based on open systems theory to compare OD with the traditional professions of law and medicine. The result is an illuminating look at the profession and practice of organization development. In their words, "the diversity of the field is at once its strength and weakness." Thus the challenge to all of us is to begin some professional development in OD. Alderfer and Berg's often provocative discourse on what might be termed "the adolescence of OD" concludes with some broad recommendations for the future of the profession.

In the first case in this section William Crockett, then in a top administrative office in the Department of State, describes the beginning of his experiences with change when, summoned to the office of Attorney General Robert Kennedy, he was told:

> Get your job straight. The State Department must be made loyal and responsive to the President. It must become more positive and proactive. It must be made to assume a leadership position in the foreign affairs community. Your job is to make this happen.

Thus began his odyssey from Theory X management to a Theory Y approach to change.

Crockett describes his early efforts to develop a system to coordinate and monitor foreign policy decisions, to develop a policy council and programming system, and to guide the Department toward leadership in the foreign affairs community. He recalls that some of his efforts were successful, "when the change was not too complex and the authority was without challenge. . . ." Others were failures "because of the *way* we went about bringing them into being . . . rather than because of their lack of merit."

Crockett's case reports the excitement and frustration, the commitment and resistance, and the success and failures of the OD effort that followed. It concludes with an incisive review of the lessons: guides to administrators, organizations, students, and anyone else interested in learning from change.

The next case is Warren Bennis' "autopsy" of a T-group change effort that terminated. Accompanied by his tape recorder, Bennis interviewed the president of a Swiss service industry, the trainers, the head of the training department, and some of the participants, all in an effort to dissect the failure. He captures their contrasting stories: between the president's management philosophy and the goals of the training effort, between the president's understanding of the change project and the training directors expectations for it, and between the excitement of some of the participants and the fears of others. Bennis begins the case with a concise review of the goals and processes of T-group change. He ends it with some propositions about the use of lab training, and concludes:

> If I have tended to highlight the dilemmas and risks, I do so with the hope that the recognition of these choice points in initiating and maintaining similar change programs will enhance their effectiveness.

In the third case in this section Susan Mohrman, Allan Mohrman, Robert Cooke, and Robert Duncan report on a survey feedback and problem-solving experience in a suburban school district. Extending the work of previous survey efforts in schools, they created multilevel problem-solving groups among teachers and principals in the district and trained some of the group members in the "process guidance" skills necessary for " 'opening' the group and ensuring that all members participate in the problem solving and change activities."

Their efforts were successful, in some schools at least, but in others the change effort was sabotaged by a hostile environment, an "old guard," and the emergence of an antiprincipal subgroup. The authors thoughtfully review these troubles, contrasting them with the successes while considering what they might have done to reverse them. They discuss the merits of school surveys, the development of problem-solving groups, and the "fit" between the teachers' values and the goals of survey technology. There is rich learning here for both practitioners and researchers.

The final case represents two researchers' analysis of job enrichment failure, "the case of change that wasn't." Linda Frank and Richard Hackman describe a change effort intended to create autonomous work groups among stock department employees of a large metropolitan bank. They consider the project with the analytic tools of researchers and with the reflective distance of observers. For those interested in the process and conduct of third-party evaluations this case provides a sound but subtle example. For those concerned with the dilemmas of work enrichment the authors describe the problems of creating semiautonomous work groups: the need for cross training, system diagnosis, and contingency planning.

In summing up, Frank and Hackman discuss the limitations of work enrichment theories, the difficulties of meaningfully enriching jobs, and the inability of the third-party researchers to "take a learning orientation to work redesign projects" by assuming the "costs of adopting an open, evaluative stance."

The essays and cases in this section give us a valuable look at past errors, but, more importantly, they define new directions for organization development and change. The beginning essay in this section calls for a new profession of change; the ending case recommends a new approach to evaluation. The difficulties of bringing change to a government agency and a school system are reviewed, tempered by an appreciation that some parts of the agency and some schools in the district enjoyed a successful period of change. That the authors in this section can learn from both their successes and failures, each in his or her own way as change agents, external evaluators, and project directors, should stimulate the current thinking and future learning of others as well.

4

Organization Development: The Profession and the Practitioner

CLAYTON P. ALDERFER
DAVID N. BERG

Essential to any serious field of human endeavor is the capacity to learn from errors. The opening chapter of this book contains a discussion of the social conditions, including norms and values, that make the public or private examination of OD failures so uncommon. It is possible to explain away this partially alienated relation of OD practitioners to their work by emphasizing the power of conditions external to the field, such as the American culture. However valid this view (and we believe it has great significance), it is not enough. There are also reasons internal to the field itself why OD is practiced as it is. This essay presents our analysis of those reasons.

We begin with an assumption—that OD can become more professional. The first section sets out our definition of "profession." This perspective is informed by our experience as scholars and practitioners. The second section presents a typology of OD practitioners. It lists and analyzes the variety of roles that today characterizes the field of OD. The third section presents a natural history of the key conflicts in the field. Here we attempt to understand how polarization around a number of crucial issues has influenced the field to become what it is. The fourth section brings a theoretical orientation for explaining the field of OD. It provides a set of concepts for understanding the nature of OD as a social system. The last section employs the preceding analysis to make some prescriptions for improving the state of OD.

Based on conversations with colleagues, we anticipate that some readers within OD will view this presentation as excessively critical. As members of the field we care deeply about the state of current affairs. There is no doubt in our minds that there is an increasing recognition that OD, *if practiced competently,* makes an important contribution to its major objectives: improving the effectiveness of organizations and enhancing human welfare of system members. There is less hope for the field, however, if it is unable to practice on itself what it seems to promote among clients. Intensive self-scrutiny is rarely easy, always painful, and never complete. However difficult it is, we hope this chapter contributes to an ongoing process of internal review and revitalization by the OD profession in full view of its several publics.

THE NATURE OF OD AS A PROFESSION

Whether one observes OD from inside or out, there is ambivalence about whether the field is or should be called a profession. Among themselves practitioners are unsure what stand they wish to take with respect to educational requirements, ethical standards, and the discipline of members. Outside observers in the larger social science community often seem quicker to recognize the potential harm that might be done by poor OD practice or to question the soundness of OD research than to encourage the development of this new field into full partnership in applied social science. Recognizing the mixed reactions to the field, we have no doubt that people who practice organization development should behave as professionals and should be able to earn the respect typically accorded to members of the more established professions.

Recognizing the complexity and conflict involved, we offer a definition of "profession." (See Cogan, 1953, Goode, 1960, and Friedson, 1970, for summaries of definitions of profession.) It is intended to be sufficiently general to be relevant for all professions. It is also written with specific attention to OD as one of the newest professions. There is potential value to the study of professions in examining the developmental problems of one of the newest. Although we are all familiar with injunctions about how important it is to learn from history, few people are really able to do so. Learning from contemporary human experience is one of the prime OD objectives (Steele, 1975). It may be that learning the current experience of the developing profession of OD will prove valuable in understanding the older professions as well.

As we view it, a profession has the following characteristics:

1. It is a field of endeavor or set of activities based on a body of theoretical understanding and empirical research intended to provide service to a set of people called clients for which practitioners may receive remuneration.
2. It includes a set of standards that defines the capacity to practice professionally, to guarantee clients a minimum level of service, and to provide a basis on which members of the profession may be censured for harmful exercise of their skills or misuse of their knowledge.
3. It is directly involved in relating theory and practice and includes the expectations that members are responsible for regularly updating their skills and knowledge and that education and training programs are to be regularly examined and revised on the basis of the latest advances in theory and practice.

The three points of our definition address successively the nature of the exchange that is professional work, the need for and application of professional standards, and the dynamic and self-renewing quality that is essential for professional vitality. What can we say about today's OD in light of this definition?

It is clearly possible to point to a body of knowledge—theory, technique, and research results—that can provide the intellectual basis of the field. Some of this scholarship goes back as many as 40 years (e.g., the Hawthorne studies), but the largest amount has been created in the last 15 years. In 1974 and again in 1977 the *Annual Review of Psychology* included a review chapter called "Organization Development" (Friedlander and Brown, 1974; Alderfer, 1977). The *Annual Review of Sociology,* in its premiere volume, carried a chapter on evaluation research which included an analysis of several studies in the OD framework (Gordon and Morse, 1975).

So the problem with OD as a professional field is not the absence of an intellectual base. Rather it is that so few practitioners conceive of their work as creating, absorbing, and transmitting that knowledge to fellow professionals and clients. Much of the training of OD professionals takes place outside formal university degree programs and is carried by word-of-mouth tradition. This pattern creates and sustains a number of problems.

It gives a misleading impression to those inside and outside the profession about how much one should *know intellectually* to be a competent OD practitioner. It discourages some very bright people from entering the field because they are "turned off" by the apparent lack of intellectual rigor. It attracts people who lack the emotional or intellectual equipment to do high quality OD work just because it sometimes appears that one can work magic by learning a few group dynamic exercises that have a powerful impact on people. It also leads people with rigorous academic social science training, but without equally rigorous preparation in social intervention theory and method, to believe that they can understand OD without adequate exposure to its experiential and intellectual traditions. Last, it supports a split in the lives of some well-trained applied social scientists who behave according to one set of values in their research lives and another in their intervention careers. As a result they help to maintain the split between theory and practice in OD.

Today those wishing to be tested for their competence to practice OD have at least two ways to do so. The International Association of Applied Social Scientists (IAASS) examines and certifies OD practitioners. It offers two routes to certification, roughly paralleling the roles of internal and external consultants. Another path to certification in the field is provided by the American Board of Professional Psychology (ABPS), which has a division for the practice of industrial and organizational psychology. Both groups rely primarily on the scrutiny of "work samples" of the examinee by "peers." IAASS requires letters of reference from both clients and peers but has no systematic method of judging the intellectual competence of examinees, except as knowledge is obviously present or absent from the work sample. ABPS requires a Ph.D. in psychology or a closely related field and five years of post-Ph.D. experience even to qualify for examination. ABPS also requires letters of reference from peers (really seniors) of the examinee and an oral examination. Both certifying bodies have procedures by which certified members may lose their certification if charges of unethical or incompetent practice can be substantiated before an impartial review board.

Thus, like the question of intellectual base, the issue of establishing and maintaining standards for professional practice can be answered affirmatively for OD; but the existence of structures for ensuring responsible professional behavior does not guarantee that they will be used. It is by no means universally accepted by OD practitioners that they *should* stand for these examinations. We have no way of knowing what proportion of OD practitioners are certified, but we suspect that it is small in comparison to the number actively engaged in OD work. Further, no sanctions are imposed by the profession or the public to ensure that members stand for examination or lose the right to practice.

If OD has any consistent value theme it is toward novelty, growth, and change. Any professional gathering of practitioners in this field is likely to produce numerous conversations about the need for or lack of innovation. As a matter of behavioral frequency, however, it would be more unusual (i.e., novel) to take in a conversation about the need to systematize the education and training of OD practitioners. We also believe that the field is regularly engaged in significant innovation. A significant amount is communicated only by word of mouth among colleagues. This characteristic makes it unlikely that careful evaluation will precede the introduction of new techniques, and it makes it extraordinarily difficult to specify what a fully competent professional should know.

Currently the education and training of OD practitioners is divided between universities and a variety of ad hoc temporary systems. The respective strengths and weaknesses of these two types of programs follow closely what one would expect. Outside the university people are more likely to be exposed to the latest innovations in practice. Inside the university programs are likely to have firmer and more systematic intellectual bases. Outside programs are more likely to suffer from inadequate or nonexistent intellectual substance. Inside programs are less likely to be current with the latest practical innovations and to provide students with the opportunity to learn from supervised practice of their skills. Although understandable and to some degree efficient in terms of division of labor, this pattern of education and training tends to reinforce the separation between theory and practice and thereby undermines the overall quality of OD as a profession.

In general, we believe that OD has all the essential ingredients to be a high quality profession, although many practictioners and institutions in the field are far from realizing this potential. Moreover, we believe that there is a great deal of undetected subpar OD activity. OD may be appropriately viewed as somewhere between a guild and a profession. The next section outlines the variety of roles taken by OD practitioners and shows how the field reflects the parts, though not the whole, of professional activity.

A TYPOLOGY OF OD PRACTITIONERS

The variety of professionals who label themselves or are labeled by others as OD practitioners is evidence that our field is eclectic. This diversity in professional training and background is at once the strength and weakness of the profession. To the extent that practitioners in universities, large and small companies, and private consulting firms maintain professional contact with one another, the field benefits from the creative and innovative fruits of such dialogue. Too often, however, the diversity lacks coherence, mechanisms for ensuring integration are absent or neglected, and the profession struggles with fragmentation which aggravates the problems of integrating theory and practice, training future practitioners, and developing performance standards.

The following typology of OD practitioners describes six categories of professionals. Each OD "type" is, of necessity, oversimplified for purposes of categorization. Nevertheless, we believe that the six practitioners identified are familiar people in the field of OD.

We have chosen to distinguish types of OD practitioner by (a) their relation to the client organization (internal-external) and (b) their present and past affiliation with an academic environment. These two dimensions correspond to the major practice-and-theory dimensions of the OD profession.

Type A. Internal OD Practitioner Without Strong Academic Roots

In many organizations, OD began as a staff function located in the personnel department. The people called on to do the OD work were, more often than not, personnel managers and former line managers who augmented their personal managerial experience with seminars on organization development and informal contacts with others in the field. Their brand of OD was and is pragmatic. Embedded in the political and economic realities of their organizations, these practitioners are constantly searching for OD techniques that work and do not threaten established political realities. As a result they are less knowledgeable about the university-based research in the field but familiar with those techniques that are well publicized and well marketed. Internal OD practitioners with this background are primarily concerned with surviving and improving the effectiveness and developing the human resources of their own organizations in line with criteria established by management.

Type B. Internal Practitioner with Academic and Professional Training

A growing number of internal OD practitioners are being trained in universities and professional schools to work with human systems. Social workers, MBA's, and psychologists of varying backgrounds and degrees are becoming members of internal OD groups. These practitioners bring their academic training with them to the job and in many cases actively attempt to maintain contact with this "side" of their professional lives through membership in professional societies, personal contacts, and journal subscriptions. More than any other OD type, they have a unique dual identity: organization member and OD professional. Much of their work is designed to bring the two together.

Type C. External Practitioner Without Strong Academic Roots

This OD type is best exemplified by internal OD practitioners who leave their organizations to get further schooling or professional training and then join a consulting firm or start one from scratch. Their survival depends on the development of a set of techniques, both diagnostic and intervention, that can be used to bring about productive organizational change. As a result they often stay in touch with one another (OD network) and with the practical and *successful* developments in the field. For the independent OD consultant "successful" often means "salable," for his or her livelihood depends on the demand for the product. The external practitioner of this type also stays in touch with the professional societies but is often unfamiliar with the theoretical developments occurring in the academic community.

Type D. External Practitioner with Strong Academic Roots

Unlike the external practitioner described above, the academically trained practitioner often starts as a faculty member as opposed to a line manager or internal OD specialist. This academic background produces a concern for and an interest in both theory and practice, a condition that produces dual, and often competing, allegiances. As an independent consultant this OD practitioner also depends on the demand for his or her services in order to survive, but instead of emphasizing a set of techniques often brings a particular theory of organization development to direct the intervention activities. This interest and commitment to theory are reflected in the contributions such practitioners make to the professional literature and in the time they devote to keeping abreast of the developments in the universities. They sometimes take "adjunct" appointments in universities.

Type E. External Practitioners with Primary Academic Affiliation.*

The part-time OD practitioner who is also a full-time university faculty member defines this category. This OD professional is committed first

* The authors fit this type. Biases in this chapter undoubtedly arise as a result.

to the development of better *theories* of OD with the belief that better theories lead to better practice and that practice is essential to developing better theories. As faculty members these practitioners are researchers who seek to combine their consultative work with their research interests in the field of organization behavior and development. Because they are applied researchers, their audience includes the academic and professional OD communities, and as teachers they are involved in training future practitioners of various "types." Their primary academic affiliation restricts their involvement with client organizations and with all but a small portion of the "internal" segment of the profession.

Type F. Academic Researchers of OD

The final OD type is not really an OD practitioner at all but rather a researcher of OD. Unlike the university-based OD practitioner, the researcher of OD has relatively little training in the theory or practice of organization development and aspires to little. As researchers these professionals are committed to subjecting OD theory or techniques to the empirical tests of field research and to evaluating OD projects in terms of their espoused outcome goals. This commitment leads them to experiment with research designs that will enable them to test theories and evaluate programs. They publish their findings in academic journals in the field of organizational behavior. Often they harbor serious doubts that social change is desirable, and they typically do not see OD as a means of generating new insights about organizations. Rather they see research as a means of exposing what they believe are invalid claims by consultants.

Our analysis of the professional types in the field of OD leads us to the conclusion that no single role definition of the OD practitioner fully captures the diversity represented in the field. What we have, then, is a collection of practitioners with varying backgrounds, skills, interests, and even occupations, who *together* approach the definition of a profession. This fragmentation often means that certain professional functions, notably training, developing ethical and practical standards, integrating theory and practice, and monitoring the quality of service, are not performed or are not performed with any regularity or consistency. We are left with a picture of a profession that is not quite a profession, often struggling against itself to be one. Interestingly, a similar case has been made for psychotherapy, a service provided by people in a variety of roles located within diverse and conflicting authority structures (cf. Henry, Sims and Spray, 1971). How did such a state of affairs come to be for OD?

KEY CONFLICTS IN THE HISTORY OF OD

Throughout its short history OD has sought to address certain conflicts in the nature of human systems. In the process of working with these issues the field itself has been influenced by the phenomena it has attempted to change. The roles taken by OD professionals, as described in the preceding section, and the nature of the profession as a whole, to be analyzed in the next, are in part a function of the several major conflicts portrayed in this section.

Inside or Outside

The base of operations for OD practitioners may be inside or outside the systems they attempt to change. Insiders face a set of assets and liabilities that differs markedly from the returns that accrue to outsiders. From its origins OD has called for the resources of people inside *and* outside client systems.

Typically, outsiders bring prestige and independence to the work of change. They are usually called in because they are "known" for possessing special knowledge or expertise and their reputations help to establish and maintain resources for the internal OD program. In the long run outsiders are not dependent on the reaction of a single-client system. They may be freer to take risks and portray system dynamics accurately than insiders, who are more dependent on a single-client system for income and the right to practice.

Insiders have rich and intimate knowledge of the client system, born of years of association. Although the client system may resist initiatives taken by an insider, it is less likely to reject the person taking action for change. The relationships built up by people who work in an organization for a number of years—especially if they do so effectively—are a source of support and credibility for weathering the inevitable storms of social change set off by OD interventions.

Outsiders may be cut off from access to needed information or people without ever knowing it is happening. Their potentially short-term relationship with the system means that they are perpetually dependent on insiders for access to organizational resources. Insiders, although far less likely to be cut off, may be depotentiated in other ways. They may be given assignments that drain time and energy away from change activities or they may be more subtly intimidated by the knowledge that their long-term organizational future is under the control of the very people they are attempting to change.

There is some tendency for insiders to become outsiders as a means of coping with the long-term dilemmas of being subject to the control of a single organization. Even insiders who work effectively in a supportive climate regularly face frustration from the fact that their professional work does not fit the normal criteria for pay and promotion. Some organizations have developed roles for OD practitioners that allow them to practice outside their primary employing organization, and others have established "individual contributor" salary tracks to escape the constraints of conventional salary schedules. Both trends reflect an increasing recognition of professionalism in OD.

Authority Relations

The relation of all OD professionals to the authority structures in which they practice is inevitably problematic. As agents of change OD professionals must exercise influence in order to do their work. Because the use of covert influence methods is unacceptable in professional practice, OD practitioners must work with existing authority systems to bring about change. Otherwise they are either incompetent or unethical.

OD practitioners inevitably sense that they are working with existing influence structures in ways that are bound to be disturbing even when the change processes take place successfully. Significant portions of the literature advocate increased participation as a goal for organizational change. Those aspects of OD based on learning from experiential group training are rooted in a conceptual position that is highly accepting of direct confrontations with authority figures. By education and training and by their work demands OD practitioners thus are in a position to work with *and* against existing authorities to alter the amount and balance of power held by individuals and groups in established social systems. Even in the best of situations, in which everyone gets more influence as a result of intervention (e.g., when the intervention "frees up" the flow of information), there is still the possibility that former low power groups will increase their influence more than former high power groups. Whenever influence exchanges take place there is an opportunity for power to be abused, including the power exercised by OD practitioners.

Several routes to OD practice are likely to draw people whose relations to conventional authorities may be more than normally problematic. In many (though by no means all) large corporations personnel departments are populated by people who "did not make it" as line managers partly because of their inability to exercise authority competently. Many private practice consultants reach that role because they could not come to terms with conventional academic authorities, as is frequently true when major innovations occur. The personal-organizational dilemmas that lead people into OD work can be a source of insight that will lead to more competent practice if those personal dynamics are examined and worked through; but without training and education that includes such self-scrutiny in regard to issues of power dynamics practitioners are likely to create as many, if not more, problems than they solve. Many training programs for OD practitioners can be faulted for their lack of explicit attention to power dynamics in the lives of OD practitioners. There are also compensatory trends: more training experiences directly concerned with power dynamics (e.g., Tavistock Conferences, Power Labs) are being developed; and organizations that make serious commitments to OD are doing so by devoting some of their best managerial talent to the task.

Another pattern that reflects the problematic nature of the relation of OD practitioners to authority is the stance taken by many toward accreditation. People generally have mixed feelings, including some significant fears and anxieties, about being evaluated. Nevertheless, it seems indisputable that individuals who exercise the kind of influence that OD practitioners attempt should be willing to have their competence reviewed by experienced peers and superiors in the field. Otherwise what protection does the profession offer to clients against incompetent or unethical practice? What response has the profession to legitimate questions from outside bodies whether it has a method of controlling its own affairs? Against the reluctance of many practitioners to accept evaluation stands the growing number of people who do subject themselves to review by formal accrediting bodies.

Intellectual Quality

One of the major insights that opened the way to a host of social technologies which make up OD practice is the deceptively simple learning principle that "experience precedes cognition." This "law" reverses the traditional design of many learning programs, especially in the behavioral sciences. It leads people to give lectures *after* participants have been engaged in an intensive exercise designed to provide concrete experience with some social process. It provides an inductive rather than a deductive approach to education, but it also has the unfortunate liability that the excitement of the exercise and the richness of the experience may seduce people away from ever getting to the demanding work of conceptualization. When experiential education in social processes was at the height of its novelty—perhaps 10 years ago—it sometimes fostered a view of experience *versus* cognition. That heritage is still with us, even though the polarization between experience (or emotions as one type of experience) and cognition is much less severe today than it was several years ago. Indeed, there are now leading practitioners who advocate the analysis of theories in practice (Argyris and Schon, 1974). There is a dearth of places to which individuals who want cognitive development in OD can go for such learning, especially in comparison to the large number of intensive workshops where people learn social technologies by experiential exercises.

The intensive workshop model for teaching and learning OD has also predominated because universities have been slow to adopt the newer educational methods or to become seriously aligned with programs that teach methods of effecting social change. In part, this is based on the inherent character of universities. Their role in society is as much to preserve tradition as to generate new knowledge. University faculty take academic positions as much to escape the turmoil and responsibility for action as to acquire new learning.

In medicine the "teaching" provides a setting in which research, training, and practice coexist. Most of these settings contain serious priority struggles among the three functions. As long as they share the same physical setting the possibility of constructive stimulation among them is more likely than if geography, as well as values and tasks, separated the activities. The closest thing to a teaching hospital for OD occurs in a very few university settings as a subsystem (not as a substantial system in its own right) of more central educational research programs. The need for strengthening these programs and for developing others if OD is to develop more robustly as a profession can hardly be overstated. We expand on this in the closing section.

The analysis of key conflicts in the history and current status of OD provides one perspective for understanding the state of the profession today. The existence of these struggles is one source of energy for the field; they provide needed stimulation for practitioners in all the roles described in the preceding section. However, mismanagement of the issues presented in this section can also lead to deleterious effects on the profession and the people it purports to serve. As a new profession OD has not yet learned how to innoculate itself adequately from the very problems it seeks to ameliorate in client systems. We turn next to an analysis of the field as a social system to explore how broader dynamics influence the nature of the profession.

EXPLAINING THE OD SYSTEM

At this point we present a conceptual framework for explaining OD. The next several pages outline the major concepts in the framework and then apply them to OD in comparison to more traditional professions. We do this for two reasons. First, we think the concepts described provide an understanding of the field of OD and the competing pressures and tensions that are part of it. Second, we have found that conceptualizing the profession in this way has helped us to think about the future and the areas in which the OD profession will have to change if it is to increase the quality of its contribution to organizations in our society.

Open System Concepts

One of the defining characteristics of open systems is that they import material, energy, ideas, and information from outside themselves, transform these resources, and then export their "products" back to the environment (Rice, 1963). Systems are distinguished from their environment by boundaries that regulate the flow between the system and its environment as well as between internal parts of the system (individuals, subgroups, and departments). These boundaries can be concrete or subjective and psychological. Concrete boundaries include walls, membership cards or lists, maps to indicate spatial boundaries, and schedules to specify time boundaries. Subjective or psychological boundaries are those feelings that are often associated with concrete boundaries or in some cases replace them: feelings of cohesion or belongingness, a sense of territoriality, or feelings about one's background or heritage.

Both internal and external system boundaries differ in their permeability. At the extremes impermeable boundaries mean that exchange is difficult and consequently infrequent; they create conditions in which the system (or its subparts) is in danger of becoming closed off from needed interaction. On the other side, extremely permeable boundaries mean that the distinction between what is inside the system and what is not becomes blurred or nearly obliterated and the system (the people in it) is virtually indistinguishable from its environment. Neither extreme is "healthy" for a human system. Alderfer (1976) summarizes evidence that suggests that system vitality is lost in systems that move to the extremes of being overbounded or underbounded. A system characterized by highly impermeable boundaries (overbounded) tends to be rigid and overcontrolled, whereas a system with extremely permeable boundaries (underbounded) is chaotic and disorganized.

In terms of boundary conditions over- and underbounded systems are nearly mirror opposites. Deeper examination of the conditions of the two systems indicates that the two kinds of pathology are not so simply specified. A number of specific parameters differentiate the two conditions more precisely: authority relations, role definition, communication, human energy, affect, economic condition, and time span of concern (Alderfer, 1976).

Both kinds of system evidence problems with *authority*. In overbounded systems the nature of authority is well defined, often profusely detailed. There is relatively little doubt about who can make which decisions or who reports to whom. The result is that overbounded systems frequently constrain initiatives from below and needed information is held only by those authorized to do so. In contrast, the nature of authority in underbounded systems is typically unclear. Sometimes it appears that several individuals and groups hold responsibility for the same thing. At other times needed work does not get done because no one has been assigned to do it.

Closely related to problems of authority are those of *role definition*. In overbounded systems member roles are too finely specified, taking away many opportunities for enlarging the use of one's abilities from naturally occurring events. Underbounded systems suffer from the uncertainty of its members about any limits or priorities in their work. As a result they tend not to plan effectively and often respond to events on a crisis basis.

Difficulties with the management of *human energy* also vary as a function of system boundaries. Typically, underbounded systems have difficulty harnessing energy to do work. People are often geographically dispersed and pulled in so many ways by conflicting pressures that they find it hard to move decisively in any single direction. Overbounded systems have trouble releasing the energy that is contained within them. Although they frequently do not lack resources, members of overbounded systems find themselves blocked from moving by system boundaries that become barriers.

Communication problems also differ as a function of boundary conditions. Members of overbounded systems have comparatively few problems meeting one another or engaging in face-to-face interaction. Their difficulties arise because of what and how they communicate. They distort and withhold information from one another and often engage in elaborate games that may give the appearance of valid exchange but beneath the surface serve mainly to enhance the self-interest of the communicator. Members of underbounded systems are more likely not to meet to discuss common problems. Diffusion of authority, role definition, and energy keep people apart in underbounded systems.

The nature of the *affect* experienced and expressed also varies under different boundary conditions. In overbounded systems member affect tends to be experienced as ego- and ethnocentric; individuals and groups are inclined to attribute positive qualities to themselves and ingroups and negative qualities to others and outgroups. Emotional expression also tends to be generally more suppressed (or repressed) in overbounded systems. Emotional expression in underbounded systems is less constrained than in overbounded and has a different quality. The affective experiences of people who belong to underbounded systems tends to be more dominantly negative than those in overbounded systems. Targets for the hostile and anxious feelings experienced by individuals and groups in underbounded systems tend to be both themselves and others. They also tend to be both intra- and extrapunitive. In this sense the members of underbounded systems tend to be less ego- and ethnocentric than members of overbounded systems.

Over and underbounded systems also tend to differ with respect to *economic* condition. Overbounded systems tend to have more certain and wealthier economic positions. Underbounded systems are typically shorter of funds and live with greater uncertainty about sources of income. This property is tied to the relations between physical and psychological boundaries. Ultimately the loss of economic support threatens the physical boundaries of a system.

Finally, both systems differ in the *time span* of their hazards. Underbounded systems continually face issues of survival. They live with a crisis-oriented mentality. Overbounded systems typically do not face short-run disaster. Their danger comes from a slowly increasing loss of capacity to cope with forces impinging on them. As time passes overbounded systems become less able to recognize and respond to problems that confront them.

Table 4.1 is a summary of the seven parameters in both systems.

Professional Systems

Conceptualizing professions in these terms provides a framework for diagnosing and ultimately changing them. Professions, like other social

Table 4.1. Characteristics of Overbounded and Underbounded Systems

	Boundary State	
System Characteristics	Overbounded	Underbounded
Authority relations	Well defined hierarchy and decision making	Unclear authority sources, overlapping authority
Role definition	Overly specified and constraining roles; strict "job definition"	Uncertainty about limits or priorities of role
Management of human energy	Difficult to release energy; dammned up and blocked resources	Difficult to harness energy; physical and emotional dispersion
Communication	Easy to convene groups; problems with distortion and invalid information	Difficult to promote communication; absence of communication
Affect	Egocentric; ethnocentric; suppression of (strong) emotions	Negative internal and external emotions
Economic conditions	Stable and wealthy economic conditions	Uncertainty about sources of funding; "tight" money
Time frame	Relative long-term security; loss of responsiveness to change	Survival oriented, crisis-oriented mentality

systems, can be characterized as overbounded (to some degree) or underbounded (to some degree). The traditional professions, such as law and medicine, have many of the characteristics of an overbounded system. Organization development, in contrast, is an example of an underbounded profession. The following comparison highlights the strengths and weaknesses of each.

In the traditional professions the authority structure and the roles embedded in it are usually clear and functional. (See Bloomfield, 1976, for historical analysis of the American legal profession and Friedson, 1970, for a sociological view of the American medical profession.) In both law and medicine, for example, there are federal, state, and local professional associations and elected officials at each level are in respected and often powerful positions. These associations are often charged with certifying practitioners and with ensuring a level of quality in its membership. As in most overbounded systems this formal and clearly designated authority structure has some dysfunctional correlates as well. The power structure becomes insulated, self-protecting, rigid, and resistant to change. The result is that the profession adapts to changes in its environment slowly, if at all, and opportunities for new people or new ideas to penetrate it are rare.

In the area of managing human energy the overbounded qualities of the traditional professions are best exemplified by the educational processes they favor. The training curricula and practices in law and medicine, for example, remain remarkably stable in the face of the swift changes that characterize both professions. Although individual areas of practice are constantly updated with the development of new research or legislation, new areas of the profession (e.g., preventive medicine and paraprofessional training) and new approaches to professional training are opened up only after a long and arduous struggle or open conflict. This situation forces many practitioners to work "outside" the profession's mainstream in order to apply their energy and skills to what they believe are critical professional problems.

The traditional professions also fit the description of communication and characteristic affect in overbounded systems. As a function of the hierarchical structure, communication flows easily "down" the profession but not up, and although it is easy to convene the established professional groups (review boards, certifying groups) the communication is often formal and ritualized when important or sensitive topics are at issue. Thus, even though communication may be frequent in overbounded systems, it may be distorted as it rises in the hierarchy or devoid of meaning in the context of *pro forma* activities.

Part of the function of the accrediting process in overbounded professions is to make it clear who is a practitioner and who is not. With the highly competitive entry process in these professions, it is not surprising that professional "ethnocentrism" is a common occurrence. The hallmark of this ethnocentrism is hostility and elitism towards nonmembers and high cohesion and loyalty toward colleagues. The former can make working relations with other professional and nonprofessionals very difficult and the latter often lead to the blind defense of incompetent or indefensible professional activities.

The traditional professions are usually economically secure, if not prosperous. Law and medicine are among the wealthiest professions in America, and this financial munificence is a stable condition. In part, the financial stability of these professions is related to the long-term, unchanging nature of the client-practitioner relations that develop in them. There is little threat of short-term disaster for these professionals and their clients are often a reliable source of income. The passage of time, however, brings with it different problems that overbounded systems like law and medicine are less able to respond to effectively (e.g., national health insurance and increases in malpractice suits), although characteristically these problems seem always to be in the future rather than the present.

In contrast to the traditional professions the profession of OD is still groping for its identity and for the characteristics and standards that will define it. Its beginnings are associated with a rebellion against the "traditional" scientific management and human relations schools of thought and practice prevalent in the late 1950s. In swinging away from the dehumanizing aspects of scientific management and the pseudohumane qualities of the human relations movement, the focus of organization development was "growth" for organizations and the individuals working and living in them and the goal of the profession was to aid organizations in developing beyond their current (and problematic) levels of effectiveness, adaptability, and responsiveness. Accomplishing this goal often meant confronting the traditional assumptions and organizing principles and most OD professionals saw these activities as central to the profession. Newness, coupled with value positions that were often confronting and reactive, produced a professional system with the following underbounded characteristics.

Authority has been and continues to be a problem for the field of OD. As we mentioned earlier, part of this problem stems from the conflicts of those individuals who choose to enter the profession, but a large part is due to the nature of the authority structure in the profession itself. Multiple sources of authority are confusing and unsettling and give rise to a host of inconsistencies and contradictions. Some of these professional associations and groups in the field offer certification (e.g., IAASS, ABPS) whereas others offer only membership and professional contact (e.g., NTL Institute, OD Network). Alongside these groups, two major sectors of the profession, university-affiliated members of the field and the full-time practitioners, are constantly jockeying for power and influence. The result of this confusion and competition is an unstable and unclear authority structure, the focal characteristic of an underbounded system.

It is also unclear what an OD practitioner's role is or should be. The typology in the second section of this chapter describes six OD roles and with them come the ambiguity and uncertainty about who is *really* a member of the profession. If the answer to this question is designed to be all-inclusive, one is forced to ask another: what are the defining characteristics, required training, and professional competencies of an

OD practitioner? The confusion alluded to by this last question and the variety of answers to it are part of the diffuse reality of our profession.

Another of the underbounded characteristics of the OD profession is the mismanagement of the human energy of its members. Again, part of this condition can be traced to the role of OD practitioners in organizations. Often OD projects are either short-term crisis-oriented activities or low priority undertakings which ebb and flow with the economic and emotional conditions of the organization. At the same time, the profession itself cannot seem to organize and coordinate the talent and experience of its members. Professional groups struggle to survive, often do not, and then attempt to reconstitute themselves, a cycle that requires large investments of time and energy but dissipates rather than harnesses the human resources of the field.

The effects of diffuse authority, ambiguous and confusing role definitions, and the mismanagement of human energy make communication difficult and often stressful. It is almost impossible to convene OD practitioners to talk constructively about the problems in the profession. The wide variety of professionals makes it hard to know whom to invite to such a discussion; and, perhaps more important, the diversity in values, practices, and goals makes communication difficult, often unproductive, and consequently something to be avoided. As a result, it is easy to understand the affective characteristics of the profession. Angry, competitive, and hostile feelings are not only directed at an environment that has little respect or support for OD (some practitioners are finding it necessary to call themselves "corporate psychologists" in order to avoid the stigma) but at other OD professionals as well.

The economic conditions in the field of organization development, although not depressed, are certainly neither lucrative nor stable, except for a very few. Client systems with an OD staff, as well as those that hire external consultants, are constantly asking the question, "Can we do without it?" and funding agencies for university-based research and practice are often reticent to support "social action" projects. Consequently money is scarce and OD practitioners find themselves fighting fires instead of doing the long-term development projects from which the profession derives its name.

In this section we have contrasted the underbounded "pathology" of the OD profession with the overbounded pathology of traditional professions. We believe that OD's current state as an underbounded system is in part a reaction against the dysfunctional outcomes of an overbounded existence. It is our view that this movement against "overboundedness" has caused the profession to slip into its own dysfunctional state: "underboundedness." But the underbounded condition has also developed because the field is so new and therefore subject to the turbulence of rapidly changing environmental conditions. The conclusion to this chapter addresses the challenge of finding optimal boundary conditions and offers a suggestion for meeting that challenge.

CONCLUSION

In bringing ourselves to the point at which it is possible (albeit risky) to give some thought to the future, we have attempted to describe the profession of organization development, its history and current dilemmas, and the types of practitioner who affiliate with it. We are not unique in our endeavor to understand the field, but our focus at the beginning, and now at the end, has been "professionalism" in the context of OD as a social system. Our conceptualization and analysis of the tensions within the profession have led us to some broad conclusions.

The field of organization development today is caught between the Scylla of the overbounded profession and the Charybdis of the underbounded state in which the OD profession currently finds itself. The former is characterized by rigid and often unresponsive authority, confining and restraining role prescriptions, ritualized and often emotionless interactions devoid of mutual influence, and elitist practices that prohibit the incorporation of new people, varied perspectives, and innovative approaches. The latter is equally foreboding, with its diffuse and often unstable authority relations, confusing and ill-defined role specifications, infrequent and haphazard communications plagued by petty competitiveness and quietly warring subgroups, and a lack of meaningful entry qualifications and procedures that robs everyone in the field of a sense of pride and professionalism.

The dilemma is all the more difficult for us because we believe that the attempts to avoid the pathologies of an overbounded system was a positive step that has borne professional fruit. The OD profession has grown quickly and has branched out into new areas and organizations—settings that continually challenge our knowledge, skills, and understanding (Alderfer, 1977). We have paid a price for this growth and expansion, and the OD profession is now caught between what we have tried not to become and what we are.

The challenge for the profession is to find itself a "center of gravity."

In the terms we have used to describe boundary relations this condition of optimal "boundedness" or "permeability" refers to a state of the profession in which there are strong and defined boundaries that identify the structure of the profession (authority roles and standards) but at the same time maintain its flexibility and responsiveness (openness to ideas, influence, and change). The goal of this change toward optimal permeability is to produce a structure for the profession that could facilitate the integration of the numerous roles and activities currently subsumed under the name of organization development. In concrete terms this would mean the development of standardized certification procedures and/or the accreditation of training programs, the formalization of an identifiable and visible authority structure to take responsibility for coordinating communication and for developing and promoting cross fertilization within the profession aimed at the integration of theory and practice. It would also include assertive actions to promote membership and leadership by all significant demographic and ethnic groups in our society.

We offer one possible approach to redesigning the OD profession as a catalyst for our colleagues. Earlier we mentioned the concept of an OD teaching "hospital." This institution, called an Organization Development Center, could provide a central and identifiable location to which prospective clients could come for service. In ways similar to a teaching hospital the Organization Development Center would support three coexisting activities: education-training, research, and practice. There would be a clinical faculty and a research faculty, both involved in the development of training standards and the supervision of OD interns. Each of the three spheres would be located at the center, thereby promoting (although not guaranteeing) communication and coordination among them.

To take this proposal a step further, OD centers would have to seek and receive financial support for training (government traineeships) and research (grants and contracts); they could provide placement opportunities for students in universities as well as for full-time professional trainees and could serve their local communities in addition to regional or national clients. With a variety of sources of financial support, these OD centers would face the issue of resource pooling and allocation but would do so with all the options in full view. Finally, and perhaps most important of all, OD centers would require administrative staffs to coordinate and oversee the full range of professional activities. The development of these professionals would be a major and crucial undertaking.

One might wonder about the role of universities, research institutes, and consulting firms in a society dotted with OD centers. The purpose of these centers is to locate power in an integrated *profession* in such a way that it can be used for professional development in the broadest and most comprehensive sense of the phrase. Each of the other organizations mentioned has a vested interest in perpetuating its own piece of the profession, the source of its power and legitimacy. Often this means competing for resources with other parts of the field, and the result is a fragmented collection of subgroups and individual practitioners. Organization development centers are suggested here because to date our efforts to coordinate these competing and diverse institutions have not been sufficiently effective. The centers attempt to draw an optimally permeable boundary around the whole profession.

We are aware of the many problems inherent in this solution. In addition to the problems of implementation, the teaching hospital analogy provides a good example of the difficulties facing a service institution with multiple goals and a diverse professional staff; yet we offer this suggestion as a stimulus for the long overdue task of exploring possible approaches to the professional development of OD. A viable and ultimately successful profession will come only with a social system that supports, encourages, and protects change while maintaining continuity in standards, training, excellence, credibility, and procedures for self-renewal and growth.

5

Introducing Change to a Government Agency

WILLIAM J. CROCKETT

Much of our contemporary thought and writing in the field of management, both in theory and practice, is devoted to the subject of change. A casual observer might therefore come to a number of erroneous conclusions; for example, he might conclude that our public and private organizations are in active, throbbing, vibrant pursuit of change.* He might conclude that all a leader has to do, if he has power, is to tell people the changes that he wants and they will then make them occur. He might conclude that all an institution has to do is to open its doors and let change flow into it. Finally, he might conclude that the people in our organizations are eager, willing, and able to embrace new procedures and concepts and to install the functional and structural reorganizations that change entails.

None of these conclusions would be totally valid, however. From my own experience in a large and traditional public institution, the U.S. Department of State, I know that bringing change to such an insti-

---

Parts of this chapter are adapted from "Introducing Change to a Complex Organization," by W. J. Crockett. In Richard Hacon (Ed.), *Personal and Organizational Effectiveness*. Copyright 1972 McGraw-Hill, Ltd.

* In all cases the masculine form of the pronoun is used for writing style but it always and implicitly means both she and he.

tution—to its processes, organization, attitudes, objectives, and way of life—is neither casual nor automatic nor easy.

In the first place managers are much too busy coping with problems, pressures, and people to have time or interest in changing things. If their operation is running smoothly, change can only mean disruption and trouble for them. Second, bringing change to a complex federal agency is complicated by the severe time limitations that any politically appointed administrator has available. Third, there is so much change in process all of the time that typical Washington managers are cynical about its validity and permanence. "Wait a while and it will all be changed back again" is their attitude. Oftentimes this may indeed by all too true!

I am therefore concerned about the easy connotations of the pat phrases we use in describing the way we organize to effect change. We call it "the management of change," as if change itself were a dynamic force knocking on our doors and all we have to do is to channel and guide it throughout our institutions. Instead, I have learned that it can be an agonizing experience for the people who are caught up in the process, and it can tear the fabric of the institution itself.

In this chapter I describe two major change efforts in the Department of State during the five years I was in charge of its management, first as Assistant Secretary of State for Administration and then as Deputy Under Secretary of State for Administration. This period started in the early days of the Kennedy administration and ended in the early months of 1967 in the Johnson administration. One of the change programs personally involved Presidents Kennedy and Johnson and Secretary of State Rusk. In that effort I served in a staff-support capacity. The other effort represented my attempt to change the operational mode of the area that reported to me directly—the Department of State's administrative apparatus, designated the "O" area.

THE BEGINNINGS

I can still feel the surprise, the elation, and the wonderment of the news when it came to me. My family and I were spending the 1960 Christmas holidays with relatives when I learned that I was being considered for an important office in the State Department by the President of the United States. At that time I was an unknown Foreign Service officer serving as the State Department's budget officer. Further, insofar as many of my colleagues were concerned, I was an FSO in name only. In 1956, during Henry Wriston's reorganization of the

State Department, I had been "wristonized" along with many other members of the Staff Corps and incorporated into the Foreign Service Officer Corps. But the Foreign Service has a long memory and most of us were never considered "real" FSOs who did not come into the service through competitive examination. Now, after a short nine years in the Foreign Service and a "phony" transition to the FSO I was to be appointed to one of the top administrative jobs in the Department of State!

When the announcement was made, I can imagine the things that were said by the Foreign Service members at their intimate Georgetown parties and in the embassies around the world. "Who is this guy Crockett? How? Why? Not only is he just an FSO 2, he's not a real Foreign Service officer! What does he stand for? He's just an administrative type! What does he know about the Foreign Service? Who can control him? What will he do to us or for us?" And so on.

INSTRUCTIONS: CHANGE

One of the first things that happened to me was a summons from Robert Kennedy, the Attorney General, to come to his office. There was no greeting, no small talk, and no chance for response by me except, "yes, sir" to his cryptic monologue. He said:

> First of all, get your loyalties straight. No matter whom you think you work for, the President appointed you and he is your boss. He will expect your absolute loyalty. Second, get your job straight. The State Department must be made to be loyal and responsive to the President. It must become more positive and proactive. It must be made to assume a leadership position in the Foreign Affairs Community. Your job is to make this happen. And thirdly, do you know how to make this happen . . .?

While I was trying to think up an answer, he held up his hand to silence my response and added, "You will make it happen by giving orders and firing people who don't produce." The discussion was ended, and although I had numerous calls from him later in which he asked for this and demanded that I never saw him in person again.

It is interesting that neither the President, who appointed me, nor Dean Rusk, who was my nominal boss, ever discussed with me whether this was my primary objective or how I might best pursue it. Neither outlined a goal or a program. Rusk's favorite admonishment to his subordinates' inquiries for direction and feedback was: "Work up to the horizons of your job. If you get too far out I'll pull you back." In the six years that I worked for him he never "pulled me back." He never gave me guidance, directions, or goals, nor did he give me much support for my efforts or acknowledgment for my accomplishments. There was one other bit of ominous warning in the beginning, when he once told his staff, "I won't support you if you become embroiled in bureaucratic dog fights with other agencies."

At the time Rusk's warning didn't bother me; neither did the absence of direction. Thinking back on those early days of my new job I now wonder at the fact that I accepted the Robert Kennedy direction so calmly. His authoritarian recipe for bringing about change didn't seem to bother me at all. Having risen from the ranks, I felt that I not only knew the problems of the Department but also the answers, and I soon set in motion the changes for achieving the results that I had in mind.

THE DEPARTMENT OF STATE—ONE PERSON'S PERSPECTIVE

Historically the Department of State has been a problem for presidents. At the beginning of the Kennedy administration it was of special concern. It was described by critics as being biased and unresponsive to domestic issues, ponderous in its deliberations, and bureaucratic in its operations—an agency well deserving of the title used by its detractors, "The Fudge Factory."

Perhaps a listing of some of the most important organizational and historical issues will help to give the reader an understanding of the complexity of its operations and the problems facing anyone who wanted to bring about change. Some of these peculiarities are the following:

Leadership in Foreign Affairs

The State Department was established in 1789 and is the oldest federal department. The Secretary is the first ranking cabinet member and, at one time, was second in the line of presidential succession. But the postwar years saw a decline in the Department's position of leadership in foreign affairs. The U.S. military, the A.I.D., and the C.I.A. all competed for leadership in this area, and other governmental agencies paid less and less attention to what was seen as the State Department's bureaucratic efforts to control them. During the Eisenhower administration, therefore, the Operations Coordinating Board (OCB) was created to pull the competing and overlapping foreign policy factions of agencies together. OCB thus caused the State Department's role in foreign policy leadership to be further reduced. State had become just one among equals and not the first at that.

The Foreign Service Versus the World

Nevertheless the Department never accepted its new position in foreign affairs. It still saw itself as owning the world of foreign policy. It was its special preserve—its territory. The Foreign Service Officers believed that they alone possessed the professionalism, expertise, and experience needed to represent the President in the fulfillment of his foreign affairs responsibilities. The Foreign Service was the self-acclaimed custodian of the U.S. foreign policy apparatus. The fact that this custodial role was not recognized by other agencies, was bypassed by the White House and the Congress in the formulation of policy, and not recognized by the President in the ambassadorial appointment process only served to drive the Service to closer cohesion and myopia around their self-elitism! It was the Foreign Service against the world.

Personnel

Historically, there has always been a caste system in the Department. First were the Foreign Service Officers (FSO's) who considered themselves the elite group and were jealous of their privileges, rank, and perquisites. Indeed, they had most of the substantive positions in the embassies abroad. In theory, at least, each was personally commissioned by the President.

Another group called the Foreign Service Staff performed administrative and consular functions abroad. Last were the federal civil servants who manned the Department in Washington. These personnel divisions intensified the problem of effective organization and leadership. As a result the Department was generally belittled as a power structure. It was old and toothless—a paper tiger.

Organizational Structure

The State Department was three organizations in one: regional bureaus, functional bureaus, and management. The regional bureaus had direct links with other countries and had charge of the day-to-day functions of our diplomatic operations. The functional bureaus (economics, planning, and so on) regarded their work as no less important, but they suffered from a second-class status. The relations between these two bureaus were made more difficult by overlapping geography and responsibility. Thus it was often uncertain who should handle a problem: the regional bureau with the territorial interest or the functional bureau with the expertise. This uncertainty created competition, secrecy, and jealousy among the rank and file concerned.

There was also the administrative side of the Department—its management. It was large in numbers but low in prestige. Yet the administrative function had power because it controlled the personnel processes for assignment and promotion, the budget allocation processes for people and dollars, the security processes for receiving and distributing messages, and the congressional liaison processes for legislation and appropriations. In fact, it was only the administrators of the Department who knew the fundamentals of management and who had exercised real leadership in our embassies.

Historically, there were recognized status differences between the administrators and the policy members. The people of the Department, and especially of the Foreign Service, placed high value on substance—making and carrying out foreign policy, maintaining diplomatic relations, conducting negotiations, and fulfilling day-in and day-out diplomacy. These were the hallmarks of a real FSO; they were substance. Anyone who did any other kind of work—consular, administration, security, and so on—had little status in "the service" because it was "administrative." There was a perpetual underground warfare between these two groups, especially when the "administrators" became strong enough to influence policy, make organizational changes, or in any way threaten the sacred privilege of the Foreign Service elite.

There seemed to be a pervasive fear among *substantive* Foreign Service officers that the administrators might one day take over:

> Retired Ambassador Ellis O. Briggs, an extreme example, referred to "administrative types" as "glorified janitors, supply clerks, and pants-pressers" who yearn to get their fingers in the foreign affairs pie. . . . Another retired ambassador, Henry Villard, wrote: "In the State Department, the administrators are no longer the servants of the policy makers—they are rapidly becoming the masters" (Mosher and Harr, 1970, p. 19).

Although there were status differences in their functions, there were differences also in the character of their jobs. The policy maker's job was research, analysis, personal contact, and reporting. It had a personal and individual orientation uncommon to most organizational functions. Consequently people in the Foreign Service were given no experience or training in leadership, collaboration, or open communication. It was a closed, private kind of society. One consultant who worked with the people of the Service said, "Most groups are pretty closed because they don't know better. The State Department people are trained to be aloof, closed and a bit suspicious." That, of course, was to some extent true.

Diplomacy has always been a personal business. From our own early days, when Franklin and Adams represented our precarious interests abroad, we have practiced a private diplomacy. The one-man diplomatic efforts of Henry Kissinger during the Nixon-Ford administration illustrates the unique personal quality of diplomacy. So the goal of a young Foreign Service officer was not to become an executive whose job it is to run a mission in an *operational sense*. His model was to be a powerful and successful "ambassador-diplomat" in a *personal sense*. Therefore the lure and exhortations of "leadership" fell on deaf ears and quite understandably so. As Secretary Rusk so perceptively said of the Foreign Service, "It's hard to get them to enlarge their management-leadership responsibilities."

Norms

All these forces—the loss of leadership, the rigid organizational structure, the status laden personnel differences, and the lack of effective management—were apparent in the organizational norms. Status and power flowed to the holders of certain positions; not only did the power that went with the position produce fear and awe but the way the person himself exercised it also contributed, as it does in all organizations. Add to this the strictly enforced, worldwide caste system called "diplomatic protocol," which gives value only to title and rank and gives no recognition to human worth or ability, and one has a norm of stilted, artificial human relationships unequaled in any other organization.

In addition, there was the pall of the McCarthy cloud that still hung over the Department personnel. Senator McCarthy's 1950 charge of widespread Communist infiltration was still a shadow that caused insecurity among policy makers. It led them to caution and careful interpersonal relations. Coupled with the bureaucratic barriers to open relationships, it produced what Chris Argyris (1967) described as the norms of the Department:

- Withdrawal from interpersonal difficulties, conflict, and aggressiveness.

- Minimal interpersonal openness, leveling, and trust.
- Mistrust of the aggressive behavior of others.
- Disguise of emotional responses and feelings.
- Emphasis on the substantive, not administrative, activities.
- Loyalties to others in the system.

A COMMITMENT TO CHANGE

In 1961, when I became Assistant Secretary for Administration, the Department's reputation for operational effectiveness in policy and administration was at a low point with both the Executive Branch and the Congress. It was, as one congressman described it, "like a ballet school of prima donnas, each doing her own thing without coordination or purpose." Another said, "It's like an insane asylum with the inmates running the place."

In other words, the State Department did not provide leadership in the area of foreign affairs, either at home or abroad. It was President Kennedy's desire that this should change, and soon after the election he appointed a task force to look into the political and administrative problems of many government agencies. Many objectives were singled out. One was to give new zest and new organization to the State Department—zest and organization needed for leadership in foreign affairs.

How, then, could I go about fulfilling this objective in such a climate? Perhaps, had I done as much reflection on the problem then as I have since, I might not have had the courage to start anything. At that time, however, I thought that I knew what needed to be done and somehow I had the energy and the confidence (maybe the naïvety) to start on the path to change. This is that odyssey.

THE DEVELOPMENT OF A PROGRAM FOR CHANGE

Soon after my appointment I made a worldwide inspection trip with Under Secretary of State Chester Bowles. We talked to ambassadors and Foreign Service officers around the world about the problems they were having in those outposts of the State Department. One of the common complaints we heard from all quarters was the lack of State Department *leadership* in foreign policy. The ambassadors complained that they had no real authority to coordinate and control properly the other agencies that were operating in their countries. Sometimes they didn't even know what was happening or being planned by those agencies until a crisis erupted after some plan went wrong. The famous U-2 incident that involved Turkey, Pakistan, and Russia was a graphic example often cited.

They also complained that the State Department gave them no support or backup when an issue or a dispute had to be sent to Washington. Who was the leader and how could State develop a new leadership style?

As a result of this trip we identified some 150 action items for changes that should be considered to improve our operations abroad and responsiveness at home. A project was started early in 1961 to develop a comprehensive list of all the subjects that had been suggested for us to look into and to establish priorities for further study. We finally identified 136 major and minor tasks that needed to be done. As one might guess, the first item on the list was State Department leadership. It read as follows:

1. *State Department leadership in foreign affairs and relationships with other agencies:* develop a program for better interdepartmental leadership in the foreign affairs field, including arrangements for general direction of certain functions transferred from the Operations Coordination Board. Time to complete: 60 days. Resources: Part time of one officer.

The list of issues involved such areas as the State Department's relations with other agencies; its leadership role in the federal government; the leadership role of the ambassadors abroad, as well as the whole bureaucratic process in State and the effect of this internal bureaucracy on the individuals and institutions it was supposed to serve.

These projects were published in a booklet called, *Work Improvement Plans for the Department of State,* dated May 1961. The two lead paragraphs in the foreword of this document are symbolic of our determination to make things happen. They read in part:

Management improvements do not just happen—they must be planned and developed systematically. . . . We have a responsibility to improve organizational structure, delegate adequate authority, eliminate unnecessary procedures and checkpoints, simplify procedures, and reduce costs through effective utilization of manpower, materials, and money.

I must confess that the method of bringing about these changes that seemed to be most approved by the new administration and most attractive to me was the use of power. As a consequence a great deal of this planned change was brought about in those early days by large doses of Theory X—power!

The efforts to change the Department were launched by a direct, authoritarian order for leadership, combined with exhortations to the "troops" about the challenges and the rewards of acting in a new style. These efforts to make the Foreign Service officers of the Department of State into *leaders* of foreign policy started at the beginning of the Kennedy administration and continued throughout the ensuing Johnson terms.

CHANGE BY DIRECTIVE

The first step in the change process was the announcement by President Kennedy of the abolition of the OCB (Operations Coordinating Board). You will recall that the OCB was established to act as a staff arm of the President with the responsibility for bringing about interagency coordination and monitoring action decisions in the field of foreign policy.

One of President Kennedy's reasons for abolishing the OCB was to give the State Department the power and authority to assume a position of foreign policy leadership. With the abolition of OCB, State was no longer an equal with other agencies nor the first among equals in the area of foreign policy—it was now *the leader*! The President made it clear that the task of leadership in foreign affairs would be the responsibility of the Department of State.

Later, on May 31, 1962, President Kennedy, in an address to the Foreign Service Association, stressed the changing and challenging responsibilities of the Foreign Service job:

> This is the great period of the Foreign Service, much greater than any period that has gone before. . . . But it places the heaviest burden upon all of you. Instead of becoming merely experts in diplomatic history, or in current clippings from the *New York Times,* now you have to involve yourselves in every element of foreign life—labor, the class struggle, cultural affairs and all the rest—attempting to predict in what direction the forces will move. . . . Those who cannot stand the heat should get out of the kitchen. . . . Personally, I think the place to be is in the kitchen, and I am sure the Foreign Service Officers of the United States feel the same way.

MacGeorge Bundy, the President's assistant on national security matters, summarized the meaning of the change: "We have deliberately rubbed out the distinction between planning and operation . . ." in other words, between substance and management.

This executive order was quickly followed by exhortations of Secretary Rusk and President Kennedy to the officers of the Department to "Seize the reins of power and of leadership!"

In the abolition of the OCB the Kennedy administration simply stated that they would look to the State Department to assume the foreign affairs responsibilities formerly taken by the board and that they would look to other agencies of government for action when a matter of policy fell in their areas of interest. So by this dramatic and arbitrary order an agency and its functions were eliminated and organizational change was indeed brought about. Whether there was an accompanying change in behavior was another matter. The mere abolition of a function does not automatically cause people to act differently. As a matter of fact, most of the agencies concerned with foreign affairs quickly sensed that State would not move into the vacuum created by the abolition of OCB. So they did! They quickly established their own independence from State and successfully challenged State's attempts at leadership. As a result the problem actually became worse because the agencies were even more independent than before. Now there was real anarchy because there was no coordination and no real leadership or decision-making authority short of the President himself. No formal system was established to assume the functions of the OCB. The appropriate Departmental officers did not "seize the reigns of leadership."

The failure of State to fill the leadership vacuum and develop a strong system of coordination was clearly evident in the Bay of Pigs crisis. During that dramatic and tragic time it was obvious that there had been a failure on the part of the agencies to coordinate their information, plans, policies, and actions; they had left all of the necessary coordination to the President himself. State was not only impotent but had been largely ignored in this entire situation.

As a direct outgrowth of the Bay of Pigs fiasco the Operations Center (located in the Department of State) was established to provide the coordinating function once performed by the OCB. This War Room or Situation Room, as it was called, had the responsibility for pulling together all communications and action bearing on a crisis. People from all of the foreign affairs agencies of the government, including the military, were brought into this center and served on an around-the-clock basis. This action, however, *did not* put the State Department or its officers in charge. The physical location of the Center was at State, but the location of the coordinating and action power was taken back to the White House! State had flunked its first test of leadership.

BUILDING ON CRISIS

Another way we used Theory X to bring about change in the State Department during this time was in taking advantage of crisis situations. Often it was not the crisis itself but the way the crisis was handled, or the deficiency in the way it was handled, that gave us the opportunity to bring about change.

To illustrate how a crisis was used to trigger change consider the second Cuban incident: the Missile Crisis. For many months we had been concerned with the antiquated communications system of the Department of State. For many months we had studied the possibility of establishing a modern worldwide communications network. We had come to the conclusion that we must take action to coordinate the systems of the Department of State with those of the CIA and the military into an integrated overseas network for all foreign affairs agencies. But agency opposition, territorial jurisdiction, and costs pushed this project into the background—until the Missile Crisis. During this crisis our communications facilities failed. It was intended that in all foreign countries our ambassadors would have a text of the President's speech to the American people in advance so that they could keep friendly nations informed. We wanted to deliver to their contacts the contents of the President's message before it was made public to the American people. Our inability to accomplish this mission was a crisis of its own. As a direct result the State Department (by authoritarian directive) developed and put into operation a multimillion dollar, worldwide computerized communications system.

CONTINUING EFFORTS

The efforts of the President and the President's Special Assistants for Foreign Policy to make the State Department assume its role of leadership continued into the Johnson Administration.

You will recall that President Kennedy abolished the OCB and ordered State to take charge, but we needed the means to make it all to happen. We needed systems. One of our most pressing priorities was to develop systems by which the Department could exercise its new leadership in making policy and overseeing operations abroad.

This had to be done with other agencies because they were operating their own foreign affairs programs quite separately from State.

We developed a number of support activities that we thought were central to making the State Department's leadership role viable.

Policy Planning Council

Each agency of the government was quite independent of the State Department in establishing its foreign policies: developing overseas programs and getting funds from Congress for their support. They operated with almost total freedom.

We believed that there should be a means of establishing one comprehensive policy for the interests of the United States in each country. The Policy Planning Council was established to achieve this objective. It was made up of representatives of all agencies of our government with a State Department representative acting as chairman.

The Council operated quite well and did develop government policy statements for each country. The interesting thing was the lack of support that the State Department's officers themselves gave this effort. They were quite open about this lack of support. One could expect the other agencies to develop their own special policies for a country, outside the master plan, but it was distressing to find that our departments and officers considered the process a useless paperwork operation. Most of the plans simply were not used by the regional bureaus in their pursuit of U.S. goals abroad.

Despite Secretary Rusk's active participation, the plans were actually only nice desk-drawer documents. We knew it and were not too surprised, but we were determined to make them a basic force for change in the system.

We decided that the best way was to measure the foreign affairs programs of all U.S. agencies against these policies; this would be done, country by country, by the ambassador in each country. In this way we envisaged that the total U.S. program in a country (all countries virtually) would be developed, funded, and evaluated against the central, agreed-on policy for that country. This, of course, would require some kind of a common programming system.

A Policy Programming System

We thought that if we could devise a programming system we could evaluate each agency's program in each country against the U.S. policy for that country. If we could do this, we could program priorities among the agencies for resource allocation by the President and Congress. To achieve this objective we designed and developed a programming concept that we called "The Comprehensive Country Programming System." We selected and trained a cadre of enthusiastic young officers to install the program at selected embassies. They were to develop input data for the system by examining, country by country, all U.S. programs.

In 1965 President Johnson directed all U.S. agencies to conduct an evaluation in 13 countries. The project was strongly supported by Secretary Rusk, but the problem was that we had no commitment from the agencies involved or the ambassadors. In most cases there was much opposition. The program was imposed on the embassies and the other agencies. We did not have enough commitment even from the State Department people to enforce the directives that were issued. Every matter was controversial. If we wanted a decision, we had to carry it to the attention of the Secretary of State or the President before we could get action. There were just too many issues that we could not get solved at lower levels because the people at those levels did not want to make the decisions required. As a result the programs never got off the ground. Despite its great potential, its high quality, and the great need for it, the program failed.

We had initiated, developed, and established the whole strategy of this change in an authoritarian, directive way. We used all the power at our command to get the system installed and accepted, and it was supported by direct order of the President to the Secretary of State. In the end our efforts to accomplish our overall objective failed to become operational, and they failed, I am convinced, because of the *way* we went about bringing them into being and trying to use them rather than because of their lack of merit.*

CHANGE DID OCCUR

A great many other changes were brought about in the Department of State by our authoritarian process, for there was no lack of problems or ideas for their correction. The only issue was to get the bureaucracy

* In one case, though, political forces prevented us from developing a new personnel system in the department. Warwick (1975) describes the development of the new personnel policies and the senatorial indifference to their reflection in the Hays bill. He comments, "Crockett's major emphasis throughout was on such values as efficiency, flexibility, and modern management—virtues with doubtful appeal to most Senators" (p. 138).

to do something about accepting the ideas. One solution that we practiced in those days was taken from the Kennedy model. We would study an idea or plan and if we thought it made sense we simply told the bureaucracy to get on it. In many cases we had enough pressure to get the job done.

In many of our direct-line operations, when the change was not too complex and the authority was without challenge, the authoritarian process worked pretty well. Our attitude then was to sweep all the opposition under the rug and go ahead and accomplish things. However, we were not nearly so effective in bringing about change by this means when the authority was not so clear and direct. In a complex organization we found that it was difficult to make changes, even by authoritarian means, when we had to move across the borders of our own line of authority and operate in a staff capacity within the authority of the bailiwick of another. The authoritarian process and the force it carried fell off greatly and opposition formed that prevented the change from coming into being at all.

CHANGE WITHOUT COMMITMENT

The experiences that I have described convinced us that the authoritarian method of changing operational responsibilities and systems in an organization was not always the most effective. It could not ensure people's acceptance of change nor their enthusiastic and effective accomplishment of tasks. In fact, change imposed in this way generated hostility, suspicion, and defensiveness and mobilized both covert and overt opposition. In the end we were not successful, despite our best efforts to make sure that real change would occur. We had top level support; we established strong follow-up systems; we set up thorough inspections and controls; and we received inputs directly from many outside sources. But I felt that there was often surface change without commitment. There seemed to be a change of organization without a change in people's attitudes. I questioned whether we were accomplishing as much as we ought to be or as much as we thought we were. I was skeptical that the changes were really being put into the fabric of the system or into the hearts of people. I doubted that the changes would endure because there was too much evidence of opposition—and we had too many failures.

I came to the conclusion that there was surely a better way of bringing about change in a complex organization than the authoritarian approach that we had used in the past. Surely there was a way that would take into consideration the feelings and ideas of the people concerned; a way that would get them involved in seeing the need for change, in wanting the change, and in planning the methods that were to be used in effecting it. We needed a style of management that would cause people not only to change a procedure but their own behavior, their commitments, their attitudes, and their outlooks as well. I needed a management system in which we would not be dependent on a crisis to act as catalyst or on power as the motive force for the change. I needed a system in which the people themselves would become the prime sources for change because they could see that it would improve their own situations as well as the institution's.

PERSONAL INSIGHTS

About this time I attended my first T-group—an NTL President's Lab in Florida. It was led by Dr. Herbert Shepard and Dr. Jack Gibb. Although I had some deferential feelings toward the businessmen who were the principal participants in the lab, I personally felt that I was one of the best administrators in the whole federal government. Frankly, I was pretty satisfied with myself. I thought that I knew all of the problems, that I knew all of the answers, and that what I primarily needed to "straighten out the Department" was a group of loyal subordinates to carry out my policies and directives.

After a few days at the lab I was surprised, to say the least, by the feedback I was receiving. I recall sharing it with my wife Verla, who was there with me at the time, and curiously enough it was much like some of the feedback she had given me from time to time (which I had pooh-poohed as being just the usual "woman's bias"). To have a group of strangers tell me these things was tough to take. Among other things they said:

> You are devious and manipulative. . . . You are authoritarian. . . . You don't listen. . . . You intellectualize all feelings and refuse to deal with people on a feelings level. . . . You are sly, and we don't totally trust you, nor would we want to work for you.

At last it began to dawn on me that perhaps the problems we were having in gaining acceptance for our new programs and philosophies in the Department of State might, to some extent at least, be because of my own personal management style and how we were trying to bring them about. It was even more important that I saw (had mirrored for me) a side of myself and my behavior that I did not like and determined to change.

A STRATEGY FOR CHANGE

I had always felt, as a matter of pride and satisfaction, that I had tried to work *for* the people of the Foreign Service as well as for the best interest of the Department of State. My intentions were to help the State Department achieve a position of leadership in foreign affairs. Despite my good intentions and the many positive things that we had accomplished over the years, change had been brought about in an authoritarian manner, with power and harshness. As a result even those things that were beneficial were often suspected and even rejected.

Dr. Alfred Marrow (1974) in his book *Making Waves in Foggy Bottom* accurately describes my strategy:

During the next few months Crockett evolved a long-range plan and, in late 1964, felt ready to begin a number of substantial reforms. He realized that a large-scale action program of such scope would need substantial assistance from people of diverse talents and abilities from both outside and within the organization.

Here is what he did. He set up five separate groups of knowledgeable, experienced advisors to help him reform the practices in the Department and to give it a new administrative philosophy.

One group of advisers had three men of respected business and scientific credentials and distinguished backgrounds in large organizations. They would meet with Crockett at regular intervals for all-day sessions. These men were neither soft-minded nor faddists. They knew from personal experience the difficult problems of introducing a more participative system of management in large organizations. These men were E. Edgar Fogle, vice president of Union Carbide Corporation, Dr. Fred A. L. Holloway, president of Esso Research and Engineering Company, and myself, chairman of the board of the Harwood Manufacturing Corporation.

A second group consisted of teams of behavioral scientists who were recruited under a contract with the National Training Laboratories (currently the NTL Institute of Applied Behavioral Sciences) to lead one-week seminars using the T-group method of training. Here the participants would be placed in situations where they could take a clearer and more objective look at themselves and become more aware of their own behavior and that of the others involved with them.

A third group was composed of internal staff and outside experts who possessed specialized knowledge and skills. These included representatives from such diverse fields as art, architecture, building construction, food suppliers, education and others.

A fourth group was a scientific task force from the Institute for Social Research at the University of Michigan. Their assignment was to measure and evaluate the effectiveness of the program. They would observe all changes initiated, record how much was accomplished, and of what value. In sum, they would document the program and assess the results.

The fifth group was a consortium of outstanding behavioral scientists and individual State Department officers who were to develop and implement the program which was known as ACORD (an acronym for Action for Organizational Development). They were responsible for the broad administration of the program and served as the direct link with the training seminars led by the National Training Laboratories. They were also to act as a central base for developing and guiding the program, serving as a clearing house for communication and coordination and a source of support for line bureaus.

These five teams worked separately but all directed their efforts to help Crockett. The broad aim was to heighten the Department's effectiveness and to lead its people to find greater personal satisfaction in their jobs (pp. 14–16).

We changed to the Theory Y style of management early in 1965. In many ways this was the beginning of the most rewarding and interesting part of my State Department career. It was the part from which I received the most satisfaction because I think it was during this period that we tried to work *with* people rather than *against* them. I believed this style of management had the best chance of achieving the objectives of change, for it was the most effective, the most interesting, and the least harmful way of bringing change to the institution and to the people in it. This new approach to organizational change was called "ACORD," or "Action Program of Organizational Development."

The ACORD program was a multifaceted program designed to bring organizational change to the Department of State, but it was also designed to expose a wide group of State Department people to a new style of management. It used the insights and knowledge of the social and behavioral sciences to help teach people that their behavior as managers was as important as their techniques and skills of management.

We decided to make the administrative areas of the Department or State, with its 2500 people and their functions over which I had direct management responsibility, into a management laboratory for this program. We wanted to be able to observe the new management process and to determine the effectiveness of our new methods and organization. We wanted to be able to observe the commitment of the people involved and the problems they had so that from this learning we could develop valid programs and methods that could be used in other areas of the Department not directly under my responsibility.

Elimination of Hierarchy

It had long been the conviction of Secretary Rusk that we should eliminate layering and establish a wide lateral organization to improve performance. His idea was that we ought to have "a great many chiefs" who knew their jobs, who had well-established policy guidance, adequate resources, and some mutually determined goals and objectives, and who as a consequence would have a great deal of operational leeway and freedom to assume leadership in doing their jobs.

The State Department process for administration, as well as for policy, was turgid and unresponsive. The excessive layering effectively prevented good ideas from getting to the top and changes in policy direction from getting to the bottom. This was one of the symptoms of the Department as a whole and the very thing that had been addressed by both President Kennedy and Secretary Rusk. Secretary Rusk once said, "New ideas have a very high mortality rate in the Department of State." Leadership simply could not function because of the bureaucratic drag. I couldn't do much about this in other people's territory, but I thought that I could in my own. So I determined to decentralize certain key functions from the administration bureau to the regional and functional bureaus and to eliminate most of the supervisory levels between me and the operating managers. Therefore the first activity of the far ranging ACORD program was the creation of a flat organization to replace the deeply layered hierarchy that was typical of State. Donald Warwick (1975) in his book, *A Theory of Public Bureaucracy*, had this to say about the activity:

> The most dramatic and controversial feature of Management by Programs was the elimination of up to six levels of supervision between the Deputy Under Secretary and the Operating Manager. The axe was applied to 125 positions ranging from middle level to top management. Among the slots eliminated were the offices of the Assistant Secretary and the Deputy Assistant Secretary for Administration—the two positions immediately below Crockett. Using the former Employment Unit as an example, Figure [1] shows the drastic effects of the reorganization on the structure of O.
>
> In June 1965 six levels of hierarchy stood between the Deputy Under Secretary

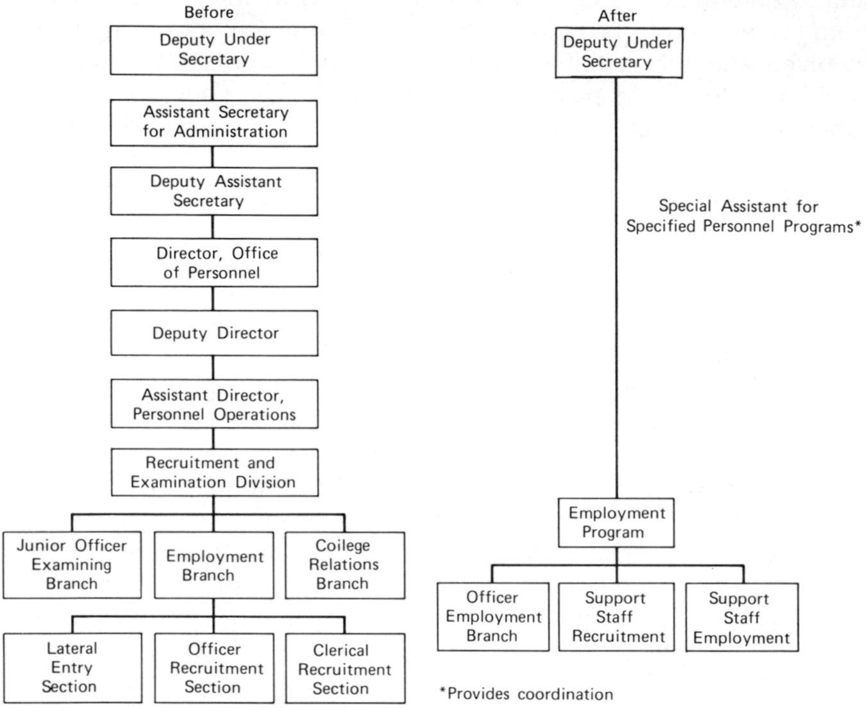

Figure 5.1 The employment unit in O before and after the 1965 reorganization. *Source*: Adapted from *A Management Program for the Department of State*, Office of the Deputy Under Secretary for Administration, U.S. Department of State, 1966.

and the Director of the Employment Program; afterward, at least in theory, the manager reported directly to Crockett. In all, twenty-seven operating units were removed in this fashion from the traditional hierarchy and were placed under Management by Programs (p. 38).

The second activity which was a cornerstone of the ACORD program was the organization of the whole administrative area of the Department of State under the concept of "Management by Objectives and Programs" (MOP). This, in reality, was an advanced version of "Management by Objectives." Warwick continued:

Management by Objectives provides the newly designated program managers with greater autonomy in operating their units. The plan was simple enough; each program manager was to specify the objectives, target dates, and resources needed for his unit. He or she would then discuss these points with the Deputy Under Secretary until an agreement was reached. The resulting program statement became an operating charter for the following year and a yardstick for measuring progress. Thereafter the manager was to carry out the day-to-day operations of the program with a minimum of supervision. Subsequent events showed that the theory of Management by Objectives was more clear than the practice. Some managers were able to draft their charter and move ahead unsupervised, but others tripped on remnants of the old hierarchy (pp. 38–39).

The organizational changes created by management of programs and objectives was not the end but the means to an end. The objective was to change the management style of the Department from X to Y—from reaction to proaction—from excessive encumbrance of bureaucracy to freedom of action—to leadership. To get at this change in style we felt that we had to help people understand the impact of their own behavior on others and help them to develop a personal change process.

I outlined this entire program in July 1965 when I spoke to some 450 management supervisors of the administrative arm (known as the O area). This was the essence of my remarks as Alfred Marrow (1974) describes them in his book *Making Waves in Foggy Bottom*:

Our challenge is to find a structure—one which releases people from the obstacles and inhibitions of our highly centralized organization, thus permitting them to feel they are their own managers, with their own operations. Is there a way of organizing ourselves so that each of us can feel that we are a vital part of the whole?

I believe that our present concept of decentralized management by objectives and programs will accomplish these objectives by decentralizing our management into self-contained, semi-independent, semi-autonomous programs, each with a manager; eliminating every intermediate supervisory level; delegating almost complete authority for daily operations to the program managers; ensuring that each program manager has the resources, the tools, the people, the money, the authority, the regulations, the means, and the conviction for attaining our mutually established goals (pp. 20–21).

I then reviewed the problems and obstacles, refuting some but acknowledging others. Next I discussed my expectations and described what they could expect from me: understanding, resources, availability, and support. Some supervisors were persuaded but many were pessimistic and a bit fearful.

Training

Providing training for our bureaucratically freed managers was high on my priority list. We believed that there were two kinds of orientation that people needed to make the new organization work: a conceptual understanding of their own roles and responsibilities and an experiential understanding of their own management styles. These two objectives were incorporated into a single training program, which consisted of off-site seminars conducted by the National Training Laboratory of Washington, D.C., and directed by professional behavioral science trainers about once every two months for State Department personnel.

Some of the sessions were "cousin groups," for which two people in the Department were selected at random; others were vertical slices of people within the same organization; still others were peer groups. By this means we spread the new management style and theory widely within the State Department as well as beyond its borders to the other organizations with whom we had to deal. These sessions were not unlike those that I had attended earlier. Many of the participants reported dramatic discoveries about themselves that they went on to change. In addition, we sent key people to outside training laboratories before assigning them to management positions in newly created programs.

More than 200 Foreign Service officers, including a number of ambassadors and deputy chiefs of mission, attended one session or another. Chris Argyris, then of Yale, Lee Bradford, then Director of NTL, and Warren Bennis, then of MIT, conducted most of the workshops.

Many officers characterized what they had learned as valuable and some said the program was the most important experience of their lives. Others were less enthusiastic and many resented the fact that they had been sent.

Team Building

Another approach used was what we called "team-building" sessions, which were short, off-site meetings of one to three days, conducted by a behavioral scientist trainer. These meetings provided a closer look at the problems of the group than had the other kinds of training and seminars, for they involved people who were working together in an organization unit.

At these meetings we considered the actual problems of the organization, both substantive and process. The agenda also centered around the difficulties group members had in working together and the things in the group that were getting in the way of effective operations. Sometimes they came together after a trainer had completed premeeting questioning of each of the group's members to discuss their problems and interpersonal relations. When this occurred, the trainer brought to the meeting a deeper perception of the group and the issues that should be discussed. At other times the teams would get together without preliminary research and in their discussion bring the issues that were bothering them into the open, thus reaching a better understanding of what it was that was holding back their effective operation.

I thought it only fair, as well as logical, that the first State Department team-building should start with me and my group. We began as near to the top of the State Department as we could, which was with my own team, for those above me were always "too busy" to be bothered with anything but exhortations about leadership. For this meeting we used Charles Ferguson of UCLA and Charles Seashore of NTL as our facilitators. I found it to be an exhilarating process which I forced on others in true Theory X style. Many of my critics called this "achieving Theory Y by a Theory X process." Unfortunately this was the case.

At this first team-building meeting I was able to carry into my management life the things that I had learned and experienced about myself in my first T-group. But everyone became involved. There were many job-related problems, as well as many personal relationships, that got on top of the table for discussion for the first time. Why do you act this way? Why don't you like me? Why do you mistrust me? What do I do that annoys you so? How can I gain your confidence? Why are you so rigid? The amazing thing to me was that the people were actually eagerly working on their own problems without getting angry, almost saying: "Get on to mine. I would like to talk about the cluster around my name, and although I don't really believe it if it's true let's talk about it and I'll try to do something about it." I would see the group, hour by hour, literally growing in trust, growing in solidarity. They were somehow involved here with one another as they had never been before. In our old back-home staff meetings they were just individuals attending a not too interesting discussion of another person's function. Here they were a real group facing their mutual problems together.

We talked about how we could work better as a group; how we could make group decisions; how we could share the problems that were coming to me; and how each member in the group could broaden his interest beyond his own territory and responsibility so that he would have a share in the whole group's problem. We discussed how the group could rid itself of its own parochialism and start a process of enlarging its interest and responsibility by working together. There were confrontations and conflict and they were handled. There were feedback and caring, disagreements and frustrations and these were handled. Personal animosities were probed and discussed and often settled or at least understood. There were also creativity and risk, and in the end there was a real sense of commitment to the principles that I at one time had thought that I might get more quickly by directive or more easily by manipulation.

A story such as this would not be complete without some description of what happened after the group went back to work in its real-life situation. Certainly it would be erroneous to say that there were no continuing problems because there were. The process did not guarantee that there would not be continuing problems. All the old animosities were not forgotten. The process did not promise that either. Conflicts and disagreements remained, but in the weeks and months that followed the group showed a highly increased capability of getting issues out into the open, of surfacing the hidden problems, and of exposing personal animosities so that we could deal with them. We worked together as a group.

It did break down the fragmentation that had existed. The process of welding ourselves into an integrated management team was started. As a result, I believe that there was a broader understanding of points of view and the total issues, a better understanding of the total problems and programs, and a greater commitment on the part of everyone to the total goals.

Team Building Downward

Several of the members of my team decided that they would like to take their own staff members off site for the same kind of team-building meetings. This was courageous on their part because they had seen how difficult it had been for me, "the boss." Yet they were willing to take the risks because of the obvious vitality of the process in bringing people together, in opening people up so that they could make contributions, in actually reducing conflict by facing it, and in the commitment that resulted when people participated and were really involved in the management process.

As a result of this experience we started forming subordinate subgroups for team-building sessions. We felt that it was important for the subordinates to be able to have such meetings of their own, and many of them later decided to go off site with their own subordinates for similar interaction. In this way, the effect cascaded downward so that there were subgroups and sub-subgroups, all down the management line, having these meetings. Each group would use a behavioral scientist as a trainer and would meet to talk about how they worked together, what their problems were and how they could solve them.

This team-building process did catch hold in others parts of the State Department; for example, Joseph Palmer, Assistant Secretary of State for African Affairs, used the same technique of going off site with his staff to better the management and decision-making processes in his bureau. The same kind of program was planned for the Latin American Bureau and other areas. It is interesting to note that it was in these two bureaus that State Department leadership was most effectively organized and developed.

In a letter to Alfred Marrow a senior Foreign Service officer had this to say about the team-building experience:

> Chris Argyris, in my judgment, is neither entirely right nor entirely wrong. Argyris, in focusing on the interpersonal problem, has put his finger on a part of the problem. He fails, however, to recognize that the alleged inefficiency of the State Department is more a function of the complexity of the world in which we live than of either organizational or interpersonal inadequacies. The most significant fact about foreign policy remains that any government's influence in dealing with foreigners, or even its own citizens, is limited. Yet we certainly do need to improve our performance, and, clearly, we should try to learn what we can from the social psychologists.
>
> Now it is commonplace to note that the principal asset of the State Department is its personnel. If exposure to the social psychologists leads to a significantly better performance by only one or two officers (to say nothing of the several hundred participants so far), it is not inconceivable that the overall savings to the U.S. will far exceed the costs. If we accept three propositions,
>
> first, that the Foreign Service has something to learn,
>
> second, that the professional social psychologists have something of value to impart, and
>
> third, that how FSO's handle or mishandle situations can have momentous consequences,
>
> the odds make social psychology at several hundred thousand dollars a year a good betting proposition for the State Department. I'm prepared to testify personally that I believe the marginal utility to me—and I hope to the Department—of the expenditure on my week of "Sensitivity Training" was higher than that of any week of FSO training to which I've been exposed . . . (Marrow, 1974, pp. 86–87).

An External Consulting Team

An important ingredient in ensuring the effectiveness of the ACORD program was building an external consulting team, a professional group of behavioral scientists that could come in to work with us as we needed them. This association of top-flight social and behavioral scientists from the NTL network with the State Department was an important part of the program.

In addition to serving as a training staff at special seminars and team-building and problem-solving sessions, these professionals worked closely with line operators to help form a strong link between *training* and *follow-up* action within the organization. They were available to attend problem-solving meetings and were on hand to observe the process of the group in other operational modes. They would often stop the group in its work to have it focus its attention on the process within the group as well as on the problem under discussion. They coached and counseled with the leader and members.

Internal Change Agents

As a part of the ACORD project we also developed internal change agents or consulting teams. Staff members of the ACORD program were identified and trained to act as internal consultants. They were assigned to our program managers and assisted them in all kinds of organizational development matters. They were available on a full-time basis to meet with operators and their staffs, to talk with them about their problems, do research with their people, and then feed this research back to the manager so that he could see what he was doing and how it was affecting his internal operations. This permitted an increased involvement and a better continuity between the individual consultants from the outside and the organizations to which they were assigned on the inside.

Changes in Organization Require Systems Development

I mentioned earlier that we changed the structure of the organization. When we established the system of Management by Objectives and Programs, it became evident that structural and procedural changes were necessary to make the whole organization function better. Just as we had learned that it was not enough to work on the structure without regard for interpersonal relationships we also learned that changes in the structure required changes in procedures and systems.

In other words, people had to work within the structure (organization) and the structure could not be effectively changed without involving the people. In all cases, however, procedures and systems had to be changed for the system to work.

Procedures of work flow, decision making, and paper processing are so interrelated with structure, interpersonal relationships, and the procedures (the system) that all have impact on the overall goal of improving organizational effectiveness and all must be given attention almost simultaneously.

Therefore a "systems approach" was used extensively. By this means we tried to take into account not only interpersonal relationships but the whole life of the organization, the way the staff meetings were conducted, the way people were promoted and compensated, the way the organizational parts were linked, the way information flowed, the way decisions were made, who needed to see whom about what, and so on. We found out very early that a significant change in one part of the system directly affected another part, which would then require systems development. We discovered that the failure to bring about a procedural revision in one part of the system after we had changed another part seriously inhibited the whole process. Therefore, as part of the ACORD program, we had a group working only on systems and systems modifications. Their job was to ensure that the system *as a whole* was linked with common procedures and that all the interfaces required to make a complex organization work were provided for.

Research

Another ingredient that played an important part in the program was research. A general body of theory, which we put vigorously into practice, required some research to give us knowledge of our progress. It also gave us quick recognition of whatever new problems our organization was causing. We felt a need for carrying on a variety of action-oriented research efforts in conjunction with the programs themselves. These activities included such things as premeeting interviews, open discussions by participants in off-site meetings, and written surveys to determine the effect of major organizational changes on people. Research gave us help in diagnosing the real-life situations we faced in fulfilling our program objectives and provided specific targets at which we could aim in our meetings to solve problems without wasting time or without beating about the bush. This research effort was carried on under contract with the Center for Research on Utilization of Scientific Knowledge, Institute for Social Research, The University of Michigan.

Public Advisors

Another important part of the ACORD program, although perhaps not so important in a business institution as in a public institution, was our Board of Public Advisors. Early on in the establishment of the program I felt that it would be useful to have a group of businessmen, experienced in OD programs in their own organizations and committed to the process, to advise me on methods of accomplishing the program in the Department of State.

Public Information—Reports on the System

Early in 1967 I released a report on the Foreign Service written by Dr. Chris Argyris. The material for his report came from numerous meetings he had held in an off-site training session for Foreign Service officers.

The purpose of releasing the report was neither to cause furor nor to punish the Foreign Service: it was meant to create an appreciation of the behavior that we in the service had fallen into and which was keeping us from attaining the leadership objectives that the President wanted us to achieve. It was meant to build dialogue and to serve as a means of developing additional change programs. The report was candid, critical, and might have been seen as an attack on the Department. Some of my colleagues urged me not to permit its publication. Once the report was written, however, I felt very strongly that it must be made available within the Department and to those outsiders who might have an interest in it. In the introduction to the report (Argryis, 1967), I said, in part:

> The Department of State has been fortunate to have had Dr. Chris Argyris of Yale step out of the academic ranks, even if briefly, to devote his wide background in the behavioral sciences and in administrative practices to serve us a kind of alter ego. And I mean an alter ego in the finest sense of that phrase; as a friend and confidant.
>
> The decision to publish a study of this kind, or to publish it without censoring the quotations, was not taken lightly. Large organizations in general are not noted for being candid about internal problems and differing viewpoints. We also recognized the fact that the sessions in which this material was developed were problem-oriented. This naturally produced a strong bias in favor of what was wrong. Consequently many of the good things about the system, including its strengths and the deep dedication of its people, or the prevalence of positive attitudes about the organization, are not reflected in the paper. It would have been much easier not to publish Dr. Argyris' work

for fear that the material might be twisted out of context or otherwise treated unsympathetically.

Several considerations argued against such a cautious attitude. The first was the realization that, if we really are breaking new ground in our organizational development program, it would behoove us to take this risk—to be open about the ambivalent attitudes, feelings, and frustrations of the people who constitute the "living system."

A second realization was that the quotations appearing in this work, with minor changes of time and place, could have been uttered by persons in any large organization; that what we are dealing with here are problems typical of all large enterprises (private and public) and not alone of the Department of State. This, indeed, is a point that Dr. Argyris himself stresses.

Finally, the most positive reason is that being honest and open about the problems dealt with in this study offers the best beginning for dealing with them effectively and constructively.

These are one skilled observer's views of a highly complex, diversified organization; an expert observer's partial sample. They are presented in the hope that they will be tested against the Department's collective experience to stimulate a continuing examination which will improve this essential institution through which we all serve the American people.

We shall need the understanding and support of all its members if we are to achieve the goals we mutually seek.

Despite the furor that this report created both within and outside the State Department, I believe it was useful. It is still my conviction that the living system of our public organizations must be exposed to public view. It is only when this is done that the public can protect itself from dangerous systems and deceitful processes, neither of which faithfully serves the real public interest. Change can be made to occur from outside pressure or will come from internal need.

THE RESULTS

By coupling all of these activities (as well as a great many others) into a program called ACORD and by earnestly using the humanistic management concepts of Theory Y, we tried to involve the people who were to be most affected by the change in the change process itself. We hoped by this means to secure more commitment to the objectives that we were seeking to achieve. We tried to make people feel that they had a personal stake in the results. We tried to ensure that their personal goals were consistent with the organizational goals, and vice versa, and therefore to avoid the conflicts of interest the individual might have had in pursuing the corporate goals versus his own.

Donald P. Warwick (1975) summarizes some of the results:

> The most striking positive effects in the first period were in the area of managerial autonomy. An intensive survey of program managers revealed a marked reduction in the number of clearances required for action, as well as in the amount of direction received from superiors. The same data showed a slight to moderate improvement in the efficiency of communication (especially upward), job motivation, and, at least in the eyes of the managers, actual performance. The following comments convey the flavor of these findings:
>
> "The big advantage is the abolition of layering. Personnel, when I arrived, was a quagmire. There were miles of people between me and Crockett. At first it was a naked but satisfying feeling."
>
> "The biggest advantage is that it tries to give each of us as much autonomy as possible, to work out our own program, give us our own facility to implement, so objectives are more easily realized."
>
> "It has cut down on a helluva lot of clearances and red tape."
>
> The impact of the changes on the clients of O was more mixed but, on balance, positive. The most important clients, the regional bureaus, reported greater speed and flexibility in their work as a result of the decentralization of functions. They also noted slight improvements in the quality and speed of services obtained from the restructured O units. The internal clients of O, those programs and divisions dependent on other O units for services, were even more enthusiastic in their ratings of the quality and promptness of services. The functional bureaus were considerably less happy with the changes than the other clients.
>
> A final positive effect was a spirit of experimentation that went beyond the original sites of change. "I gained personally from being part of the experiment," one supporter commented. "I borrowed some of this to apply to [unreorganized unit], but structured it in a different way." A division chief observed: "The last five years have been a period of great turmoil in the philosophy, organizational structure, and attitudes of O. This has been good, for there has been progress in the turmoil—a modernization." Others added that even though Crockett went too far too fast, he was to be commended for launching a frontal attack on the inveterate problems of layering and clearances (pp. 46–47).

In all honesty things did not work so smoothly as we had hoped. No matter how carefully a plan is made, no matter how wide the participation, and no matter how well the communications are done, there are still those who can legitimately claim that they neither had adequate knowledge nor enough participation in the process. And some just plainly did not like the new system. Again, to quote Warwick:

> Still, the first year was far from organizational bliss. The reforms were hobbled from the outset by the initial suspicion and resistance of those most intimately involved. The hastiness of the changes, the narrow base of participation, and poor communication about its scope and intent also generated concern and resentment in other parts of the Department. The acceptance of MOP was further stymied by the long history of reorganizations in the department, leading to the feeling that "we've seen it all before"; by its glaring departures from managerial orthodoxy; by a string of other reforms undertaken at about the same time; and by perennial bad blood between O and the bureaus, between "substance" and "administration." Some of these difficulties were surmounted during the first year; others persisted (p. 47).

LAST DAYS

I retired from the State Department soon after these research inquiries were made. My successor did not like the organization I left, disapproved of my management style, and had no stomach for change except to get the State Department's organization back into its traditional bureaucratic boxes as quickly as possible. The grand design, despite the efforts of many outside people to keep it alive, succumbed to the pressures of traditionalism. There is no evidence that Secretary Rusk ever responded to a letter written after I left the Department by Dr. Chris Argyris, dated on February 21, 1967:

> The program that Bill Crockett began (ACORD), with careful nurturing could become the finest example of genuine change in a large governmental organization, initiated, guided, and successfully executed by members within the system. In addition, the program makes a modest beginning to induce people to take on more responsibility and take risks. Moreover, this program has within it the ingredients to provide a viable basis for establishing and integrating PP & B [planning, programming, and budgeting], plus the other recommendations of the Hitch Committee into the living system of the State Department.
>
> The progress of the ACORD project, and more important, of the attempts being made by high ranking Foreign Service officers to unfreeze the system and make it more effective could be greatly accelerated with some more visible support by you and others at the highest levels.

Drs. Alfred Marrow, Rensis Likert, and I have been working together trying to be of help to the State Department to change its internal system. If you would find it convenient to meet with any one or a combination of us, we would appreciate the opportunity to inform you further about our work.

ACORD was dead and with it died the chance of the State Department to seize the reigns of leadership in Foreign Affairs.

LEARNINGS

Some of the things that I learned from that period have come to me in recent years. They were not so directly apparent to me then. So the learnings are chiefly retrospective.

1. *Organizational change does not guarantee behavioral change*

The most obvious learning from our experience is that organizational change may not bring about a change in organizational behavior.

There is no doubt that leaders have the power and the authority to change organizational functions and responsibilities. Our experience amply revealed that fact, but it also showed that the real power and authority for achieving the spirit envisaged for the change lie with the people themselves.

The two presidents wanted the people of the Department of State to exercise leadership. They moved boxes around and issued orders to make leadership emerge. It did not emerge because the people concerned, for whatever complex reasons, did not behave like leaders. The organizational changes did not affect changes to the living system —the people system—of the organization.

This ultimate power of the people to do or not to do seems to be one of the most illusive and difficult lessons of organizational life for leaders to learn. The history of organizational failure is replete with examples of this most basic mistake.

In retrospect, we made the same mistake time after time with the same dismal results. Our attempts to bring change to the State Department were in fact the imposition of the view of others—outsiders—on the people of the Department. The Kennedys, President Johnson, the task forces, and even the Crocketts were seen as unfriendly outsiders. The diagnosis of the problems of State was well stated in a report made by Chris Argyris and published by the Department in 1967, but being an external source it was hotly denied and strongly denounced by the people of State. They could not accept it as an accurate perception of themselves.

The only means of ensuring that data and diagnoses are accepted is to involve the people in the process itself. In this way they own the problem and will take over the solutions. It is on the issue of *ownership* (of the problems and their solutions) that the fate of change hangs —whether it is to be lasting or transitory; to be implemented in fact or to be window dressing to fool the power that is forcing it depends on the degree of ownership that people feel.

2. *Too much*

Another obvious risk for a change effort is in attempting too much, too quickly. The foregoing is a recounting of just the major change efforts that we had underway.

It is of little import that there was a grand design and that all the changes fitted together neatly into the mosaic of the final objective. The important thing is that far too much was attempted. We did not have the time to oversee them all. We did not have the energy to nurture them all. We did not have the power to push them all. We did not have the insight to involve all the people who should have been made a part of them. It was far too ambitious an effort for the organization to digest and implement.

If I were to do it over, I would be more patient with the process. I would involve a great many more people and groups. I would include all the interested constituencies from the inception of the problem and try to make it their problem for their solution. Instead, I thought that I knew all the problems and had all the answers (which I probably had), but this attitude does not elicit broad support. I met my needs—not theirs.

I would have started earlier to ensure that my personal assistants and those responsible with me for bringing about change also worked through the participative mode instead of the authoritarian: "the boss wants so-and-so to be done." I suspect that there was much of that by fine, loyal subordinates who fell into this trap as a means of getting things done for me.

3. *Theory Y style is difficult*

Theory Y management is neither a traditional nor a "natural" way for leaders to behave and for decisions to be made in most of our organizations. This humanistic style must be strongly supported if it is to survive. After I left the Department of State the management programs, organization, and reforms that I initiated dwindled out of existence. This is not necessarily discouraging. It only illustrates the fact that the Theory Y management style cannot long survive in a hostile climate. It is not some kind of magic. People can share, risk, care, handle conflict, and handle confrontation by these techniques only if it is their management's desire that it be that way. If management does not want it, then people can also be managed by the old techniques of authority, power, and fear. People are resilient, versatile, and facile in adjusting their personal survival to the various modes and styles of management.

Despite the seeming fragility of Theory Y concepts, it is neither soft-headed nor "easy." It is much easier to sit in the big office and issue directives. It is much easier to avoid personal confrontation by issuing orders.

I am convinced that a program of organizational change, no matter what its specific agenda of action, is best for the living organization and the people involved when it works *with* people in the spirit of Theory Y. This means trying to bring about changes in the structure of the organization, in methods and procedures of operation, outlook and climate, job design, and managerial behavior, by working *with* people. People have the data. It is their problem. If we can work with people rather than arbitrarily making decisions for them, they will solve their own problems. Too many of us try to force our decisions on people when we have little knowledge or understanding of what it is all about. It is easier to avoid personal involvement and conflict with people by smoothing over the surface. Theory Y management is for those managers who are willing to take the gut punishment of a truly toughminded approach to management. It is for those who believe that conflict can be handled best by confronting it openly. It is for those who understand that the real commitment of their people can be secured only by their participation in the development of making plans and setting objectives.

4. *Introduction to Theory Y concepts by Theory Y methods*

The authoritarian method of change creates emotional disturbances, animosities, and schisms within the group that are never healed. It builds up distrust, resistance, and fear, which can mean that the change is never effective and never implemented. It is my conviction that a good OD program gives people an opportunity to work together in groups to solve their own problems and those of the groups. This is the only way that a change that depends on the overt support of the people affected can succeed. There is indeed dry truth to that old midwestern farm adage—"You can lead a horse to water but you cannot make him drink."

Most of the reform programs I started in the Department were top-down directions from me. This was also true of the presidential reform. There was little participation in the launching, even though participation was one of the goals. To create a Theory Y organization with a Theory Y climate and Theory Y managers, no doubt a Theory Y means of getting it all started is an essential part of the process.

Perhaps the most serious mistake I made was in trying to inject the programs as a top-down reform, using tough Theory X methods and relying too much on the diagnoses of *outside* experts and *outside* task forces, study groups, and advisory bodies. I am sure their diagnoses were accurate and their prescriptions for change, correct. However, the patient did not even admit to his illness; thus the diagnoses were strongly denied and the medicine, when administered, was not only bitter and punishing but mostly rejected.

Because change is slow and painful, it must be well planned, well coordinated, and well communicated. Above all, the people affected must be involved. The lessons from the two major efforts that I have described—giving the Department of State leadership over policy and the new style of management for administration—both indicate the same conclusion: top-down reorganization will not necessarily change the attitude and behavior of the people involved. If the behavior is not supportive of the new structure and objectives, then no real change will have occurred. In both cases the objectives were legitimate but the process was authoritarian, therefore suspect.

5. *Involvement and support from the top*

Major change efforts need the continued involvement and support of the top of the organization. The top officers of the Department of State, and even the presidents (Kennedy and Johnson), contributed occasionally but were lacking in consistency and constancy in their follow-up support when it was most needed. The programs took on the image of a Crockett Crusade, which left many people in doubt of their motives and validity.

This failure to get the "top" involved created uneasiness among some of the managers. It gave them the impression that the whole program was lacking in sincerity, purpose, and commitment. This caused it to lose some of the validity that it might have had if top management had been more personally and directly concerned.

Rusk was not particularly interested in helping to implement the organizational reforms that his own concept of State Department leadership required. Perhaps they smacked all too much of the "bureaucratic infighting" that he had warned us many years earlier that he would not support. As an ambassador later said, "When the Secretary says 'Go' loud and clear and makes everyone understand that he means to have it done, then we can fit the pieces together without much difficulty. But until then, why pass our time planning for something that will probably never happen?" In discussing disagreements with representatives of other agencies in his country, the ambassador remarked that "when it comes to an open confrontation, in most cases if I try to make an issue which will be carried upstairs it is pretty likely that I will lose. They know it. And I know it." Secretary Rusk urged his departmental assistants to assume leadership at the very time he urged against bureaucratic conflict with other agencies.

6. *A supportive management style*

I believe that efforts must be made to help people acquire a management style that is supportive of the new organization norms and objectives. The T-group is a valuable tool that helps people to get started and provides a focal point for disseminating information about the program and its objectives. It did help us to create a receptive attitude and a climate of trust and commitment that somehow must take place in an organization before it can move forward effectively in its own renewal. This must occur if its living force is to change.

The laboratory training laid the foundation for subsequent team-building and problem-solving meetings that were essential to the success of the program and perhaps did as much as any single thing in contributing to it.

I do not believe that sending people to strange labs or training sessions outside the living environment of the organization is the most effective way of bringing about organizational changes. This alone will not create a change in the climate of development. Personal and group learning and development can best be accomplished by common group experience. Growth, the creation of new norms, and changes in personal behavior can be achieved by a work group that experiences the new concepts and moves forward together.

T-group learning does help people to deal with ambiguity and change. Our organizational development program had to be flexible enough to meet the new situations and new problems that people faced and to move to any new situation that emerged. We needed people who could accommodate themselves to these changes.

CONCLUSION

The various efforts to achieve a more effective Department of State that I have described in this chapter were not developed at any one time. Some of them were ideas that had been in progress in the Department of State for a number of years. They did not occur in the orderly sequence in which I have placed them. Often many were in progress at the same time, but all put together indicate a consistency of approach, a unity of purpose, and a climate for inquiry that, to me, was impressive.

Many of the objectives were so illusive, albeit important, that they will probably never be fully achieved. Others, although temporarily achieved, will have to be redone as conditions, environment, and management change. All our efforts toward this organizational renewal were important for the simple reason that if people—management and staff alike—do not make an effort to improve themselves and their operations their operations will become outmoded and archaic. Management, like all other activities and disciplines, is not static. Management, in various organizational programs, must endeavor to be ready to take advantage of the new concepts and theories wherever they emerge. It is hoped that it will be in the vanguard testing, experimenting, and even creating the new. Then, when change is introduced with the involvement and help of the people concerned, lasting effects will be felt.

In our experience there were irritations because the old ways of getting the job done were no longer effective. There were frustrations because the new systems needed to nourish the whole took time to develop and install. There were mistakes because we were people, but there was excitement, fun, commitment, enthusiasm, and a sense of freedom that I had never experienced in a large institution. The involvement of people in their own change was a tremendously exciting adventure in a new management and organizational style. It was worth the effort.

6

A Survey Feedback and Problem-Solving Intervention in a School District
"We'll Take the Survey but You Can Keep the Feedback"

SUSAN A. MOHRMAN
ALLAN M. MOHRMAN
ROBERT A. COOKE
ROBERT B. DUNCAN

Many of the organization development or planned change efforts conducted in schools have been based, at least in part, on the "feeding back" of survey data. These *survey feedback* interventions generally involve collecting data on a standardized questionnaire from members of organizational work groups. The results are then compiled for each work group and returned to it for the identification of problems and the development of solutions. These survey feedback and group problem-solving efforts typically are supported by process guidance in which an internal or external consultant facilitates the difficult process of group problem solving by, for example, "opening" the group and ensuring that all members participate in the problem-solving activities. Although data-based programs have not always proved to be effective, various interventions—including the one that is the focus of this chapter—have used survey feedback techniques, and this approach to organization change has often been considered to be particularly appropriate for educational systems (Coughlan and Cooke, 1974; Zaltman, Florio, and Sikorski, 1977).

The survey feedback approach seems to be relevant for schools because it has the potential for promoting change and improvement in both individuals and organizations. Valid and "objective" information provided to organization members (teachers or administrators) can stimulate change by pointing out the need for corrective behavior and by promoting the search for new behaviors (cf. Nadler, 1976; Vroom, 1964). When feedback data are analyzed in groups, change is further facilitated as members build on one another's suggestions and as the group becomes committed to implementing solutions (Mann and Likert, 1952). Assuming that various groups in an organization participate in survey feedback and problem solving, change at the organizational level can be achieved. The implication is that valid data about the organization, in terms of products and processes, can be instrumental in correcting the way the system is operating.

Data feedback can be used to promote two different types of change in organizations. First, it can provide information that identifies failures to achieve existing goals and therefore can stimulate changes that will bring the system back "on target." This type of change corresponds to "single-loop learning" (Ashby, 1952). The theories in use—the existing individual and organizational values and strategies—set the boundaries for action and provide programs for reaching objectives (see Argyris and Schon, 1975). Second, data feedback processes can generate information that is the catalyst for more basic changes in the system. These changes center around the goals themselves and the "model" that members hold for defining the strategies available to individuals and organizations. This type of change corresponds to "double-loop learning"; that, according to Argyris and Schon, opens the organization to more fundamental changes. Data can be an effective catalyst for this type of learning if they are fed back in a context in which individuals are aware of and responsive to alternative "theories-of-action" and are able to practice behaviors that differ from those prescribed by the organization.

Survey feedback has the potential for stimulating both types of change. Only limited evidence exists, however, that data-based interventions help organizations to reach their present goals and even less evidence that they bring about the changes associated with double-loop learning. Given the "track record" of survey feedback (and organization development in general), the results of a data-based intervention we recently conducted in a school district are not surprising. This survey feedback program, although moderately successful in many regards, was unsuccessful in other respects. In this chapter we review this intervention from a "failure perspective" in an attempt to identify problems and mistakes that might otherwise go unnoticed. We begin by presenting the intervention model and examining the assumptions underlying survey feedback in general and our model in particular. The survey feedback intervention is then described in the context of these assumptions. We conclude by discussing some of the knowledge acquired in this organization development experience.

THE DESIGN OF THE INTERVENTION

Our survey feedback organization development model was designed specifically for educational systems. The intervention was intended to be consistent with the environment in which schools operate, the somewhat uncertain and interdependent nature of educational processes, and the professional orientation of the teaching staff. Survey feedback techniques were to be used to promote the structural modification of schools; that is, to develop collective decision structures for faculty problem solving and change initiation. The intervention was an expanded version of an earlier survey feedback program which, in a previous field experiment, was shown to be associated with organizational change and improvements in faculty work attitudes (Coughlan, Cooke, and Safer, 1972). The present action-research program, funded by the National Institute of Education, was conducted to provide an in-depth evaluation of the program's effectiveness in a medium-sized urban school system. The intervention differs somewhat from other survey feedback programs and, as such, is reviewed here in terms of the *data* used for feedback, the *group structures* in which the data were analyzed, and the *change model* that guided the feedback and problem-solving activities.

The Data

Two versions of a work-attitudes questionnaire, the *School Feedback Survey*, were used to collect and return data to elementary and secondary school teachers. A similar survey was prepared for the principals in the district. The questionnaires consisted of 155 task-oriented items that tapped 14 dimensions of school functioning, including the environment, input, process, and output of the school (Figure 6.1).

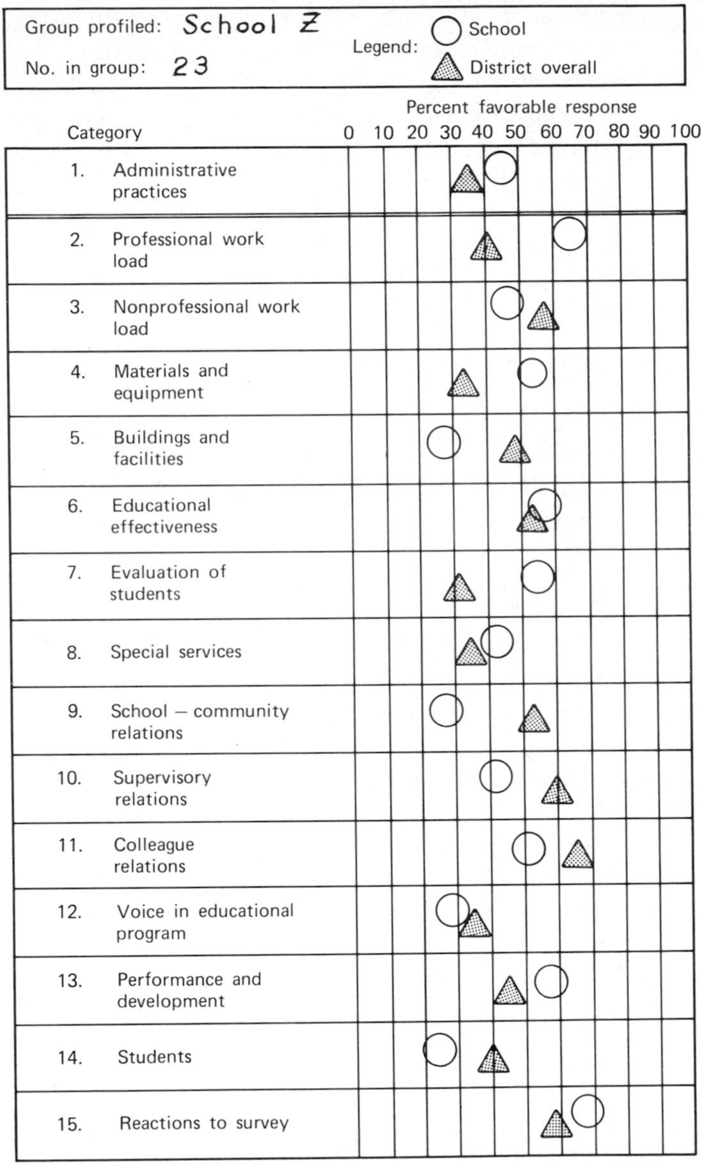

Figure 6.1 Elementary school survey—general profile. Adapted from R. J. Coughlan, *School Survey Program Feedback Guide*. Chicago: The University of Chicago, 1967. The data presented in these diagrams are simulated for illustrative purposes.

Members of the school district helped to modify and add items to the basic questionnaire before its administration.

As illustrated in Figure 6.1, the teachers received summary scores along the 14 dimensions for their own schools and for the entire district. More specific feedback which focused on the individual questions constituting each dimension was also provided. These detailed profiles were relatively complex and included data on the percentage of favorable responses to the question, the percentage of unfavorable responses, the mean response, the percentages of "undecided" responses, and the percentage of respondents who felt that the item was not applicable. The statistic emphasized for group feedback was the percentage of favorable responses. (The complexity of the feedback form was partly in response to district administrators who felt that less complete forms would be misleading.) The feedback surveys were administered at the beginning of the program and again a year later, and the groups received feedback after each administration. Another instrument, the *School System Description Questionnaire*, was administered for evaluation purposes and was not fed back until after our project ended.

The Feedback Groups

The survey data were fed back and analyzed in *program groups* that included all the faculty members in each elementary school. In addition, a *principal group* was formed so that the administrators could analyze their own survey data and deal with problems of mutual concern. Our intervention was designed around these peer groups, even though family groups (consisting of a superior and his or her subordinates) are more commonly used in survey feedback programs. Peer groups were used because they have been shown to be associated with open communication (participants do not have to be concerned about being evaluated by their superiors) and with high-quality solutions (Bridges, 1967). Furthermore, an important objective of our intervention was to develop a professional decision-making capability for dealing with problems related to the technical activities of the schools. We felt that this could be accomplished best by establishing a collegial decision-making structure that was separate from, but integrated with, the existing authority structure of the district. The peer group approach seemed to be consistent with this collegial orientation. As would be the case in many districts, however, these peer groups had to be "created" in the intervention district, for neither teachers nor principals had been holding meetings without their superiors.

The members of each program group elected a *group leader* and a *group monitor* who served as internal change agents. The group leaders received three days of training and were expected to feed back the survey data, lead problem-solving discussions, and "teach" the group the change model and procedures that were included in the training. The group monitors attended a one-day training session that was designed to prepare them to observe and assess group processes and to work with the leaders to improve the groups' problem-solving effectiveness. In addition, the principals received training in survey feedback and group problem-solving techniques.

The program leaders' training included necesssarily brief instruction and practice in the rudiments of feeding back data, group processes, problem-solving skills, planned change techniques, resistance to change, and the structures and procedures of the organization development program. The training was designed to enhance the likelihood that the program would be self-sustaining after the termination of the experiment. Our objective was to provide personnel in the system with the necessary skills and abilities to make the intervention work—thus reducing their dependence on us to supply these capabilities. We provided the training and were available for consultation but generally tried to maintain a low profile in terms of the day-to-day functioning of the program.

The Structure

The program groups were integrated with the existing authority decision-making structure of the school district by means of a series of committees with overlapping memberships (Figure 6.2). A *review committee*, consisting of the principal and the program leader and monitor was established in each school. Review committee meetings were

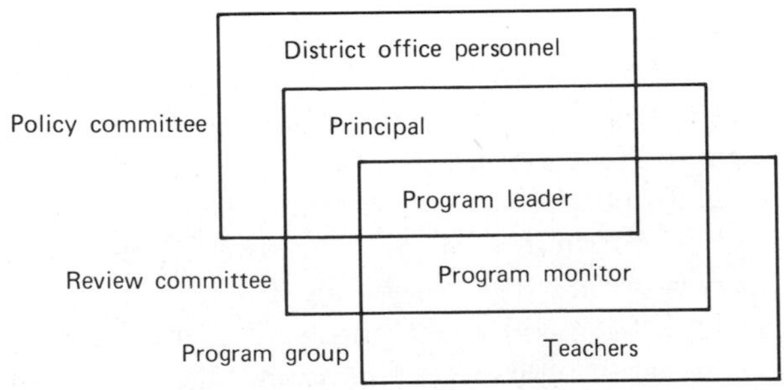

Figure 6.2. Diagram of the overlapping groups.

called to present the principal with the problems and solutions identified by the program group and, when appropriate, to gain the principal's approval or to modify proposed changes. If district level sanction were needed, a *policy committee* meeting could be arranged, to be attended by the principal, the group leader, and the appropriate central office representative. The principals could also call policy committee meetings to review suggestions emerging from their groups.

We tried to facilitate the functioning of these committees by formalizing them and by clearly specifying their activities and responsibilities (see Table 6.1). In addition, special forms were developed so that intercommittee communications would be documented. Principals and/or district office personnel would receive (when the forms were used) a fairly complete description of the problems identified by the program group along with proposed solutions, a rationale for them, and an implementation strategy and timetable. Special forms were provided for review committee reactions to program group proposals.

The Seven-Stage Change Process

The feedback data, the program groups, and the committee structure were designed to establish collegial decision-making and change processes in the schools. To facilitate this type of change our training centered around a seven-stage process of collective decision making which included evaluation, solution generation, internal diffusion, adoption, legitimation, and routinization subprocesses (Coughlan and Cooke, 1974). The components of the intervention itself were designed to aid in the successful utilization of this collective decision-making process (see Figure 6.3).

The feedback data were used to initiate the collective process and to provide a focus for the *evaluation*, or problem identification, stage. The program leader training was explicitly designed to facilitate the *solution generation* stage by providing the groups with skills and tech-

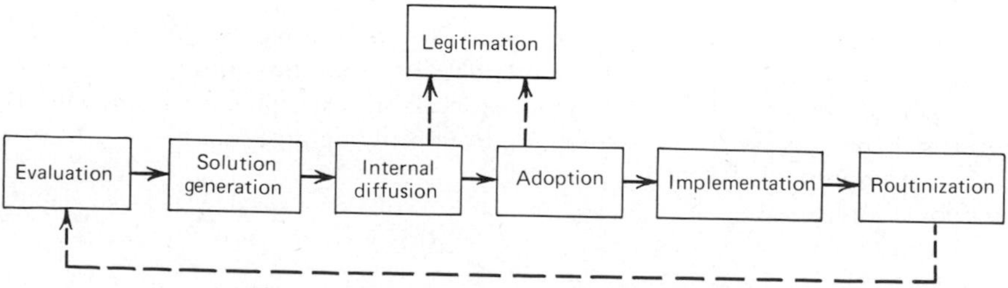

Figure 6.3. The collective decision process.

Table 6.1. Committee Membership and Activities

Group (and Composition)	Functions
Program groups (program leader, monitor, and faculty of the school)	1. To interpret survey results for their own group. 2. To identify the group's key work problems and needs. 3. To diagnose the basic reasons and causes underlying work problems. 4. To determine what action can be taken at the school level in solving problems and meeting needs. 5. To discuss problems and possible solutions with other members of the system who might be affected by the problem or proposed changes. 6. To communicate to the review (and/or policy) committee the group's thinking and recommendations regarding alternative proposals for solving problems and meeting needs. 7. To obtain from the review (and/or policy) committee reasons and explanations for existing top-level policies, programs, procedures, and action. 8. To plan for the implementation of solutions.
Review committee (principal, program leader, and monitor)	1. To plan and schedule survey administration, feedback, and problem-solving meetings. 2. To approve proposed changes and innovations proposed by the program group. 3. To explain why proposals for change cannot be approved and to suggest modifications of proposals for further consideration. 4. To facilitate upward and downward communication between the policy committee and program group.
Policy committee (superintendent or district representative, principal and program leader from the school(s) interested in the particular problem)	1. To respond to questions, suggestions, and recommendations of program groups. 2. To sanction and suggest changes in innovations emerging from program groups.

niques that could lead to high-quality solutions (Maier, 1968). The program groups served as a forum for *internal diffusion*; that is, the communication of problems and solutions to other interested members. Leaders were encouraged to invite to the meetings any people in the district who could assist in solving a problem or who might be affected by a proposed change.

Many of the changes suggested by the program groups required sanctioning by district officials. The committee structure and the communication forms we have described were designed to facilitate these *legitimation* activities and to coordinate the collective and authority structures. The *adoption* stage was to be accomplished as an outcome of the group activities in collectively deciding on a preferred solution both in interaction with one another and with other members of the system. *Implementation* was expected to be facilitated by commitment to the solution, timetables, and clear assignments regarding who was to be responsible for effecting the change. Responsibility for implementation could be assumed by program group members or by superiors in the authority structure. At the *routinization* stage the changes could be evaluated by the program group to determine whether the problem(s) had been dealt with effectively.

The principals, group leaders, and monitors were familiarized with this seven-stage process during training. The importance of going through a systematic and thorough change process was stressed throughout the training, and the various forms of resistance to change that might be encountered at each stage were examined.

SOME ASSUMPTIONS UNDERLYING THE SURVEY FEEDBACK TECHNOLOGY

The expectation that survey feedback will promote organizational change is based on certain assumptions concerning the organizational context and the behavior, beliefs, and values of the persons in the organization. In this section we discuss some of the assumptions that are implicit in the survey feedback technology in terms of the *data*, *groups*, and *process*. We also review some of the assumptions underlying the *design* of our particular survey feedback intervention.

The Data

Survey results are expected to serve as a catalyst for the identification and solution of problems by work groups. This expectation, however, is based on at least three assumptions. The first is that *members of organizations value systematically collected questionnaire data*. Arguments for survey feedback often stress the *objectivity* of data that are aggregated over the entire work group, the *openness* of respondents who believe that their anonymity will be preserved, and the *motivation* that results as members compare their perceptions with those of their (and other) work groups. Only the individual members, however, know how open and honest they were when filling out the questionnaire and they formulate their attitudes toward the credibility of the results on the basis of their behavior as respondents. Similarly, perceptions of the seriousness and thoughtfulness with which other work group members responded to the survey will determine the credibility and motivational potential of the data.

A second assumption is that *the model of organizational effectiveness and functioning inherent in the design and content of the questionnaire is acceptable to organization members*. The theory on which the questionnaire is based may be compelling to the interventionist but divergent from the client system members' concepts of the functioning of their organization. If this is true, interpretation of the data becomes difficult and, if members are reluctant to change their beliefs, the data will not seem useful for identifying specific problems that need to be solved.

Another, somewhat similar, assumption is that the *questionnaire taps areas that are perceived as relevant and important by organization members*. The value of a questionnaire in motivating group members to engage in problem-solving activities would be limited if it did not provide feedback concerning aspects of the organization that are perceived to be relevant by members of the group. Knowledge of failure to achieve desirable levels of performance can stimulate effort only if the area of performance is considered important.

The Groups

The survey feedback technology is also based on assumptions regarding the groups that use the data. Meetings of the work group for the purpose of analyzing data, identifying problems, and determining the direction for change are believed to lead to the "unfreezing" of attitudes, to the emergence of superior decisions, to increased motivation to change, and to improvements in work group effectiveness (Huse, 1975, p. 173). The problem-solving and change potential of the survey feedback technology is therefore based on the fundamental assumption that organizations *are comprised of "work groups" made up of members who share common experiences, goals, and problems.* Feedback at the work group level requires that the organization can be viewed as a system of relatively stable groups, that the members see themselves as belonging to a group, and that the group members share a mutual stake in the decisions and changes made. Another important assumption is that *the work group is perceived by the members of the organization as an appropriate place to solve problems.* If either management or work group members do not see problem solving as an appropriate activity for the group, survey feedback would be a meaningless and perhaps dysfunctional exercise.

Other assumptions regarding work groups and change are implicit in survey feedback, not the least of which is that groups are better than individuals for promoting all types of change. Similarly, feedback interventionists generally have assumed that family groups or peer groups are more appropriate than, for example, committees made up of representatives from subunits in the organization. The work group approach is also based on the assumption that collectively members possess the knowledge to deal with problems and have access to relevant information. The latter assumptions, however, become moot issues if organizational members cannot identify with a group or do not see problem solving as a legitimate activity for their group.

The Process

Members of work groups generally have not had extensive experience or training in group processes, problem solving, and change strategies. Process guidance has therefore emerged as the third major component of survey feedback interventions. Change agents provide process guidance in feedback and problem solving with the expectation that this guidance will help the group to learn to function effectively. This expectation is based on at least three assumptions.

First, it is assumed that *with process guidance a work group can become effective in analyzing data, identifying problems, and generating solutions without extensive training.* Few feedback interventions provide training for work group members and some include only minimal training for group leaders or internal change agents. The assumption seems to be that with process guidance group members can learn to use data (even if they are not accustomed to using numbers or are uncomfortable with data) and can learn skills that may have taken the interventionist years to develop. Another assumption is that *the feedback group attributes legitimacy and expertise to the change agent.* Without previous exposure to and experience with a group facilitator members may not be responsive to his or her process assistance. This may be complicated by the fact that members may see an *external* agent as an "outsider" who is not sufficiently knowledgeable about their organization to provide meaningful assistance. An *internal* agent may be accepted as someone who is familiar with the idiosyncracies of the system, but members may doubt that the internal consultant has developed sufficient skills to help the group.

A third assumption is that *members of the work group are motivated to expend effort to work through the interpersonal, organizational, and task-related barriers to quick and easy problem solving.* Being motivated to solve problems and being motivated to go through the long and difficult process of group problem solving are two different things, especially when the latter entails learning a new organizational role and new skills. Members may derive little intrinsic satisfaction from undertaking the whole process, and the organization may provide few extrinsic rewards to motivate members to build their skills. Without this motivation process guidance is unlikely to be effective even if the consultant is accepted as someone who could provide assistance.

The Design of Our Intervention

Our particular intervention was based on assumptions in addition to those underlying traditional survey feedback programs. The first is that *it is more likely that change will occur if all stages of the change process are performed.* Survey feedback programs have tended to emphasize the initial stages of the change process, particularly problem identification and solution generation. Although these stages are important, it also seems critical to consider the later stages of the process, including legitimation and implementation. The assumption is that even creative solutions may have little impact if provision is not made for their implementation.

Second, we assumed that *the survey feedback process works best if it is carried out in the context of clearly defined supporting roles and structures.* Rarely does the group itself have the requisite skills, knowledge, resources, and authority to effect all desired changes. Thus we assumed that the role of the group should be clearly defined and that the group should be integrated with other segments of the organization with clear procedures and channels of communication. We stressed not only the need for supporting structures but also for highly *formalized* (i.e., clearly defined and documented) structures and roles. Third, we assumed that *these structures would be most effective if internal change agents were given the skills needed to lead the problem-*

solving groups. We felt that internal change agents (i.e., specially trained teachers and principals) rather than external consultants could run the problem-solving groups more effectively and economically and keep the change effort going after the experiment ended.

A fourth, and very important, assumption was that *the problem-solving and change process is initiated most effectively by using task-oriented surveys*. We expected that feedback data that related directly to school organizations and the activities performed in schools would circumvent focusing on personality and interpersonal problems in and of themselves. Such issues when they appear would always be in the context of some task-oriented problem, which we assumed would remove some of the reluctance people seem to have to deal with interpersonal issues. Interpersonal problems were therefore to be confronted in the structure and process of the intervention itself instead of being identified by the data.

A risk inherent in this task approach is that feedback groups could avoid dealing with interpersonal issues even if the task-oriented problems identified by the surveys were the result of poor interpersonal relations. The groups were encouraged, however, to treat the task data as symptoms and to search for the underlying reasons for problems. The task-oriented surveys may therefore have minimized the extent to which our intervention predetermined the types of underlying problems on which the groups would focus. School personnel were expected to decide for themselves the causes of their task-oriented problems, no matter whether the causes were structural, technological, or interpersonal. This approach is different from that of other organization development programs which assume that poor organizational functioning is due to interpersonal process issues. We assumed that interpersonal relations may or may not be a problem in any particular school but that the structure we were establishing needed to be reinforced by proper processes. Therefore we confronted interpersonal process issues *not* as an existing organizational problem but as a necessary component of the intervention design.

Last of all we made the assumption that *our program would be more or less relevant to all schools*. The need for more professional interaction and problem solving in public schools has been stressed by many observers (e.g., Dreeben, 1970; Hawley, undated), and our intervention seemed to be responsive to this need. Nevertheless, the intervention is generic in design and may not be appropriate for certain schools or school districts. In some schools professional problem solving may already be the norm; in other schools there may be a felt need emerging for a program to facilitate professional interaction; and in still others the idea of group problem solving may be so inconsistent with current organizational practices that it would be difficult if not impossible to initiate this type of activity. Such differences among schools would not only have implications for the adoption of our program but also for its impact. For example, the program might be rejected by those schools whose "theory-in-use" is highly incongruent with the design of the intervention, yet potentially the program could have a great impact on them. In contrast, the intervention might be easy to implement in schools in which professional problem solving is already ongoing; however, the use of the program would imply only minimal change (i.e., change based on single-loop learning) in these organizations.

Our assumptions concerning the general applicability of the intervention are addressed throughout the remainder of this chapter. Particular emphasis is placed on the congruency (or fit) between the schools in the experimental district and the intervention model. In addition, our discussion centers on the other assumptions underlying the design of our program and the assumptions underlying survey feedback in general.

THE INTERVENTION: ENTERING THE SCHOOL SYSTEM

The intervention was carried out in a school system serving a midwestern city of medium-size. We selected the district because it was of sufficient size and heterogeneity to contain all the problems associated with urban education but small enough to make the intervention manageable within the budgetary and manpower constraints of the research grant. The district consisted of 17 elementary schools and five secondary schools (junior and senior high schools). The total professional staff numbered slightly more than 900.

The Initial Entry

We first approached the district concerning the organization development program in March 1974. Coincidentally, the superintendent was at that time considering seeking the help of a consultant to correct a rather unwieldy committee system and to improve communication and decision making in the district. He voiced hope that the structure of the proposed intervention would be helpful to his district.

What followed was a drawn-out series of presentations to various "groups" in the district, during which it was never clear to us which of them had the authority or responsibility to decide whether to adopt the survey feedback program. There also seemed to be considerable opposition or at least skepticism among some members concerning the worth or "workability" of the program. Many of the administrators appeared to be threatened by the idea of peer-group problem solving and decision making, and some of them apparently feared that "trouble-makers" would take over the program and use it to make things even harder for the administration. They said they had made "enough concessions" to the union. As a result of union negotiations several district committees had been established with faculty representation, and the administrators perceived many of the teacher-representatives as adversaries. They also felt that the problem-solving groups would further complicate a complex committee structure and that our program would duplicate their system of "faculty advisory committees" which had been established in each school. Moreover, they were skeptical that teachers would exert effort to solve school problems. The administrators' image of teachers, which was related to adversary union-management relations, was that they were interested in putting as little time as possible into their teaching activities and would refuse to attend problem-solving meetings.

Despite the reservations voiced at these meetings, the superintendent informed us that the "cabinet" (assistant and associate superintendents) and the principals had voted to go ahead with the program. What we believed to be the last of the series of entry meetings was held in June 1974 with a "representative" group, including teachers, subject matter coordinators, and assistant principals, none of whom had been included in presentations up to that point. This meeting, which the superintendent also attended, made it clear that the road ahead would not be smooth. The district members in attendance, although not particularly opposed to the concepts of the proposed program, wasted no time in stating clearly that it did not seem to fit in very well with the way the district was run. These members spent much of the meeting pointing out to the superintendent that he had not appeared to be particularly supportive of previous "committee" efforts or teacher decision making and that the lower levels of the organization had almost no influence in the district. The subject quickly shifted to the show of administrative commitment that would be needed to get the teachers to accept the program. The conversation focused on such issues as "released time" from teaching for faculty members to attend problem-solving meetings and whether the district office would respond to the efforts and requests of the program groups. The teachers were reluctant to get involved in any new programs that would be given a low priority by the administrators. An important point was made at this meeting which we were to hear over and over again during the next two years: the district had started many programs and hired many outside groups, but nothing seemed to come of any of the programs because the district office appeared to attach little importance to them.

The spring ended with the administrative component of the district having decided, under some pressure from the superintendent, to adopt the organization development program, but with clear indications that gaining real acceptance would be difficult. It had become apparent by this time that the "model" underlying the program differed substantially from the "model" operative in this district. Although both the administration and the union had sponsored many changes in the district, change processes were generally unstructured and specific efforts "fizzled" for reasons not completely understood by anyone. Because the facts underlying these failures were never apparent, the various factions in the district attributed "malice" or "laziness" to one another. The existing committee structure and decision-making roles in the district were neither clearly defined nor understood, and the general feeling was that time devoted to committee efforts was not well spent. Committee recommendations were often ignored and committee members received little feedback concerning their efforts.

The teachers hesitated to accept our program because of the anticipated lack of administrative support and the administrators were predisposed against it because it might lead to increased "teacher demands." In addition to the misgivings of these two groups, a more subtle problem emerged in regard to a third group of district members. District representatives kept asking how the large contingent of special services personnel (i.e., educational specialists in areas such as learning disabilities, speech, and reading) would be included in the program. We were forewarned by the associate superintendent in charge of these services that his staff might be effectively cut out of our program and that this would be detrimental because they were so central to the school district. We did not fully appreciate the significance of his statements. Given the emphasis on building faculty-level problem solving at the school, we expected that special service teachers would participate as members of the program groups in the buildings in which they worked. It was not until the program began to function and friction between "specials" and regular classroom teachers became apparent that we became sensitive to the extent to which the special personnel were in dual chains of command or were in many cases virtually independent of the principal's authority. Furthermore, many of the "specials" traveled to several schools and attendance at meetings in all of them would have been difficult.

As it turned out, the problem of integrating the special services sector into the program was solved successfully in some buildings. In several schools improvement of the level of coordination between regular classroom teachers and "specials" became an expressed focus of the program groups; in others, however, friction between the two groups became a detriment. This issue is an example of the kind of problem that emerges when a generic organization developemnt design is implemented in a particular organizational setting. Given a more cooperative working relationship with the district office at the time of our entry, we would perhaps have modified the intervention to facilitate the participation of the special service personnel. As it was, we developed through experience a sensitivity to this and other aspects of the program that did not fit the district's organization. The special services problem, however, was a myopic failure on our part. Although we had some experience with schools as consultants, teachers, and administrators, we were still trapped by the perspectives of these particular roles and were not fully attuned to the needs of district members in other organizational roles.

The Second Entry

Over the summer it was announced that the superintendent would be leaving the district in December and that an interim superintendent would be appointed. In early September we met with a "steering committee" composed of a representative group of district personnel to decide how to implement the program. (The members of this committee had been told of the imminent departure of the superintendent.) What was to have been a meeting to plan implementation became instead another forum for explaining and "selling" the program.

Fortunately the circumstances of this session were such (e.g., sufficient time and separation from organizational demands) that perhaps for the first time we were able to present the program completely and respond to individual concerns. By the end of the meeting the steering committee was sufficiently in favor of the program to proceed with its implementation. The future interim superintendent agreed to cooperate but without enthusiasm. The program was never given the type of formal endorsement that was needed to instill a feeling of district commitment among the teachers.

After another round of meetings it was agreed that the decision to participate would be made on a school-by-school basis. We met with representatives of the faculty of each school to discuss the intervention and subsequently visited most of the schools in the district to explain the project to the teaching staffs. The same hesitation we had noted earlier was evident and the same fear that this project, like all the rest, would turn out to be "a waste of time" was expressed. Some teachers felt that their schools were functioning well and that any problems they had were at the district level. The district office, however, did not seem to be open to requests or suggestions from below. In addition, teachers were justifiably skeptical of embarking on a new program with no assurance that the incoming superintendent would be supportive of or responsive to their efforts.

Another attitude we detected was "what's in it for you?" Teachers seemed skeptical of our intentions and felt we were using them as "guinea pigs" to get a couple of publications and doctoral dissertations. Because there was an element of truth in this accusation, we could not deny it. It seemed most proper to counter this argument by focusing on the fact that in exchange the district was getting some very real services. We accentuated the point that we would be providing the system with a problem-solving structure and process and that district personnel would gain expertise in carrying out the process. Our assertions, however, had little effect until after the intervention got underway (and even then some members doubted that the district was receiving any real services).

The personnel of some schools, nevertheless, were genuinely interested. Eight elementary schools and one high school decided to adopt the program. It was clear at this point that the districtwide impact of this intervention would be severely limited, given this lack of total participation and the temporary status of the superintendent. Consequently one focus of our research became a comparison of the participating and nonparticipating schools (Mohrman, Cooke, and Duncan, 1975). The majority of the teachers were willing to take the survey; many of them, however, simply did not want the feedback.

ISSUES IN TRAINING

Having gained admittance to the district, we proceeded to set up training sessions for the principals, program leaders, and monitors. The training centered on the presentation of the organization development model and on the development of the skills necessary for its implementation. Given this focus, the reactions district personnel had to the training became an indicator of the degree of congruence or incongruence between the model of our intervention and the theories in use on the district and participating schools. Some of the general impressions we developed regarding this "fit" are discussed in the following section.

Principal Training

We initiated the program with the principals in order to acquaint them by first-hand experience with the functioning of the program. This strategy would allow the building administrators to analyze data from the *Principal Feedback Survey* and to solve problems as a principal group before the faculty program groups were assembled. We hoped that in their experiences with the process the principals would understand and value the intervention model and be less threatened by program group activities in their own schools.

The principal component was functionally independent of the school level program groups and optimally required the participation of principals from all schools in the district. Therefore training was scheduled for the entire group of 22 principals for two days in November. The day before the training, however, the interim superintendent had second thoughts about having all principals absent from the district at one time and decided to send only those of the schools in which the faculty had voted to participate as a program group. A second training session was scheduled for the others. This decision had the effect of dividing the principals into "in the program" and "out of the program" groups. The second group of principals never did fully participate in the problem-solving activities.

The training of the principals of participating schools was interlaced with expressions of anxiety concerning the faculty component of the program in their buildings. Some of the principals felt trapped between a faculty that had decided to embark on survey feedback and problem-solving activities and a district office that was, at best, lukewarm toward the project. They felt that they were in a high-risk situation in which attention was focused on them simply because their faculties decided to be in the program. For several principals this was especially threatening because, as the data revealed, they were faced with various problems in their schools.

It became apparent during the training that the model inherent in the program was quite different from the assumptions and management style of many of the principals. For example, some principals did not agree with our assumption that teachers, as professionals performing the technical tasks of the organization, have the legitimate authority and necessary expertise to solve problems and to initiate certain types of change in their schools. One principal made the straightforward claim that there was not a single decision that his faculty had the right to make and that he had a principal's handbook to "prove" his point. As he put it, "Everyone can't be boss; and it just so happens that in my school, I am." Other principals, however, appeared interested in the program and felt that it provided a way to tap the interest and professional skills of their staffs.

Another assumption underlying the program was that problem-solving activities could be carried out by work groups consisting of members with common goals and problems. Some of the principals, however, believed their faculties to be divided in their philosophies. They voiced the fear that the program group would make more work for them, for they would constantly have to mediate between factions. Some of this divisiveness may have been caused by the principals themselves; several of them admitted that they maintained control in their buildings by "dividing and conquering" or by "keeping the faculty off balance." The teachers were further divided because their collective bargaining representation was being contested by locals of both the National Education Association and the American Federation of Teachers. (This conflict also implied, at the district level, a generally antagonistic employee-management atmosphere characteristic of situations in which the need is to be militant in order to attract and please the constituency.)

Besides the unfortunate splitting of the principals into two training groups, another failure was perhaps even more detrimental to the success of the principal group. The principals elected as their leader a man who had neither a management philosophy compatible with the program nor a strong desire to fill the role. We had held off on the election until training was almost completed so that the demands of the position would be clear to all principals and their subsequent choice would be an informed one. The election was by secret ballot with first, second, and third choices. There were to be no nominations or interpersonal campaigning. Unfortunately we had set the stage for sabotage. If the principals knew what type of individual was necessary to make the program work, they also knew who would ensure failure. As the ballots were being distributed, another principal whose reactions to the program were erratically ambivalent loudly, and with a cavalier dismissal of our stated procedure nominated the eventual and, of course, inevitable winner of the election.

Our hope that the principal group would get started first to become acquainted with the process before their faculties began meeting did not materialize. The principals decided not to meet until the day of the first faculty program group meeting two months later; they felt obligated to convene during the released time secured by us from the district. These meetings were relatively successful, largely because the elected monitor was a forceful individual who strongly favored the program. In the second year, when meetings depended on the initiative of the leader, none was called, although a few principals indicated willingness to attend.

Leader and Monitor Training

Training for the teacher leaders and monitors began amid controversy. To alleviate the administrative and practical problems that would be caused by a three-day absence of the trainees from their classrooms, the district administration preferred a training schedule that would include two Saturday workshops. Although they were to be paid by the project budget for their attendance on these days, the trainees saw this move as a deliberate slight to themselves and the program and refused to participate unless the administration agreed to schedule training during the school week. This position was taken in part, because the teachers wanted some assurance that their efforts in the program would be supported by the administration. Furthermore, they were extremely sensitive to the issue of power in the district and were not willing to sacrifice the principle of negotiated agreements concerning the scheduling of meetings and hours of work. The professional-bureaucratic tension was closely related to the labor-management tension, and the desire for "professional autonomy" became highly consonant with "protecting the contract." If the administration wanted professional problem solving, it would have to provide the time for it.

Although the training sessions were rescheduled, it took a while to overcome the bad feelings that had emerged. Some teachers felt that we were tacitly, and perhaps unknowingly, acceding to district strategies to keep the faculty in a subordinate role. At the same time we were in a difficult position because of our tenuous status and marginal power in the district. We felt that the continuation of the project depended on our willingness to present as little administrative inconvenience as possible by insisting only on arrangements critical to its implementation. To some extent both the teachers and the administration were using the interventionists as a buffer, expecting us to work out arrangements that were satisfactory to both sides. As researchers we were dependent on the district to carry through with the program, and at various times this entailed performing "middleman" functions that its members were unwilling to assume. (As the year progressed we took a less active stance in the district, and to some extent the success or failure of the program in the various schools depended on whether the program personnel were willing to assume the new roles and responsibilities necessary for its continuation.)

During the three days of leader training we covered the relevant topics in short lectures, discussed issues raised by the teachers, and conducted a number of group exercises and role-playing experiences. The training, however, was too short to prepare the leaders thoroughly for all the tasks they would have to perform. Our "training evaluation surveys" indicated that most of them felt adequately prepared to guide the group in interpreting the feedback data, but several of them were uneasy about their group process and problem-solving skills.

The one-day training for the program monitors was inadequate to prepare them for their tasks of evaluating group processes and filling out the communication forms. Although these training sessions were too short, a more serious problem resulted from the fact that the monitors and program leaders were not trained together. We expected the leaders and monitors to work as a team, yet we had not provided them with an opportunity to develop mutual role expectations or a cooperative working relationship (this mistake was rectified in the second-year training program). In addition, the principals were still trained separately and possibly never fully understood the roles of the leaders and monitors. Our program was based on clearly defined roles and structures, but our approach to training did little to promote the necessary role expectations among the major program personnel in each school.

During training the teachers voiced concern that in many schools the survey feedback program represented a strong departure from current attitudes and practices. The leaders felt that a major task would be to persuade their faculties to expend effort on the program. As one teacher voiced it, "Our teachers have been *taught* by the district that their efforts are ignored." The leader and monitor from another school said they thought that their faculty would try this program, but if it fizzled it would probably be the last thing they would try. As the leader put it, "The group of teachers who are apathetic becomes larger with each failure."

Many of the trainees were concerned about how they could get *all* the teachers in their schools—and not just the usual vocal groups—to participate actively in the problem-solving meetings. Some teachers anticipated trouble in getting the various factions in their schools to work together.

Another concern was that the faculties would be unwilling to go through the orderly and somewhat slow process that the seven-stage change model implied. Many teachers were "solution-oriented" and viewed time spent in meetings as a waste. The leaders feared it would be difficult to maintain their interest as they tried to utilize the resources of the group in arriving at accurate problem definition and the best solution.

The program leaders were also worried about a more basic issue—their own source of legitimacy. Although they had been elected and trained, some of them felt that their faculties would attribute legitimacy neither to their roles nor to the process. They doubted that they could take the model we had provided and "teach" their colleagues how to operate within it. In several cases they were also concerned by the apparent failure of their principals to attribute legitimacy to their roles.

Finally, the data itself was problematic. The teachers had in some cases been negative about filling out the questionnaire. They complained about its length, the wording, the response codes, and our request that they identify themselves for project evaluation purposes. Several teachers had begrudged the effort required to generate the data and mistrusted its potential use. Many had no faith in the value of the questionnaire or the validity of the responses. In general, it became clear during the training experience that some of the assumptions underlying our program were not valid. Evidence began accumulating that, at least in some of the schools, the program was being implemented in a incongruent environment.

THE USE AND IMPACT OF THE PROGRAM

Despite the issues raised in the first round of teacher training, survey feedback and problem-solving activities were initiated (early in 1975) in eight elementary schools and one high school. Five program groups were established in the high school because of the size of the faculty. Six of the elementary school groups and four of the high school groups met throughout the spring, well past the three meetings for which the district administration had provided released time from classes. Teachers came to school early or left late in order to meet. Although individual teachers or groups of teachers in some schools refused to participate, it seemed that the district administrators' predictions that faculty would not exert themselves were inaccurate. Two elementary schools did stop meeting when released time was no longer provided. In one case this was a result of conflict in the group; in the other school the teachers did not identify any new problems that generated their interest after the first three meetings.

The Durability of the Program

At the end of the first school year seven elementary schools had decided to continue the program through the upcoming year. The high school subsequently dropped out because leaders and monitors could not be found to replace those who had been transferred or those who did not want to continue. The principal group, which had solved a pair of problems that produced changes in district procedures, was not reconvened in the new school year partly because of the lack of leadership and the feeling that the group included only those principals whose schools were engaged in program activities.

At the beginning of the second year of the program (September 1975), a full training session was held for newly elected leaders and monitors in three schools in which the previous leaders and monitors had chosen to resign. A one-day brush-up session was held for all leaders and monitors to regenerate enthusiasm and cover areas that had surfaced as problems in program functioning. Particular areas that received attention were (a) the resolution of conflict within the groups; (b) the procedures and structures for linking the group efforts to the authority structures of the district, that is, the review and policy committees and the use of the communication forms; and (c) the roles and responsibilities of program personnel. A quick review of techniques for promoting open communication was held to address an issue that was important in several schools; namely, the difficulty of encouraging participation by the "silent" members of the group because of the domination of the vocal few.

Program groups in five of the elementary schools met throughout the 1975–1976 school year. During this second year of the program a new superintendent arrived. Although he was philosophically quite sympathetic to the program, he gave only the necessary support to see that the project could be completed. As a new superintendent he was really not in a position to assign high priority to an on-going organization development effort, especially one that involved so few schools. During this year, however, the central office personnel became noticeably more responsive to the requests of the various program groups.

The five elementary school groups decided to continue meeting in the 1976–1977 school year, despite the scheduled termination of the research project. A one-day training session was held in late spring for new program personnel in three of the schools in which the leaders and monitors were stepping down or in which they felt the program would have a better chance of succeeding if more members of the staff received training. It became evident at this training session that even in the schools in which the program had functioned smoothly and all the components had been fully utilized the new trainees were not cognitively aware of the model of the program. It would have been difficult for group members to have assumed positions of leadership without some training. With no prospect of continued training in the future, it appears that personnel turnover among leaders and monitors quite possibly will result in termination of the program.

The Differential Implementation of the Program

Although the program was initially adopted by eight elementary schools and one high school, there was great variation among them in terms of the extent to which the program was fully implemented. Complete implementation of the program would imply that the members of the schools used the feedback data, attended group problem-solving meetings, and facilitated these meetings by means of process guidance. An overview of the extent to which school members utilized the components related to these three major aspects of feedback intervention (data, group, and process guidance) is presented in Table 6.2. This tabulation indicates that some of the groups at both school levels did not do so even during the first year of the program.

Data. The intervention design provided for feedback of survey results to the various program groups by their respective program leaders. In the first year the feedback session was held during released time and was the first component of the intervention to be used. The program began in the middle of the first academic year and continued through to the summer. The program groups reconvened in the fall with the continuation of problem-solving activities. Feedback of the second round of data occurred during the middle of the second academic year. This was done to ensure comparability between the two sets of data in terms of the yearly school cycle. During the second year, therefore, the feedback component took place sometime after the problem-solving activities had begun. (The sequence of components in Table 6.2 reflects this chronological order.)

The entries in the table under the various groups show whether the data were fed back by the leader in a group situation as prescribed by our design. Although all the groups held feedback sessions during

Table 6.2. Use of Program Components by Participating Schools

Components	School Program Groups												
	Elementary Schools								High School Groups				
	A	B	C	D	E	F	G	H	1	2	3	4	5
First Academic Year													
Data													
Feedback Session	yes	yes	yes	yes	yes	yes	yes	yes	yes	yes	yes	yes	yes
Groups													
Program Group													
Number of Meetings[a]	6	11	5	9	7	6	4	5	12	12	12	12	3
Percent of Attendance[b]	75	100	90	75	50	80	95	75	50	25	20	20	—
Review Group	yes	yes	yes	yes	yes	yes	yes	no	yes	yes	yes	yes	no
Process Guidance													
Seven Stage Model	yes	yes	no	yes	no	no	yes	no	yes	yes	yes	yes	no
Forms	yes	yes	yes	yes	no	no	yes	no	no	no	no	no	no
Second Academic Year													
Groups													
Program Group													
Number of Meetings	3[c]	11	5	15[d]	13[d]	12	0	—[e]	—[f]	—[f]	—[f]	—[f]	—[f]
Percent Attendance	95	100	100	60	50	75	—	—	—	—	—	—	—
Review Group	yes	yes	yes	yes	yes	yes	no	—	—	—	—	—	—
Process Guidance													
Seven Stage Model	no	yes	no	yes	yes	no	no	—	—	—	—	—	—
Forms	no	yes	yes	yes	yes	no	no	—	—	—	—	—	—
Data													
Feedback Session	no	yes	yes	yes	no	no	yes[g]	—	—	—	—	—	—
Third Academic Year													
Status	—	cont.	cont.	cont.	cont.	cont.	—	—	—	—	—	—	—

[a] Includes three initial released time meetings provided by research contract funds. [b] Percent refers to those participating *after* the initial three released time meetings. [c] Monitor left and was not replaced; the program was not really continued, although the leader was asked to call meetings regarding a particular problem. [d] Change in program group leadership. [e] Group formally voted to drop the program. [f] Failed to replace leaders and monitors. [g] Attended by principal.

the first year of the program, some of the elementary schools (including two that had continued their problem-solving activities) held none during the second.

The Group. Schools differed greatly in the extent to which the idea of a program group took hold. This variation in the implementation of the program group component is illustrated in Table 6.2 in terms of (a) the number of meetings held during each year; (b) the average percent of faculty members attending these meetings; and (c) whether review committee meetings were used to coordinate the program groups with the authority structure. This third indicator of the acceptance of the program groups is included because feedback and problem solving took place in peer groups. When a peer group rather than a family group is the locus of feedback, failure to coordinate its efforts with the authority structure of the organization would be strong evidence that the group was not yet viewed as an appropriate vehicle for organizational problem solving. The review committee—the most critical program component for bringing about this coordination—was used in many of the participating schools, indicating at least some acceptance of the peer-group approach to problem solving.

Process Guidance. Our intervention model included various components that could be used by the program leaders and monitors to guide the group problem-solving processes. One was the seven-stage change model, which was emphasized during training as a conceptual framework for planning and sequencing group problem-solving activities. Another important component was a set of forms developed for the program groups; these forms were to be used to record problems and solutions identified by the groups, to schedule implementation activities, and to facilitate communication between the faculty groups and the review committees. The use of this component would represent not only the adoption of the process guidance aspect of the intervention but also the acceptance by program leaders of their internal change agent roles. Table 6.2 shows that these forms were not utilized by all the program groups; the high school groups, in particular, seemed to reject this aspect of the intervention.

THE DIFFERENTIAL USE AND IMPACT OF THE PROGRAM: SOME LEARNINGS

It is evident that the extent to which the program was fully implemented varied among the schools in the district. There were other, more qualitative differences from school to school. These variations seem to be related, at least to some degree, to the program's impact in terms of such criteria as the number of changes initiated by the faculty groups and improvements in teachers' attitudes toward their schools' decision-making processes. Furthermore, certain factors may explain why the program was relatively successful or unsuccessful in these schools. Some of them are explored in this section, which focuses on the *high school* and *school B*—two schools that differed markedly in terms of their initial congruence with the change model and their eventual use of the intervention components. These case studies, supplemented by data regarding the other schools in the sample, suggest a number of learnings relevant to feedback interventions.* They are discussed in the remainder of this chapter.

Program Implementation and Impact: Two Case Studies

The most complete implementation of the program occurred in *school B,* which was also the school initially the most congruent with the assumptions on which the survey feedback intervention was based. Questionnaire data indicated that this school, compared with others in the district, had before the intervention supported the greatest amount of problem-solving activity.

The members of school B were able to implement the program fully and to use it to initiate a flexible individualized reading program, to increase the use of the school library and resource room, and to develop measures for improving the coordination between the special educational services personnel and the regular classroom teachers. Interview and survey data revealed that in addition to solving problems the faculty had indeed adopted a new "model" of behavior. They had begun to take responsibility as a group for their own professional development and for improving the quality of education provided at their school. Program group meetings replaced the traditional "faculty meetings," and the teachers elected to continue the program for a third year.

The *high school* was significantly larger (130 teachers) and more complex (e.g., five program groups) than any of the other schools in which the program was implemented. Given this size and complexity, the high school experience brought into bold relief the problems that

* The results reported in this chapter are based on interviews, questionnaires, and informal observations and most of our conclusions are based on multiple sources and methods.

can emerge in the implementation of a survey feedback program. In addition, a number of differences were apparent in the way the five program groups functioned—a variation that helped toward an understanding of the dynamics of the survey-feedback process, for all these groups operated within the same authority structure and organizational context.

Questionnaire data indicated that before the intervention the high school was the second "lowest" of the participating schools in terms of ongoing problem identification and solution-generation processes. Furthermore, various assumptions underlying the survey feedback intervention simply were not valid in the case of the high school. Intact work groups were not readily available for survey feedback purposes and many faculty members were unwilling to assume the responsibility for solving school problems. Nevertheless, at least one group (group 1 in Table 6.2) took advantage of almost all components of the program. This group was able to bring about changes in space utilization on the building and to introduce specific steps designed to make the school more effective in detecting and responding to student deficiencies in basic skill areas. One other group (group 2) introduced measures designed to increase interdepartment exchange of information. Groups 3 and 4 expended a great deal of effort trying to cope with the problems of truancy and class cutting but were unable to generate any concrete suggestions for solving these problems. The fifth group canceled their meetings early in the first year of the intervention.

The program in the high school was terminated after the first year. Relatively few teachers were interested in seeing the program continue, and the principal was unable to find teachers who were willing to commit the necessary time and effort required by the monitor and leader roles. This early termination of the high school program is in sharp contrast to the situation in school B (and in some of the other elementary schools) in which the program was continued for a second and third year. The factors accounting for the continuation/discontinuation of the program, and some of the knowledge gained can be identified in terms of the three major aspects of feedback intervention: the data, the group, and the process guidance.

The Data

In school B the data served as an important focal point of the initial efforts of the group. The leader and monitor both reported high faculty interest in the data and little skepticism concerning its validity.

The members of this program group devised a procedure for circulating the data so that each teacher had a chance to review it at leisure. The first problems dealt with were identified from the data, and both the leader and monitor felt that it was this "objective" stimulus that enabled the group to find a direction and proceed in unity.

There were great differences among the five groups in the high school in the way the data were received by the teachers. In some much interest was shown and the teachers generally attributed validity and relevance to the information that was fed back. Two of the groups (3 and 4) became immediately sidetracked by complaints about the format of the questions and the ambiguity of the feedback scores. Members dismissed much of the data as irrelevant or as dealing with matters peripheral to the real problems of the school. Others were skeptical of the value of the feedback data because they disagreed with the way in which responses to certain questions were labeled as "favorable" or "unfavorable" (i.e., they took issue with the model of effective organization functioning on which the questionnaire was based). Both groups ignored the program guideline to start with a fairly straightforward and readily solved problem. They proceeded directly to difficult problems, that is, truancy and class cutting, and spent the entire spring of the first year in the solution-generation stage. Although the members of these groups were highly motivated (the less interested teachers stopped attending the meetings), they had defined a task that ensured failure, at least in the time frame of several months. They experienced a great deal of frustration in defining the underlying problem and finding a solution. The school year ended without a concrete change and left members of these groups dissatisfied.

As in the high school groups there was great variation among the remaining seven schools in terms of their use of the data. Teachers in two schools in which the program continued in the third year never even bothered to hold a second feedback session. In contrast, faculty members in school G, in which the program terminated after the first year, held a meeting to feed back the second year's data and used them to identify major areas of faculty effort for the upcoming year. This school was the second highest in terms of a questionnaire measure of problem-solving activity at the beginning of the program, and it appears that they were able to use the data effectively in their preexisting faculty meeting structure.

The experiences of these groups suggest that individual members differ in their willingness to attribute value to survey data. Some teachers had no faith in the validity of the results because of their own experiences in responding to the questionnaire. Many had found the feedback survey difficult to fill out because of the negatively worded items and the wide range of response options. The measures that researchers employ for methodological reasons may be sound in a research context but may also lead to subjective experiences on the part of respondents which will cause them to reject the data. Furthermore, these individual reactions can have synergistic effects in group feedback settings.

Although our feedback surveys were designed specifically for school personnel, some members of the district did not see the questionnaires as relevant. Perceived relevance of the data seemed to have been dependent on the extent to which the questionnaire items directly tapped areas that were already on the minds of the teachers. Another important factor was the extent to which the teachers understood the purpose of the questionnaire as a stimulus to the evaluation of problems rather than their identification. It took a skillful leader, and one whose role was considered legitimate, to be able to overcome the tendency of the group to say, "We already know our problems, and we don't need a questionnaire to tell us what they are."

The feedback surveys, though task-oriented, were nevertheless value-based. The model of school effectiveness inherent in the questionnaire attached a positive value to faculty participation in decision making, professional interaction and cooperation, and self-improvement efforts by the staff. For teachers who had been socialized in a school in which this was not the general model of functioning acceptance of the questionnaire data was often just as difficult as acceptance of the organization development project itself.

We can state tentatively several learnings that concern data relevant to survey feedback programs. Although these observations are not completely new, they reflect issues often overlooked in the design of feedback intervention.

The extent to which individuals attribute validity to survey feedback data depends on their own experiences in taking the questionnaire and their perceptions of the reactions of others to the questionnaire.

The extent to which individuals attribute relevance to the questionaire results depends on

(a) their understanding of the entire survey feedback process and the role of the data;
(b) the inclusion in the survey of questions which focus directly on areas of felt concern by the respondents and

(c) the congruence of the values inherent in the questionnaire with the values of the respondent.

The forces that determine the relevance and validity attached by individuals to data can become inordinately important to the functioning of a survey feedback program, for they are directly related to the individuals' inputs into the group process.

The above learnings have to do with the way attitudes determine the use and interpretation of the data, but there are also ways in which the data can help shape attitudes. Some of the program groups, after taking an initial look at the feedback results, never returned to the data as a group. Nevertheless, interviews indicate that the data had some continuing saliency. The explanation for this minor paradox seems to lie in what it was about the data that was salient. Many groups seemed to be as much impressed, in the long run, by the scope and content of the areas the data made salient as they were by the way their schools were rated in those areas. In effect, the areas of organization functioning covered by the questionnaire were legitimated as "fair game" for group problem solving once the results were fed back (Mohrman et al., 1976):

> The content of the survey acts to define and, more importantly, to legitimate the domain of issues available to the feedback group for consideration.

The Group

Four factors worked in favor of the creation of an effective program group at school B. First, the principal let the teachers know that he was highly in favor of the program and carefully cooperated with and reinforced their problem-solving efforts. Second, the fact that attendance at meetings was optional was never stressed in this school; the principal considered these meetings as replacements for regularly scheduled faculty meetings. The result was 100 percent attendance. Third, the leader and the monitor took special measures, such as distributing agendas in advance of and minutes immediately after each meeting, to make sure that no one felt left out and that program group issues were salient to each teacher. Last, the school was relatively small (18 teachers) and not characterized by divisiveness. Any conflict that did exist tended to surface at the meetings and did not act to erode the membership base by outside maneuvering. This contrasted greatly with some of the other elementary schools, notably D, E, and F, in which divisiveness among teachers resulted in the identification of the program group with a subgroup of the faculty.

Although the establishment of program groups in the elementary schools was relatively straightforward, it was difficult to create workable feedback groups in the high schools. In consultation with school representatives it was decided that the composition of the program groups should be based on the teachers' "preparation periods." Given this arrangement, all faculty members who were not teaching at a particular time of the day would constitute a group, regardless of departmental affiliations. This approach avoided the unsolvable problem of finding a time when all members of each department could meet and set the stage for the type of cross-departmental problem solving advocated by some of them.

These artificially created groups included members who did not necessarily share a common perspective. Most of the groups, however, experienced attrition and were left with a core of teachers from the larger departments who held compatible views. This limited the extent to which the program groups represented the entire faculty and increased the need for communicating problems and solutions to nongroup members. Although some groups did a fairly good job of integrating their efforts with the rest of the organization, much time and effort was required of the leaders. In addition, the small number of teachers who were left had difficulty maintaining enthusiasm in the face of the many uninvolved, and in some cases antagonistic, nonparticipants.

Although the principal of the high school cooperated with the groups, he was nevertheless sensitive to the fact that only a portion of the faculty was participating. He therefore made no outward gestures to indicate that he would grant official status to group decisions or requests. This situation made things difficult for the leaders, who had to compete for his attention with the many other groups and individuals who sought his time.

The feedback technology assumes that work groups, comprised of people with common perspectives, can be identified in organizations and are available for problem-solving activities. The program was more readily implemented in buildings in which work groups already existed and in which there was little divisiveness among the faculty. In schools in which informal factions and/or formal departments cut across the problem-solving groups the program generated overt conflict that sometimes resulted in participation from a smaller and often unrepresentative group of teachers. By bringing together (often for the first time) teachers with different viewpoints and philosophies latent conflicts surfaced. In some schools these conflicts resulted in the identification of the program with one element of the faculty. The program therefore served to differentiate certain groups formally from the rest of the faculty. Even when the program group represented a fairly unified faculty, it was a "new" group and as such its effectiveness depended on its coordination with the entire organization; that is, on the smooth functioning of the integrative groups and procedures provided for in the intervention design. These observations suggest two "learnings" relevant to groups:

A work group cannot be effective in the survey feedback and problem-solving process unless it can achieve the integration of the viewpoints of its members and can coordinate its efforts with the authority structure of the organization.

A "new" group that is created for the purpose of survey feedback is likely to encounter conflict in achieving both internal integration and coordination with the larger organization.

We expected that a work group could utilize the survey feedback process effectively only if it were considered a legitimate problem-solving body. In the high school the extent to which teachers saw their groups as legitimate varied, and this may explain why the activities of some groups were more effective than those of others. Among the elementary schools differences in the perceived legitimacy of the groups resulted from differences in the attitudes and behaviors of the principals as well as the faculties. In schools in which the principal was threatened by the program (particularly in schools D, F, and H) disunity among the faculty was a handy excuse for dismissing their efforts as nonrepresentative. Some of these principals, however, never clearly indicated that they viewed the program groups as legitimate problem-solving bodies, and this may have been the cause of the unwillingness of certain groups or individual teachers to participate. Even when teachers were neither divided nor predisposed against the program, negative or uncertain attitudes of the principals led the faculties to doubt the legitimacy of the problem-solving groups. This suggests a conclusion reached by many other interventionists:

Survey feedback and problem solving is unlikely to achieve changes if either the members of the feedback group or their immediate superordinate question the legitimacy of the group.

The experiences of "artificial" groups in the high school served to point out another conclusion also suggested (but more subtly) by the "natural" work groups in the elementary schools. Evidence shows that the homogeneity of the group dictates the content of problems identified and solved. The extremely heterogeneous high school groups inevitably dealt with universal school-level problems, such as truancy, or focused on organization-level problems, such as interdepartmental relations and communication. Problems of the first type are universal perhaps because, given pragmatic organizational and societal constraints, they are intractable. Problems of the second type may or may not be pertinent to the organization, and heterogeneous groups may be of little use if they are not. If, however, organizational problems are relevant, the scope of these problems may be beyond the capabilities of the group.

The breadth in membership of survey feedback and problem-solving groups will correspond to the scope of the problems which are identified. Therefore broad-based groups should not be convened if broad-based problems are not pertinent.

The members of the group must also be given (if they do not already possess) the authority, expertise, and resources which are necessary for dealing with problems of the predicted scope.

Process Guidance

The leader and monitor in school B were a competent team in guiding their group through effective problem-solving processes. They were highly respected members of the faculty and were not identified with any particular subgroup. In addition, the principal of the school attributed legitimacy to their roles and provided them with support and encouragement when they led the group through the difficult stages of the problem-solving process. (This contrasted with the principals in several other schools, notably D and F, who wanted to take things over or stop the groups' activities if disruptions occurred because of their efforts.)

The leader in school B utilized the seven-stage problem-solving process, making sure that each phase was adequately carried out before moving on to the next. The group spent a long time in each problem area, arriving at a consensus concerning the preferred course of action after weighing alternative points of view. By beginning with a relatively simple problem the group developed skill and experienced success in group problem solving before proceeding to others more complex and controversial. The monitor was especially conscientious about carrying out her communication tasks and providing the leader and group with process assistance throughout the program.

In contrast there was little teamwork between the leaders and monitors in the high school. The monitors rapidly lost interest and left most of the work to the leaders, who differed substantially in the extent to which they were able to "train" an effective problem-solving group. One leader followed the guidelines completely and made sure that the group knew exactly which "model" it was following. That group (group 1 in Table 6.2) began with a simple problem and progressed to the more complex, experiencing success and consequent reinforcement with every solution. Other leaders were less effective in teaching the model to their groups. Although this effectiveness depended partly on the skill of the leader, it also seemed to be related to the group's "personality." Some of the groups (especially 3 and 4 in the high school) were initially made up of many impatient cantankerous individuals who were unwilling to complete a long and systematic problem-solving process. Ironically, because many of these groups focused immediately on "important problems" that were also extremely complex and laced with philosophical issues of education, they ended up immersing themselves in a literally endless problem-solving process that offered little prospect for achievement. The result was that the leaders felt powerless to direct their groups, and many members dropped out because of the lack of progress.

The personalities of the various program groups in the elementary schools also differed substantially. Their characteristics seemed to interact with the characteristics of the leader in determining whether the members were willing to "learn" the process and were motivated to carry it out. The perceived legitimacy of the leader and monitor as process analysts and facilitators depended on their not being highly identified with any faction in the faculty and on their ability to demonstrate their knowledge of the model by working hard and systematically following the change process. Highly contentious groups were less likely to allow the leaders to demonstrate their knowledge and to be patient enough to follow an orderly process. (This seemed to be the case in schools E, F, and H.) Thus they were unlikely to experience reinforcement for successful problem solving and to develop the motivation to continue to learn the process.

The ease with which a group can "learn" to be effective at problem solving depends on the unity of the group and on their motivation to solve problems.

Process leaders are more likely to be attributed legitimacy if they are not strongly identified with one element of the organization, and if they demonstrate a competence in the processes they are trying to teach the group.

These experiences in the high school and elementary schools reinforce our belief in the need for a systematic change process and clearly defined roles and structures to support the survey feedback effort. The groups that successfully implemented change were those that utilized all the components of the program and followed a thorough but often slow change process, invariably accompanied by a great deal of personal effort by the leaders. Leading the feedback groups was essentially an extra and voluntary task, however, and there was little organizational reinforcement for performing the role well. In schools G and A this seems to have contributed to the breakdown of the program. The leaders in both schools were highly capable, enthusiastic about the program, ambitious, and engaged in many activities outside teaching which included coaching, union activities, graduate work, and community politics. We believe that the programs in these schools were not stronger because these key people declined to give it the necessary effort. Their program roles were less important to them than their other obligations and, during busy periods, they could not devote much time to program activities. Their peculiarly demanding situations point out a general flaw in this program: there was no institutionalization of the program leader role and no organizational support in terms of time or money. The following learning is suggested:

> The effectiveness of internal change agents will depend on the extent to which their roles are clearly specified, rewarded, and supported by the organization.

In-depth interviews with the leaders and monitors revealed that the most useful aspect of training and of the program in general was the seven-stage change process. An understanding of that model enabled them to lead their groups more effectively in the problem-solving process. As one leader put it:

> That process allowed me to understand what the task of the group was at any one meeting, and to make sure that it got accomplished. That way people didn't leave with the feeling that time had been wasted.

This finding supports one of the assumptions underlying our intervention:

> Feedback groups are more effective in implementing change when they follow a systematic change process.

In the high school the existence of five groups magnified the problem of integrating group efforts with the rest of the organization. Even after a group had come up with a solution the internal diffusion, legitimation, and implementation stages all involved a great deal of time and effort simply because of the size of the school. The various groups also experienced some uncertainty about their relations with one another, especially groups 3 and 4 which were working on the same problem. At least one meeting with the research team was held at the request of the leaders to devise procedures for intergroup coordination. A similar problem occurred in several elementary schools in which leaders were not sure how to go about calling a review committee meeting. Several schools simply did not hold meetings until more explicit procedures were specified for them. These observations suggest:

clearly specified procedures can increase the probability that feedback groups will carry out a systematic change process.

Explicit procedures seemed particularly necessary in schools in which there had been little problem evaluation and change initiation by the faculty before the intervention. Failure to specify procedural aspects of the program afforded an opportunity for recalcitrant individuals, especially principals, to impede implementation of the program.

Several of the learnings refer directly or indirectly to the emphasis that our intervention model placed on structure. Specified and documented roles and procedures were conceived as necessary support mechanisms for the behavioral processes necessary for survey feedback and problem solving. Structural arrangements and procedures, however, became surrogates for the behavioral and cognitive skills which are prerequisites for organizational change but are difficult and expensive to develop. We realized that we were giving leaders, monitors, and administrators only minimal behavioral skills. Nevertheless we underestimated the extent to which the success of the program depended on the personal commitment and skills of the leader and monitor in using (and going beyond) the structures and formalized program procedures. Our training component simply was not sufficiently extensive to provide district personnel with a thorough cognitive understanding of the new model of functioning and the necessary skill base for implementing that model.

Accepting the conclusion that more comprehensive training is needed it could still be argued that our learnings suggest that more specific structures and procedures be built into the program. This increased specificity would imply a more complete and complex and possibly less flexible intervention. It is unclear whether improvements of this type would, beyond a certain point, increase the effectiveness of the intervention. One of our original assumptions was that our generic program for educational systems would be relevant to all schools. Our experience in this district does not support this assumption and it seems that it would be even less valid if the intervention were more structured and specific.

Earlier in this chapter we speculated about the way in which the "fit" between an OD model and an organization might predetermine the effectiveness of an intervention. The theories-in-use of some of the schools in this district were fairly compatible with our intervention, but other schools were operating in ways that were highly inconsistent with the program. Although the latter potentially could have derived the greatest benefits from the program, many of them declined to participate in our experiment. It is possible that this rejection rate would have been higher if the program had been more structured and the inconsistencies between the program and the *modus operandi* of the schools, more apparent.

Implementation of our survey feedback program was most difficult in participating schools that did not match our assumptions in regard to data, groups, and process guidance. Those schools that were able to create conditions compatible with the program opened the possibility for basic changes in the functioning of the organization (i.e., active professional problem solving on the part of the faculty). In schools that were having difficulty creating compatible conditions the efforts of the staff have not yet achieved a new model of functioning. Several schools (e.g., C, E, and F), however, are still using the program and may be moving toward that end. It is unclear whether more of these schools would be moving toward a new model had the intervention been more structured. A more structured intervention may have increased the potential magnitude of change in these organizations but may have decreased the probability that the program would have been accepted and implemented in the first place.

FAILURE VERSUS SUCCESS: SOME CONCLUDING THOUGHTS

The perceived success or failure of an OD program is largely a function of one's frame of reference. For example, our survey feedback program might be viewed as somewhat effective if change associated with single-loop learning were the criterion; the program would be seen as less effective if evaluated in terms of the more basic changes associated with double-loop learning. In writing this chapter, therefore, our objective was not to evaluate the overall success or failure of the program. Instead, our intention was to analyze and evaluate the intervention from a *failure* (rather than a *success*) perspective in an effort to identify its shortcomings and to test the validity of its underlying assumptions.

Reviewing our organizational development program from a failure perspective was at times somewhat disconcerting and seemed to be at variance with the prevailing sociology of "the science" of organization development. The process of writing this chapter, although illuminating, has produced some dissonance, given the time and effort we devoted to the intervention. The possible dysfunctional consequences of having written this failure-oriented review have also been bothersome. We feel that our intervention was unique in design and, in comparison with many other OD programs, relatively successful. Casting the program in a negative light may, however, unnecessarily and irreversibly damage the possibilities of further development and implementation. Furthermore, respected colleagues have viewed our intervention as one that has produced important changes in schools and have advised us against including it in a book about failures.

Nevertheless, there were compelling reasons for writing this chapter. An important factor is that the quality of OD research has been less than optimal and this has interfered with the advancement of intervention theory. Argyris has argued convincingly that the intervention field is "populated by practitioners who have little interest in conducting research and even less concern for theory" and that it has become easy for researchers to use "second-rate criteria" for evaluating OD programs (1970, pp. 12–13). Besides retarding the theoretical development of the field, the reluctance of OD researchers and practitioners to evaluate their programs critically and to analyze their failures may be reducing the public's acceptance of organization development. It is evident that the members of our experimental district were predisposed against our intervention because so many of the "staff improvement" and "organizational change" programs they had tried had failed; it is less clear to us that the consultants who directed these programs recognized these failures and learned from their mistakes.

The problems associated with evaluating organizational development programs are numerous. In conducting this study, we experienced many of the dilemmas associated with conducting field experiments in formal organizations, including the conflict between scientific versus ethical and practical considerations (Seashore, 1964). We found that the demands of the intervention combined with the evaluation created tensions for the research staff and district members, and these tensions may have reduced the effectiveness of both the program and its evaluation. Our efforts to avoid the problems of self-selection by inviting a district to participate in the project (rather than publicizing the program and waiting for a district to approach us) also led to problems. A significant minority of the people in the system preferred to cooperate with neither the implementation nor the evaluation of the program. Furthermore, the size and complexity of the school district, along with the difficulties of implementing a quasi-experimental design, severely restricted the completeness of our evaluation. The point is that even when efforts are made to assess interventions the results are often incomplete and inconclusive. If these results are then interpreted solely from a "success" perspective, the potential contribution of the research effort is further reduced. Although few guidelines are available on how to analyze a project from a failure perspective, we have tried to review our intervention from this negative vantage point. The "learnings" gleaned from this effort are not necessarily new, but at least they provide an empirical basis for questioning some of the implicit assumptions underlying data-based change strategies.

7

Bureaucracy and Social Change

An Anatomy of a Training Failure

WARREN G. BENNIS

Almost no one save for some cynics and cranks would argue with the *goal* of humanizing bureaucracy, and certainly some improvements have been made, if not always in practice, then at least in theory. Such terms as "participative management" and "two-way communication" reflect this tendency. These terms also reflect democratic values held by most social scientists toward their research subjects and lay clientele. But *values* are only one and perhaps not the most important consideration. There is a *pragmatic* issue at stake as well, for as organizations grow in size, as they increase their complexity and scope, and as they diversify and spread into sprawling behemoths the problems of leadership, coordination, collaboration, and communication force themselves on our attention. We can put the problem this way. How can the virtues of bureaucracy—its speed, precision, predictability, and efficiency—be maintained while preserving an adaptability to change and a climate of creativity, growth, and satisfaction for the work force?

A small portion of this manuscript is adapted from *Changing Organizations* by W. G. Bennis. Copyright 1966 McGraw-Hill. Used with permission of McGraw-Hill Book Company.

Many of us share a bleak melancholy in our outlook toward the potentiality for "change," at least socially desirable change. Pessimism, as well as politics, breeds strange bedfellows and, whatever else divides them, students of psychoanalysis and bureaucracy view their relevant units—people and organizations—as being mulishly resistant to most forms of alteration. Freud once said that he would be satisfied, indeed delighted, if he could transform neurotic despair into normal unhappiness; for social scientists and actionists the infusion of democratic values in bureaucratic mechanisms remains as unconquered promise.

This pessimism I speak of is nowhere better stated than in Gouldner's essay, "Metaphysical pathos and the theory of bureaucracy," in which he claims that for those intellectuals "who have erected a theory of group organization on Weberian foundations, the world has been emptied of choice, leaving them disoriented and despairing" (Gouldner, 1955, p. 498). Is it "metaphysical pathos" or "reality" that blinds us to the democratic potentiality of bureaucracy? The evidence adduced, I believe, tends to support Cassandra more than Pollyanna; it tends to challenge Gouldner's hope more than his colleagues' sullen despair. Indeed, the available evidence from social science research is far from promising.

Let us take some examples from research, admittedly selective, and state them unconditionally and without qualification. Concerning people: they tend to conform to the group even when their senses dictate a nonconforming response; and this tendency to conform is intensified to the degree that there are no operational referents for decisions, a state that exists frequently in bureaucracies. People are dependent, and even when they have the opportunity to participate many would prefer to remain passively obedient. People, when structured in a completely connected communications network, a democratic prototype, will revert to a more hierarchical and restrictive network. Leaders, that is, those who exert task influence, often tend to draw hostility rather than positive reactions. In fact, it is a rare event when a leader is liked at all (c.f., Asch, 1951; Bavelas, 1950; Festinger, 1954; Kelman, 1961; Leavitt, 1951; McMurry, 1950).

Concerning organizations: authoritarian organizations are more effective in task performance than democratic structures. Although democratic organizations enjoy generally high morale, there is a real question whether "closeness," interpersonal sensitivity, and analysis are functional for bureaucracies. Furthermore, the most effective organizations, ranging from basketball teams and survey crews to industrial work groups, are led by men who prefer distant and remote, rather than close, personal relations with subordinates. Add to these woeful findings Argyris' *Personality and Organization*, in which a research-based argument is made for the basic incompatibility between formal organization's structure and individual health (c.f., Blau, 1961; Argyris, 1957; Fiedler, 1964; Likert, 1961; Lippitt and White, 1958).

These references are obviously slanted to emphasize the bleaker side of democratic prospects and illustrate at least some of the foundations of "metaphysical pathos." Other data could be cited that contradict or question these studies, although keeping a "box score" of empirical research rarely resolves doctrinal disputes. The point, nonetheless, should be clear. Research provides no consensus or answer to the problem of democratic potentiality; at best, it points to a dilemma.

While granting the problematical nature of the evidence, our optimism is far from dimmed, particularly if notice is taken of an important change program. I am referring here to a group of social scientists who have had moderate success in inculcating democratic patterns and values in more traditional bureaucratic structures by employing a variation of what is called laboratory training, known also as T-group or sensitivity or group dynamics training (Bradford et al., 1964; Schein and Bennis, 1965). Promising work of this sort has been carried out in a number of institutions, mainly in industry but also including hospitals, health and welfare agencies, social service, school and university systems, and government.

In the remaining pages a brief description of laboratory Training is presented. Attention is focused here on identifying those learning goals that demonstrate leverage for social change; I call them the "meta-goals." Following this, a situation is described in which this form of training was employed ineptly and unsuccessfully. My hope here is not to discourage the use of such programs but only to exemplify the difficulties in creating socially desirable change and to point out what is essential for success. In the last section I propose some prerequisites and conditions for advancing democratic change programs.

LABORATORY TRAINING AND TRAINING "META-GOALS"

It is unnecessary to dwell on this topic, for there is already a substantial literature on laboratory training. Originating in Bethel, Maine, in 1947 under the guidance of Lewin, Bradford, Benne, and Lippitt, heavily influenced by social psychology, group dynamics, psychotherapy, and adult education doctrines, and with an overriding concern for the application of social science to practice and policy, laboratory training has become one of the main instruments for organizational change. Generally speaking the training takes place in a residential location—a "cultural island" away from the individual's home and work place—for varying periods up to two or three weeks. During the course of training the participants are exposed to a wide range of applied social science concepts: personality theory, group dynamics research, organization and social change theory, usually transmitted on lectures or seminar discussions. Role playing, demonstrations, and simulation experiments constitute another segment of work, but the bulk of the time, at least one-half to two-thirds, is spent in small unstructured T-groups in which the main focus is on self- and group analysis under the guidance of a staff member, usually a social scientist.

The T-group ("T" stands for training) is a deeply personal, intense, involving process by which the participants attempt to examine their interpersonal relations in group settings. The training process relies primarily on the *experienced behavior* of the participants; that is, the group itself becomes the focus of inquiry. The trainer fosters this approach by introducing the experience, at the first meeting, as a learning vehicle that attempts to study group process and interpersonal behavior in groups by examining the data generated by individuals as they form a group. The trainer provides no structure, no rules, and few norms of appropriate behavior and steers clear of interfering with the natural unfolding of the group formation. The trainer's role, as explained to the participants, consists primarily in promoting conditions in which group members can learn from their experience together. The situation itself adds to the ambiguity: the participants are often strangers to one another; the goals, although stated by the staff members, are vague and intangible to the participants; the reward system is unclear; a normlessness exists; there is a "strangeness" and "newness" to examining behavior and feelings.

All of these factors together, plus the participant-observer emphasis, creates an initially tense, uncertain environment that tends to activate the defensiveness and security concerns of the participants. With the help of the trainer, the group moves toward an existential examination of its "reality" and from this experience generalizes about other "realities" back home: family, community, and organization. T-group training, then, can be viewed as an attempt to learn about human behavior by exploring one's relations with others in a "here-and-now," existential setting.

Although the stated goals of these laboratories vary, depending on staff composition and institutional needs, they generally include objectives such as these: (a) self-insight, or some variation of learning related to increased self-knowledge; (b) understanding the conditions that inhibit or facilitate effective group functioning; (c) understanding interpersonal operations in groups; (d) developing skills for diagnosing individual, group, and organizational behavior.

Beyond these explicit goals there rests another set of learnings referred to as "meta-goals." These meta-goals transcend, underlie, and shape the articulated goals mentioned above. More crucial, for our purposes, is the realization that the meta-goals, if internalized, lead to a set of values that may run counter to those prevailing in the sponsoring organization. More is said later about the tension resulting from this conflict of values, as it has direct relevance for the case study. For the moment let us look at the pivotal meta-goals.

1. *Expanded consciousness and recognition of choice*

Extracting people in organizations from their day-to-day routines and preoccupations and transplanting them into a culture where they are urged to observe and understand personality and group dynamics creates conditions in which "givens" become choices or at least create potentials for choice. I must emphasize that laboratory training is a device that deroutinizes or slows down and lifts up for analysis processes that are "taken for granted." It is a form of training that questions received notions and attempts to "unfreeze" the role expectations of the participants (Schein, 1964). The impulse for this cognitive restructuring comes about primarily because the control mechanisms present and taken for granted in institutionalized behavior are decisively absent in a laboratory. I am referring to control mechanisms, such as mission, authority patterns, norms regulating intimacy and control, decision apparatus, communication, traditions, and precedents, which serve to regulate behavior. The ambiguity and confusion of norms, behavioral constraints, and anticipatory rewards create what Lewin referred to as a "primitivization" of behavior due to the regressive climate. The happy necessity of this human existence, to paraphrase T. S. Eliot, is for men to find things out for themselves; that is, to create order, clarify one's identity, and establish norms and a sense of community. In fact, one can look at laboratory training as the formation of norms and structure that build a community, except that, unlike most communities, the constituent members are present at its birth.

Laboratory training, then, realizes its meta-goal of "expanded consciousness and recognition of choice points" by way of a complicated process: extracting participants from their day-to-day preoccupations, cultural insulation, and deroutinization. Parallel to and combined with this "unfreezing" process is an emphasis on awareness, sensitivity, and diagnosis, all of which encourage the participants to think about their behavior or, most particularly, about how they choose to behave.

2. *A "spirit of inquiry"*

Closely related to the meta-goals of choice—and, in fact, only conceptually separable—is an attitude of inquiry most often associated with science. It is a complex of human behavior and adjustment that has been summed up as the "spirit of inquiry" and includes many elements, only two of which are considered here. The first may be called the hypothetical spirit, the feeling for tentativeness and caution, the respect for probable error. The second ingredient is experimentalism, the willingness to expose ideas to empirical testing, to procedures, to action. The exigencies of the laboratory situation help to create this orientation in the participants, for the ambiguous and unstructured situation creates a need to define and organize the environment. In addition, the participants are prodded and rewarded by staff members to question old and try new behaviors; they are reinforced by concepts to probe, to look at data and realities unflichingly—to ask "why."

In laboratory training all experienced behavior is subject to questioning and analysis, limited only by the participants' threshold of tolerance to truth and new ideas.

3. *Authenticity in interpersonal relations*

An important imperative in laboratory training has to do with the relatively high valuation of feelings: their expression, their importance, their effects. The degree to which participants can communicate feelings and, in turn, evoke valid feelings from other group members is regarded as an important criterion of group growth. One theory, for example, postulates that "group development involves the overcoming of obstacles to valid communication among the members"; that is, where valid communication is defined as interpersonal communication free—as humanly possible—of distortion.

Authenticity, "leveling," and "expressing feelings" constitute an important part of the laboratory argot, all of which can be summed up in a passage from *King Lear*: "Speak what we feel, not what we ought to say. . . ."

This tendency toward authenticity should not be surprising when we consider that so much time and attention is devoted to the analysis of interpersonal behavior, to understanding the effects of a participant's behavior on other group members. Measurements of changes during these training programs indeed suggest personal growth resembling that seen in psychotherapy; that is, the participants, as they know themselves, will be much the same person as they are known to others.

4. *A collaborative conception of the authority relationship*

Permeating the atmosphere of laboratory training is a conception of the authority relationship that differs substantially from the legitimacy of position. The contractual elements in the authority relationship are understressed, and the collaborative and interdependent elements are accentuated. In McGregor's writings we can identify the major elements in this conception of authority. (a) Management by objective; that is, the requirements of the job are set by the situation; they need not be seen by either party as personal requirements established by the superior. Thus the authority relationship is viewed as a joint, collaborative process in which superior and subordinate attempt to develop ground rules for work and productivity. (b) The recognized interdependence between subordinates and superiors. (c) The belief that subordinates are capable of learning *self-control*; that is, to internalize and exercise standards of performance congruent with organizational objectives without reliance on controls that emanate from external sources.

How this conception of authority is transmitted and internalized during laboratory training is beyond the scope of this chapter; moreover the process is not altogether clear. Readings and lectures cover the material somewhat and identifications with staff members undoubtedly contribute, but most important is the realization that *the teaching-learning process of laboratory training is a prototype of the collaborative conception of authority*. Putting it differently, we can say that learning is accomplished according to the requirements of the situation and as a joint, collaborative venture between the trainer and participants. Also, there is the belief that participants can exercise self-control in the learning process; that they accept influence on the basis of their own evaluations rather than reliance on outside controls such as rewards and punishments. Internalization, by credibility rather than compliance, is the type of social influence employed in laboratory training. It is precisely this form of influence that holds for the collaborative conception of authority we have been discussing.

These four meta-goals—expanded consciousness and recognition of choice, spirit of inquiry, authenticity in interpersonal relations, and a collaborative conception of authority—represent what I think are the most important results gained from laboratory training.

Emphasizing the meta-goals has analytic importance for what is to follow. First of all, they represent what the participants internalize and what they ordinarily transfer to their organizations. "Everything the child learns in school he forgets," goes an old French maxim, "but the *education* remains." Similarly, the meta-goals remain. Second, these internalized learnings have profound implications for the individuals and for their organizations because they deeply affect and modify the value and motivational commitments that determine the individuals' orientations to their roles. We have to keep this in mind as a prelude to the case study that follows.

In general, the case exemplifies two sets of institutionalized values in conflict: one generated by laboratory training, the other, by the parent institution. This tension could be resolved in one of two ways: changing the normative patterns of the organization, particularly those related to authority relations, or checking, if not destroying, the laboratory training. The latter course was taken, which leads us to the case.

THE CASE OF AN ABORTIVE CHANGE PROGRAM

It might be helpful to state at the outset how I learned about the incident reported here. During the academic year of 1961–1962 I was a Visiting Professor at IMEDE, a management development school for middle management in Lausanne, Switzerland. Early in the year I was visited by a Swiss industrial social psychologist who was eager to discuss the prospect of laboratory training for management development in Europe. He explained that there were so few people who "really understood" these techniques and he very much wanted to obtain my point of view on these various matters. Subsequently he revealed the following story:

He was hired around the middle of 1960 by a large international Swiss service industry to develop and execute a human relations training course for first- and second-line supervision.

Heavily influenced by the Harvard Business School case-method approach (by working as a teaching associate in an American business school in Europe) and a group dynamics approach (sponsored by a European center), he persuaded his immediate superior and a colleague to inaugurate laboratory training for all first- and second-line supervision. Accordingly, nine one-week laboratories were held in a mountain resort with better-than-expected results. In addition, my informant's colleague conducted seven one-week programs along the same lines with equally good results. All in all, both men had offered laboratory training to about 180 men and women, averaging about 14 individuals per session.

In the middle of the ninth week of the course, while the laboratory participants were having their breakfast, the president of the company arrived, unannounced and quite unexpectedly, and asked Berger (my informant) if he could observe the day's activities. Berger had never met the president before. At first, he tried to dissuade him but yielded when he became more insistant. During the day the president observed two T-group meetings; he also attended an unstructured planning meeting at which participants decided on their next day's activities, a lecture on leadership theory based on McGregor's *The Human Side of Enterprise*, and an "application group" in which attempts were made to think through the transfer of laboratory learnings to the company.

Later on in the day the president returned to company headquarters, and the following Monday, at the weekly top management meeting of vice-presidents, proposed that the laboratory training program be terminated. The reason given was financial difficulties. Further effects of the president's visit can be seen in the following actions: Berger's contract was allowed to expire at the end of the year; Berger's colleague, Kreutz, who conducted a parallel course, asked for and was granted a transfer to another section of the personnel department; the vice-president of personnel left the company for a high government post; and Berger's immediate superior, who was in charge of all management training, was asked to add hiring, selection, and recruitment to his functions, which left virtually no time for training programs. In short, the training department was virtually destroyed.

This sketchy outline cannot possibly convey the emotional release and bitterness that accompanied Berger's narrative. Berger urged me to talk with him about this again and asked me to consider writing up a case study of the incident. For somewhat vague motives, curiousity perhaps, but mostly compassion for what seemed like the victimization of a colleague, I agreed to collaborate with him. We decided to tape record the interview, after which I was determined to see if I could collect more data on the case. I adopted this approach because I have always been particularly intrigued by the clinical pathology conferences used in diagnostic medicine at which evidence from an autopsy is presented to a diagnostician and, working backward, he or she attempts to reconstruct the cause of death. In this case, I conducted an "autopsy" of the change, believing that if the main issues surrounding this failure could be understood more progress in installing democratic change programs would result.

I was able to interview the main actors involved in the incident. They included the president of the company, the former vice-president of personnel, the chief of the training department, Berger's colleague, and two participants who were present during the president's visit. No one appeared unwilling to discuss the incident and all but two of the interviews were tape recorded. Each interview was completely unstructured save for two questions: "Could you describe what happened (or what you heard happened) on the day the president visited the laboratory? What do you think caused the termination of the training program?" Berger's interview lasted over several meetings and about 10 hours of tape; the others lasted between three and four hours.

What follows is a selection of excerpts from these interviews made with an eye toward showing discrepancy in perception and interpretation. In general, most of the reports of the president's visit and decision were similar, although there were wide differences in interpretation. I should also say that all informants felt genuine regret at Berger's dismissal and the termination of the training program.

INFORMANTS

Berger —The social psychologist who originated the change program.

Kreutz —A colleague of Berger's in the training department who conducted a similar course and who transferred to another department in Personnel shortly after the program collapsed.

Maier —The head of the training department and the immediate superior of Berger and Kreutz.

Trogler—Vice-president of personnel and Maier's immediate superior, now a high official in the government.

Linz —President of the company. Linz has been president since 1950.

Anton —A first-line supervisory who participated.

1. *The president's visit*

Berger. I explained to the president what the general lines of the course were and what we were going to do today and I was wondering how I was going to tell him that it would be most undesirable for him to join the group during the T-group session. So finally I told him that I have to make a remark which I am exceedingly unhappy about and that is that probably it would not be very interesting and illustrative for him to join in at the meeting. I tried to explain that that kind of activity involves people so deeply and so personally that they probably will freeze up when he comes in and will not speak. He replied that he had visited the case study discussions the year before and saw no reason why he shouldn't sit in this year. I tried to explain the differences to him, but not very successfully, and I became quite agitated because it was time for the group meeting to start. Finally he said, "Well, am I the president or am I not the president? Alright then, I want to see this T-group. After all, that is the reason why I am here. If you have something to hide, then it is still more important that I really come and see what is going on here. If you do not have anything to hide, well, there is no point in arguing about it." He also added: "If you are refusing my request to come into the group meeting, this will be the end of the courses." So, I thought that in the interest of the course and its continuance it probably was worth taking the risk and letting him come in. I then suggested to him that I would like to go to the group and inform them about the purpose of his visit and that they should carry on their activities as if it had been the normal pattern. But he refused this, too. He said, "There is no point in informing people; let's go in together."

At the beginning of the meeting, I felt very uneasy about it, but then I forgot about the president and toward the end of the two-hour session I realized what an excellent meeting it had been and I felt very confident. I told him that it was probably a unique situation when somebody from the outside could drop in as he did and get a realistic picture of what usually would go on. He noted this and smiled at my remarks and expressed astonishment about the lack of structure in the group. . . .

After the meeting, while having coffee, he seemed a little surprised about my rather passive attitude and my not exercising any leadership function. So I started to explain to him that that was the heart of the matter but I had the feeling that I could not really communicate with him; that there was an enormous wall of prejudice which I could not get behind. He kept a very polite surface, but I realized that there was considerable doubt behind it. . . . I then gave a lecture to the group on leadership behavior drawing my material from McGregor's *The Human Side of Enterprise*. Following that we had a special activity. I had asked the participants to use this time in order to plan some activity which they would have on one of the last days of the week's program. I thought that giving them such a realistic task would be an excellent activity inasmuch as it resembles the more routine work activity. After that meeting the president asked me if that were the usual way things happen here. By this question I understood that he again expressed his astonishment about the apparent confusion and lack of guidance from me. I told him that this was the usual pattern, in fact, very much so. I also expressed my great satisfaction over the results which had been achieved. We then went to lunch and he ordered some wine and we had a nice chat and I felt at that moment that probably he enjoyed it and was a little bewildered but probably realized that there was something valuable in this whole thing. When he had finished lunch he said, "Well, I'm feeling that the ice is broken."

In the afternoon, right after the T-group was ending and people were on their feet to leave, the president stepped to his feet and said, "Wait a minute" and then delivered a 20-minute speech. He first said that supervisory training was an important thing and that the company had already spent a lot of money on this. He thought that the participants were getting something from the company which was not at all self-evident that a company would do for its people. He said how important this thing seemed to top management and this was the reason he came to see us. He went on to say that our hesitation in the morning to receive him was in a way understandable but regrettable. Then he went on to repeat what he already had said on New Year's Eve in his annual speech to the personnel; namely, that difficult times were ahead requiring the greatest effort of everybody, calling for close cooperation and asking for people's understanding of the present situation. How this could be achieved, according to him, was by working hard and by following exactly the given orders—all the requisites of a paternalistic management. Then he came back to my short lecture and said that there was one point which he did not at all agree with. (One of the participants asked me if a subordinate always has to follow strictly given orders. I answered in a qualified way, trying to show the conditions for obedience and the conditions for questioning a superior.) He said that he most strongly wanted to emphasize that "A subordinate had always to follow the orders of his superiors. There was just no question about that." And then he went into some detail about leadership philosophy which all ended up in a flat contradiction of the whole underlined philosophy of the course. People were rather baffled by this sudden speech and there was a certain amount of confusion about it—especially among the more alert participants. They realized that here were two exponents of two different philosophies. . . . When I drove the president to his train before the evening meal he told me that I gave the impression that people might do whatever pleases them and that I tried to counteract discipline and the hierarchical line command in his organization. He felt that it was necessary to stop such revolutionary thinking. . . .

After returning to the laboratory one or two participants expressed their view about the president's visit. I particularly remembered one who said that he felt ashamed of the events of the day because here was a group of people working together in a way which he felt was one of the most rewarding things he had ever gone through. He said, "I felt that you should not have let the president come into the room. I felt that this was a deception. At the moment, I felt it was almost a treason of the group to admit the president and for you not to protect us from this visit. You told us at the beginning of the course that whatever would be discussed here would be strictly confidential and under no circumstances would it be passed along to top management. And here comes the president and takes notes during our session. How could you permit this?"

Let us turn to the two other eyewitnesses present the day of the president's visit before returning to Berger's interview:

President Linz. I was genuinely impressed by our methods used in our management development programs—simply thrilled with it. I visited the training site from time to time in years past (when case studies and lectures were used) and would come away lyrical—really thrilled about it. Now I have heard—getting back to Berger—many rumors about what was going on there. So I decided to go. It was the first time I met Professor Berger and he acted strangely—as if he didn't want me to visit the group. I told him that I am used to inspecting courses. I am, after all, the president and there is no good reason why there should be a barrier erected here. Well, he submitted and I went into the group and then someone made the same suggestion as Dr. Berger; that is, take me for a walk and explain the training to me. I said to the group "No, no" that I came to see what was going on. After all, I said, "management development is part of my responsibility." Well, they soon forgot I was there and seemed to talk about what was on their minds. . . .

They were discussing group relations, I guess. They were sitting in a circle and they would sit silent for a while and they would sit and discuss group relations. Every once in a while someone would ask, "What is your impression of me and what do others make of me and what do I make of others." Then there would be silence and the pressure would build up and then it would explode and everyone would start talking at once about impressions people were making on each other. I suppose that one can learn a lot about how one feels and sees, but I did not think this kind of discussion was foremost for management training and development.

I want to tell my key people how to guide their subordinates and what the goals of the company are and what they will be. However interesting this experiment is, I can tell you frankly it just isn't foremost. As far as the people who went there are concerned, well, some people had nervous breakdowns, others seemed to enjoy it and even improve in their operations. . . .

You see, we Swiss, in our schools, in our land, rarely get any instruction in guiding people. Our main doctrination—our main orientation—is the army. This is primitive, but at least they come to certain conclusions. Anybody who controls other people must have the courage to interfere when they are not doing their job correctly. It's so easy to overlook lacks in behavior on the part of subordinates. You see many officers in the army averting their eyes rather than telling a man to change. Even at the American Management Association, which I respect very much, I said to them last year, "Maybe you forget one thing: that every organization has its hierarchy, has its goals, has its leaders, and authority needs enforcement. This one point, you seem to neglect here." And they recently told me that they think I am right.

But back to this group training for a minute. If we could teach skill and techniques, and if we have the financial position, we'll go ahead. Right now we have to tell our people how and what our ideals and goals are and how our organization should be run and how they should handle their people. After this we could go on to psychological things, like group relations.

Anton. We were having breakfast when he arrived, I overheard the owner of the hotel where we were staying ask him why he hadn't told them of his visit so he could have prepared a decent welcome. I heard Dr. Linz reply, "There are two sorts of inspection in military service: one, you will never forewarn and the other you will. When you forewarn, you find everything O.K. When you do not, you might find something you never will see." We all heard him say this. Before Linz and Berger came into our meeting room we were having a heated discussion over whether we should permit him to join us. Two or three of us were against it, but the rest thought it would be better. In my opinion it is typically Swiss: we have no courage to tell what we think. The whole thing was against my principles. I still think we should have thrown him out.

The speech he gave after our T-group meeting convinced me that he never will understand what our work was all about. If he understood our work at the laboratory, he could never have talked to us the way he did. He only wants to control us. But it's not only a thing of the head, but also of the heart."

2. *How the program was communicated to and accepted by top management*

Berger. One of my objectives for this course was that top management should be fully informed about what we were doing. I was completely covered by the O.K. I had received from my boss, Maier, the chief of training. Right from the beginning I had told Maier to make sure that top management knows what we are doing because unless they do, this whole thing could explode. Maier tried, I know, to get the vice-president of personnel, Trogler, more actively interested but he found that difficult—for different reasons. Trogler took the view that management education was basically not a worthwhile thing; at any rate, he was not very much interested in details of training. Furthermore, I had expressed a wish to Maier that top management should not make their usual inspection visits of our training program. I thought it would interfere with the process if a high ranking company officer would visit for a day or two. Then, when President Linz asked Trogler, the vice-president of personnel, for detailed information about the course, Trogler said he knew very little or nothing about it. The president insisted that the vice-president should attend part of the course, but Trogler said that this was not desirable. Then the president said, "O.K., if you are not going, I will go myself."

Meanwhile, another development had taken place which had made it important for the president to come and visit us. (A woman in the firm) overheard a conversation by a previous female participant who was trying to tell another girl about her experience in our training program. She said, "This course was the deepest experience I have had in my life so far." The other girl wanted to know more about it.

So she told about her experiences and among other things she said, "Can you imagine, there was one man who took off his clothes completely?" The German expression is *Ausziehen* which has a double meaning. It can be either the physical sense of taking off your clothes or revealing yourself. Well, she meant "reveal" but the other girl understood her to mean "striptease." The woman who overheard this then went to her superior and said, "Since this kind of strip-tease is going on there, I don't want to go to these courses." So, as I understand it, the superior told her two subordinates that they should go there and find out what is really going on and that they should leave the course immediately if things got too drastic.

President Linz. I was under the misapprehension that they were conducting case analyses. The method they were using—group relations—I'm not so sure about. After all, they introduced the whole thing without telling me . . . without telling me. I should have known about this program beforehand and I got a bit cross. They then tried to hide it from me and I didn't like that a bit.

Vice-President Trogler. There was simply no point of contact between the president and Berger or Maier. The methods they were using were completely unknown to top management. I told Maier and Berger that it was dangerous to undertake the project without explaining what will take place. There was simply no rational discussion of the program. The important thing was that Linz was never informed. If he had been, his reaction would not have been so violent.

Maier. I am responsible for the T-group experiment having lived through the ordeal before and was convinced of its merits. But I was skeptical of introducing it and it was only after Berger convinced Kreutz that I went along with it. We felt we should inform our vice-president, Trogler. He is an extraordinary man and is a trained psychologist. After 15 or 20 minutes of discussion he seemed to understand perfectly, and agreed with what we were doing. After the "striptease" incident the president asked our boss, Trogler, if he knows what is going on in those courses. Trogler said he did. 'Have you ever been there?' and Trogler replied that he had not. "Why haven't you?" Trogler said that Berger and Maier felt it was unwise to visit this type of course and he was satisfied with their answer. "It is unwise to go into the courses," he explained, "because the group integrates so quickly that any visitor is thrown out, mentally rejected." But the president didn't understand

and said, "Well, if you don't do your duty and inspect these courses, I will."

Kreutz. Another element we have to notice is that Berger had never met the president before his visit. Berger, not knowing Linz, had to explain to him in three or four minutes what this whole thing was about. The president was very enthusiastic about our case courses. He did have confidence but not that strong when those things I have mentioned happened. (Kreutz is referring here to the "striptease" incident and the psychotic break of a participant.)

Now Trogler was always sponsoring our project but he didn't know exactly the methods we were using. He was perhaps a bit of a pessimist and didn't really think you could change a man. Naturally he couldn't explain our program to the president because he didn't know it himself. Maier always stood behind the program and still does. But he doesn't claim to be a specialist and I don't think he knew exactly what Berger and I were doing. . . .

So the president arrives at the training site with anything but an open mind. He had heard rumors and he had heard that people up there deal with something like psychology, sociology and that people are in group dynamic sessions where nothing happens. Well, all this was very strange to him. . . .

3. *The causes of failure*

Berger was particularly bewildered by the chain of events that led to the termination of the program and his own dismissal. He inferred that he was victimized by the president's prejudices and used as some sort of a scapegoat, but beyond that he was perplexed. In fact, shortly after the program was terminated he distributed questionnaires to all the participants in his group and of the 140 participants about 100 responded. The data showed that 84 percent of the respondents were "highly satisfied" with the course.

Only 8 percent of the responses were unfavorable and were from predominantly female participants. All negative responses included some criticism of the "overpersonalized nature of the training and its inapplicability to the company."

The participants' superiors were also asked for their opinions of the course on the basis of perceived changes in their subordinates. Few superiors returned their questionnaires, and of the small total who did the responses were noncommittal or negative. (It should be pointed out, however, that these questionnaires were distributed *after* the program was terminated; moreover, they were distributed and returned through official channels and with some concern about their confidentiality.)

Kreutz. There were a number of reasons for the breakdown of the program. First of all, in order to have group experience in group dynamics you have to have groups without structure; that is, people who have had no former relationships with each other. That is practically impossible in a company. And in a few courses we had some people, particularly women, who had known each other and brought all their rivalries into the group. So, it wasn't a group without a structure. In fact, there was one group of women, old-timers, who were threatened by all of this training and they spread the rumor that people were doing a striptease. That's completely silly, but it was believed. The fact was that there was a great mystery about the course.

Then there was the president's visit. I think Berger could have handled the situation more tactfully and diplomatically. He should have gladly invited the president to join in the activities and changed the program for the day; he should have used more structured exercises and lectures.

The third point was this man who was mentally ill and had been in treatment before he came to the course without our knowing it. Also there is a fourth reason. That is the financial picture of the company. But most important is the fact that in order for any management training program to be a success you have to have the program 100 percent supported and understood by top management. But this is impossible to get, particularly with a course of this kind because it is virtually impossible to tell anyone about it without going into psychology and sociology.

President Linz. The chief reason was the financial condition of the company. When you have to struggle for survival, when you are in a difficult competitive situation, then I felt we could no longer afford this program. From now on, we'll have to conduct our management development program on the job. We simply cannot afford to send people away for a week on something which may be psychologically important but without relevance for our company. This is the whole story, the whole story. . . .

Trogler. As I said earlier there was inadequate communication to Linz. He was never informed fully enough. Berger also deserves some blame. He is not free enough to face a new situation. He's a bad man to be surprised. I think another man could have avoided the conflict with Linz. Also, I feel he went too far in his group dynamics.

I also think that the program should have been billed as completely voluntary, and I'm not sure that was done. At any rate, top management should have taken part in the first place.

Maier. Well, the whole trouble started when a female supervisor heard someone who had returned from the course say that the participants had unrobed. She had said "entblösste sich"—he undressed. This was repeated and the rumor spread in a matter of days.

Then the president—alarmed by this and other rumors—dropped in on the course in progress. Berger told me later that he had thought it was a model demonstration of good group work. But of course the president doesn't understand a word of it. This is quite natural, I suppose. I mean people concerned with finance and production aren't used to hearing people talk about themselves. So the president reported to his staff that people there had gone "crackers." He felt that they were wasting their time and the company's money. Then after the session, Berger talked with the president, and here is a problem. Everything went badly because as our vice-president put it afterwards, "the president didn't like Berger's nose." Trogler said that if any other man had been there instead of Berger, it wouldn't have gone that way. I admire Berger very much, but he is a stubborn fellow and if he is convinced of a good thing, he would go through a concrete wall. He is absolutely inflexible in this respect.

Now Linz, our president, watched everything. He watched them play ball after lunch and he watched Berger ask the participants to plan their next day's activities. At the staff meeting, where he proposed the termination of the program, he was reported to have said, "They (the participants) are playing ball games and moreover Berger asks them to prepare tomorrow's program. *He*, the course leader, asks the participants—his subordinates!—to work out the program and he says he will accept their suggestions. That is the world upside down. Is this the purpose of our training—to teach anarchy?"

I like our president very much and admire him but I think he is rather convinced of authoritarian methods. He is an army colonel and he believes in the principles of the army. He tells me now and then, "Maier, you see what the army does. You cannot do any better in management training than if you adhere to the principles of the military." And so that was the end. This kind of program has to be backed up by top people. Top management must know what it is all about. Even if the president does believe in me, he may still have some fears that if I start playing with what he calls psychology, I may discover something he doesn't want disclosed. I don't blame the president. The same thing may happen to me or to anyone. But this is the explanation for the attitude of top management on that decisive meeting when they abandoned our project. I am absolutely convinced.

Anton. My impressions of that week were very good and I never had such a week in my life. It's an impression or feeling, perhaps; something which is inside and which can hardly be explained. There was something to learn: that you are not alone and that it is very complicated to live together. Perhaps I learned that the other man is as important as I am or as you are, and that it is not only you who exists but also another human being. I can't express it differently, but for me it was just something that goes direct to my insides.

I think it was a silly thing to stop those programs. I am sure it's right. Now I am supervisor of 60 persons and I always remember that week when I am working with them. Even at home I use what I learned there. I think the course was stopped because from that visit Dr. Linz thought we may be some anarchists or such things. I think I learned to "be myself," not an anarchist. Perhaps there is some feeling that the members of those courses will become too independent. But this is important, and perhaps elsewhere you have another orientation. But here in Switzerland, one doesn't like to supervise a man who is too independent.

SOME PROPOSITIONS ABOUT THE USES OF LAB TRAINING IN EFFECTING SOCIAL CHANGE

This case of "failure," because of its dramatic aspects, should not blind us to the fact that it may be the exception, not the rule. On the other hand, unusual as the case may be, it would be a mistake to regard it only for its pathological interest. What I should like to do now is consider the failures and develop some propositions about social change:

1. *In undertaking any planned social change using lab training, the core of the target system's values must not be too different from the lab training values.*

Every target system has a core of values that characterizes it and determines a good many of its decisions. Lab training also implies a system of core values, discussed earlier in terms of legitimacy of interpersonal phenomena, concepts of control, and so on. This case indicates that the target system's values should be somewhat in accord, or *potentially* congruent, with lab training values. When the two systems of values are widely discrepant and rigid and the value system of the target cannot yield without vitally endangering the target system's core values, then change induced by lab training will probably not succeed.

Let us be specific. In this case it is obvious that the institutional base was perceived by men in power as seriously threatened. The values, the normative patterns, and the set of shared expectations were all in flux because of the training endeavors of Berger and Kreutz.

Perhaps the central issue here concerns the definition of "training." Webster defines it as follows: "1. To subject oneself or to be subjected to instruction, drilling, regular exercise, dieting, etc. 2. To form habits or impact proficiency by teaching, drilling, etc." Most "training" affirms these definitions; that is, training is a process by which individuals learn the skills, attitudes, and orientation congruent to a particular role. Training, viewed in this way, has a conservative connotation. It takes organizations as they are and attempts to shape individuals to them.

What we have been calling training is probably misnamed, for certainly a program that aims to change the very structure of the organization by modifying a role orientation is not training in the usual sense of the word. This is not only a semantic issue. Training, in its dictionary sense and in the sense in which most personnel managers use it and top management construes it, is viewed conservatively: fitting people to roles. Training in the sense in which it was employed in this case signifies a *fundamental* change: an alteration of the values, norms, and patterns of expectation. In this sense President Linz was completely correct in viewing lab training as "revolutionary." It was revolutionary to the extent that the core of institutional values Linz was striving to preserve was basically threatened by the lab training change programs.

Putting it a bit differently, most organizations agree to various training and development programs insofar as they strengthen the core of institutional values and facilitate the functioning of the organization. When programs are seen as imperiling the institutional base, we can expect the strong resistance evinced in this case.

Most social-change programs, certainly lab training, attempt to alter institutional values. How, then, can the inevitable and powerful resistance be reduced?

2. *In undertaking any planned social change, legitimacy for the change must be gained by obtaining the support of the key people.*

This is not to say that lab training should start at the top; it does mean that a careful and deliberate effort must be made to gain acceptance by the top management group. Without this acceptance lab training is constantly in peril. Indeed, if the vice-president of personnel had been able to tell President Linz what was really going on, it might not have been necessary for him to make the surprise trip.

In any case, an effort must be made to provide top management with a picture of lab training that is as clear and realistic as possible. This is done not only as an acquaintance process but also to test top management's commitment to the potential changes. If the commitment is weak at the top level, then a total reevaluation of the strategy is required. It is far better to discover this early. In this case, partly in fear and mostly from futility, the training staff worked surreptitiously with the faint hope that the training effects would be accepted. The outcome produced an unstable situation in which the lowest levels of management maintained values that were in conflict with those at the top. The tension created by this value conflict was reduced by removing Berger, its source, and restoring the old orientation.

Obtaining hierarchical acceptance, no matter how painstaking and difficult, provides at least some guarantee that management can understand, hence manage, the change without undue tension.

3. *In undertaking any planned social change, the process of installing the change programs must be congruent with their process and goals.*

We are talking here of a fairly simple, but crucial, matter. The change agent should know what he is doing and should act congruently and authentically. Although we are not absolutely confident that this proposition will hold in every situation (e.g., installing a totalitarian system), we are sure that it is essential for a democratic change program. For reasons that appeared sensible at the time, Berger operated more as an "undercover" agent than as an agent of change. It is doubtful that he understood the consequences of his decisions: the fact that he viewed lab training as a simple substitute for the case method gives rise to this question. Were the goals and meta-goals of lab training clearly understood by the change agents?

It is not obvious that they were understood. Berger, in particular, violated the meta-goals to some degree: authenticity was abandoned by the underground methods used to start the program, action was taken without a "spirit of inquiry," and the nature of the change program was far from collaborative. The way Berger dealt with President Linz was not an example of "authentic and collaborative" relations.

Unanticipated consequences can jeopardize any change program. Only the omniscient can be blamed for those, but in the case of this Swiss firm many of the consequences could have been foreseen and avoided if Berger himself had used the processes of lab training in installing the change program. What we observed instead was the blind use of a "tool" in a way that contradicted its essence.

4. *In undertaking any planned social change, the employment security of the change-agent must be guaranteed.*

Blau (1961) points out that one of the prerequisites for adaptation in bureaucracy is the minimum employment security of the personnel. In terms of the brutal reality of existence, this means that most people would not risk their jobs in order to create change. Given the lab training approach to organizational change, minimum employment security is essential for the change agent, particularly if he is a member of the organization. The training staff must maintain their separateness from other company employees and must develop some discretion and autonomy insofar as training functions are concerned.

For Berger there was no real alternative but to let the president "sit in"; it was either that or dismissal. If a similar situation had occurred in which the trainer had maximum employment security or was an outside consultant, employed temporarily by the company, there may have been a different outcome.

5. *In undertaking any planned social change that utilizes lab training, the voluntary commitment of the participants may be a crucial factor in the success of the program.*

The difficulty of describing lab training by verbal orientation, plus the problematical aspects of organizational legitimacy to influence interpersonal behavior, leads to only one conclusion with respect to participant attendance at labs. This is that all delegates must undertake lab training in a completely voluntary spirit. It is hightly doubtful that they will learn if this condition does not prevail.

6. *In undertaking any planned social change that utilizes lab training, the legitimacy of interpersonal influence must be potentially acceptable.*

The spread and belief of the "striptease" rumor shows, if anything, the desirability of an orientation for prospective participants. But it shows more than that. We must ask how much and in what way can (should?) an organization influence the personalities of its employees? It is not exactly obvious that interpersonal competence is correlated with effective role functioning; in some specific situations there may be no, or an inverse, correlation. Indeed, the theoretical foundations of bureaucracy are based on *impersonality*. Even with the modern role conception of the modern manager, which includes social-system management and responsibility, the prevailing norms of legitimacy or organizational influence must be explored and understood fully by the target system.

7. *In undertaking any planned social change, the effects on the adjacent and interdependent subsystems related to the target system must be carefully considered.*

This case, and many others, demonstrates this principle, but whether it is "doctors" or "headquarters" or "colleagues" or "bosses" a complete diagnosis of the total effects on all relevant parts must be made before not after the training starts.

8. *In undertaking any planned social change, the state of cultural readiness must be assessed.*

Here I have in mind relations between the organization and the wider society within which the target system is embedded. It would appear that Berger failed to comprehend completely the normative structure he was attempting to alter. The values of President Linz, known well in advance of the training failure, reflected those of the Swiss community he served.

Cultural readiness, then, depends to some degree on the normative structure of the wider society; a clear diagnosis cannot be made without understanding those forces.

The preceding eight principles provide only a partial view of the complex elements that enter into social change. This complexity, along with the drama of the failures, probably tends to make social change seem more hazardous than it need be. If I have tended to highlight the dilemmas and risks, I do this with the hope that recognition of these factors in installing and maintaining similar change programs will enhance their effectiveness.

8

A Failure of Job Enrichment: The Case of the Change that Wasn't

LINDA L. FRANK
J. RICHARD HACKMAN

Advocates of job enrichment as a strategy for organizational change have been living through a time of excitement. As originally formulated in the pioneering work of Herzberg and his associates (e.g., Herzberg, 1966, 1968; Herzberg, Mausner, and Snyderman, 1959) job enrichment was seen primarily as a device for increasing the motivation, productivity, and satisfaction of people at work. Now, as reports of its success are multiplying, job enrichment is being acclaimed by some as a cure for problems ranging from inflation to drug abuse.

Others are finding reasons for skepticism about the technique (e.g.,

---

Reproduced and adapted from *The Journal of Applied Behavioral Science,* "A Failure of Job Enrichment: The Case of the Change that Wasn't," by L. L. Frank and J. R. Hackman. Volume 11, Number 4, pp. 413–436.

We acknowledge with great appreciation the help of the consultant who made this research possible and the cooperation of members of the organization in which it was conducted. Clayton Alderfer and Daniel Feldman commented helpfully on an earlier draft of this chapter. The research reported here was supported by the Office of Naval Research (Organizational Effectiveness Research Program, Contract No. 00014-67A-0097-0026, NR 170-744) and by the U. S. Department of Labor (Manpower Administration Grant No. 21-09-74-14).

Hulin and Blood, 1968; Gomberg, 1973). Reports of "job enrichment failures," although almost never published in management or scientific journals, are now beginning to circulate among operating managers and organization development professionals (Hackman, 1975). We believe it is unfortunate that systematic accounts and analyses of such failures are not more widely available—for at least two reasons.

First, and most important, it is through failure that we often learn the most about the strengths and weaknesses of behavioral science techniques and discover previously unknown factors that must be accounted for in their implementation. Second, many managers and practitioners who are seeking ways to solve organizational problems are never alerted to the pitfalls associated with the change strategy they choose. As a consequence they proceed to implement the strategy as if they were the first ever to use it, unwarned by the unreported failures of others and unarmed against the problems in implementation they are sure to face.

The numerous reported successes of job enrichment as a change technique (cf. Davis and Taylor, 1972; Ford, 1969; Maher, 1971) make a convincing case that work redesign can, in the right circumstances, significantly improve both the satisfaction of individual employees and the productive effectiveness of organizational units. The problem is to determine what the "right circumstances" are and how to bring them about.

By documenting and analyzing the reasons for a seemingly clear *failure* of job enrichment we attempt here to show how the success of work redesign interventions can be critically affected both by the nature of the changes themselves and by the characteristics of the larger sociotechnical system in which the changes are installed.

THE SETTING

The Stock Transfer Department

The work redesign project was carried out in the stock transfer department of a large metropolitan bank. This department is responsible for two distinct operations in changing the ownership of securities. The first is the legal and mechanical transfer from one owner to another; second, the change of ownership is officially recorded on the books of the corporation involved.

To remain competitive with stock transfer operations in other banks the entire transfer process must be completed within 48 hours. Department employees perform 16 different functions, many of which are directly involved with the operation of a data processing system. The computer system prints new stock certificates, files changes in ownership, and maintains various records. At the time of our study about 300 employees worked in the stock transfer department.

The change project involved employees who worked on the six most central jobs:

1. Preparation clerk. Sorts and tickets incoming securities.
2. Processor. Checks certificates to ensure that they have the proper signature guarantees, transfer taxes, assignments from brokers, and so on.
3. Operator. Types the names and addresses of stock transferees on a console for processing by the computer.
4. Legal clerk. Deals with all questions relating to the law; for example, death inheritance taxes, verification of testamentary letters, affidavit domiciles, and corporate resolutions.
5. Correction clerk. Corrects errors made by operators and processors, answers outside inquiries from customers, and checks incorrectly delivered stock, confirmations, and billings.
6. Typist. Types and mails all correspondence, such as notifications to clients of corrections that have been made.

Eighty-five percent of the employees working on the focal jobs were female. Their average age was 33 and most had attained a high school degree.

Each employee in the department reported to a "work coordinator" (first-line supervisor) who was responsible for 8 to 12 employees who performed the same work function. The work coordinators reported to one of four second-line managers. These four managers, headed by a vice-president in charge of operations, formed the "management team" of the stock transfer department. The vice-president reported to the executive vice-president in charge of the entire corporate trust division of the bank.

Line managers in the stock transfer department were advised on personnel issues (including matters of employee morale, training programs, and work design) by two members of the bank personnel staff. At times personnel staff members were assisted in conceiving and carrying out change projects by outside consultants contracted for by the corporate personnel department.

THE CHANGE PROJECT

Impetus and Design

The idea for the job enrichment project originated with the corporate personnel department of the bank. For a number of months its staff had been watching for an appropriate site for a job-enrichment project. The executive vice-president for corporate trust also had expressed a long-standing interest in job enrichment and other behavioral science interventions. When signs of employee dissatisfaction and work inefficiency (e.g., excessive overtime) were detected in the stock transfer department, the executive vice-president contracted with the corporate personnel officer to explore the possibility of undertaking a work redesign project.

An external consultant, who had been meeting periodically with the personnel officer, was invited to meet the management and staff members of the stock transfer department, and a series of workshops was held for department managers about job enrichment and its implementation. After about three months a concrete design for a job-enrichment project was formulated.

The basic plan was to create 10 to 13 "modules," each of which would be a "miniature stock transfer department" in its own right. Each module would have its own work coordinator (supervisor) and would function as a semiautonomous work group (Gulowsen, 1972; Herbst, 1962; Rice, 1958). The modules would be given complete responsibility for a specific group of corporations whose stock was handled by the bank—in contrast to the previous arrangement in which workers arbitrarily handled whatever work happened to be channeled their way by a supervisor.

Each module was to include one preparation clerk, two processors, six operators, one legal clerk, one correction clerk, and one typist. Each was to learn and eventually perform all the functions of the module, thereby increasing the skills of the individual employees, the variety of their work, and the flexibility of the module as a whole. In addition, some of the specific jobs in the module were to include "enriching" tasks.

It was hoped that the assignment of a specific set of corporations to each module would increase the workers' identification with and commitment to their work. These feelings of identification were to be strengthened by allowing workers in the module to leave work together when the security transactions from "their" companies had been handled (rather than with other employees who performed the same work function as before).

Furthermore, members of each module were to be provided with increased knowledge of the results of their work by three new feedback mechanisms that were to be built into the modules: (a) the presence of a corrections clerk in the module on a continuing basis, to show members immediately when they had made a mistake and to help them correct it; (b) the pairing of experienced operators with those less experienced to allow the former to verify the latter's work; and (c) programming of the data processing system to provide individualized reports of performance to module members on a weekly basis.

The module was to be managed by the work coordinator who would be broadly trained so that she could advise and supervise competently all the workers in the module—in effect, manage her own small stock transfer department.

It was expected that the modular operation would produce a general increase in the overall quality of the working experience and the work satisfaction of stock transfer workers. It was also hoped that a reduction in work flow delays (because of the increased flexibility of the module) and an increase in the quality of service provided (because of the additional feedback provided to module members and because of increased employee commitment to the work) would become apparent.

Implementation

Modules were scheduled to be introduced one at a time, with a six-week interval between the start of each. Because the first module was set to begin before employees in that module could be cross trained, it was decided to train them (and their work coordinator) after the system had been introduced and things had settled down. The remaining workers (i.e., those not scheduled to be in the first module) would be cross trained before entering their modules. The three new feedback channels (i.e., direct input from correction clerks, pairing of operators for work verification, and computerized feedback of performance) were scheduled to be installed immediately after Module One was begun.

Corporations were to be assigned to each module so that the number of securities to be processed would approximate the quantity done by a similar number of employees before the change. The appropriate quantity could not be computed with certainty; it therefore was deliberately decided to underload Module One at the outset and gradually increase the workload as the work capacity of the module became clear through experience.

One member of the management team was assigned the major responsibility of supervising the modules, both as they were introduced and after they were functioning. He was relieved of many of his previous duties so that he would have ample time to manage the change process.

THE EVALUATION

Design and Implementation

About five weeks after the first module had been introduced, and just before the start of the second module, we were invited by the external consultant to undertake an outside evaluation of the change project to document its effects. It was agreed that we would have no involvement in its change aspects and that we would not provide feedback on findings until all changes were completed or the project was terminated.

A research design was devised that called for data to be collected just after each module had been installed, at which times data would be obtained not only from the members of the newly formed module but also from employees working in previously created modules (to assess the long term effects of the change) and from others who had not yet become part of a module (to assess any possible effects of shared history on the work group as a whole). Table 8.1 displays the chronological flow of the change process and the data collection.

Several types of quantitative data were collected as part of the evaluation: descriptions of the characteristics of the jobs and the reactions to these jobs by the employees were gathered with a standardized questionnaire; measures of employee performance, effectiveness, and absenteeism were drawn from company records and supervisory ratings; and observations and interviews with employees and managers were conducted to monitor the overall change process and its effects.

Job Characteristics. Measures of the characteristics of jobs involved in the change to work modules were obtained from employees using the Job Diagnostic Survey (JDS), which is described in detail elsewhere (Hackman and Oldham, 1975). The instrument provides scores for the

Table 8.1. Chronology of the Case

Module 1	→ Job enrichment activities	→ M_1*		→ M_2	→
Module 2		→ M_1	→ Job enrichment activities	→ M_2	→
Control		→ M_1		→ M_2	→
Time		→ October	→ Nov.-Dec.-Jan.	→ March	→

*M_{1+2} = measurement (job characteristics, attitudes, performance, interviews, and observations).

following five "core" job characteristics, each of which is viewed as contributing to the capacity of a job to motivate the person who performs it.

1. *Skill variety*. The variety of activities required in carrying out the work and the extent to which different skills and talents are used.
2. *Task identity*. The completion of a job from beginning to end with a visible outcome, that is, a "whole" and identifiable piece of work.
3. *Task significance*. The impact of the job on the lives or work of other people, either inside or outside the organization.
4. *Autonomy*. The freedom, independence, and discretion the employee has in scheduling the work and determining the procedures to be used in carrying it out.
5. *Feedback from the job*. The amount of information about the effectiveness of performance an employee obtains from doing the activities required by the job.

An overall Motivating Potential Score (MPS) can be computed from the scores of a given job on the above five dimensions. The MPS is a summary indicator of the overall "richness" of the job. (The computation of this score is discussed in Hackman and Oldham, 1975). In addition, the JDS provides scores on two other job characteristics: (a) the degree to which the job requires significant involvement with others in carrying out the work (dealing with others) and (b) the degree to which employees receive feedback about their performances from supervisors or coworkers (feedback from agents).

Satisfaction and Motivation. Measures of a number of other employee reactions were also obtained from the JDS.

1. *General satisfaction*. An overall indicator of employee satisfaction with work.
2. *Specific satisfaction*. A number of subscales that tap satisfaction with "hygiene" factors, pay and benefits, coworkers and clients, supervision, and the chance for personal growth and development on the job.
3. *Internal work motivation*. The degree to which the employee is *self*-motivated to perform effectively on the job.

Performance and Attendance. The questionnaire data were supplemented by two measures of actual behavior at work:

1. Work performance effectiveness. Supervisors rated each individual in the study on (a) the amount of effort exerted on the job, (b) the quality of the work, and (c) work quantity.
2. *Absenteeism*. Absence data were collected from company records (the number of unexcused days absent from work during the preceding year).

Interviews and Observations. Interviews were conducted with employees and members of management throughout the period of evaluation, and employees were observed extensively as they worked on their jobs (both before and after the changes) to develop an understanding of the reasons why observed changes in the modules were taking place and how people were reacting to them. Minutes of all meetings of the departmental management team for the evaluation period were also obtained.

Findings

Analysis of these data across the entire scope of the evaluation project confirmed the expected relationship between job characteristics and employee attitudes and behavior: jobs rated high on the five "core" dimensions were associated with high employee satisfaction, motivation, performance, and work attendance (for a more detailed discussion of these data see Frank and Hackman, 1975). These findings suggest that the job characteristics measured in the research are good indicators of the degree to which a job motivates and satisfies employees and leads them to perform effectively and come to work regularly. Therefore the job characteristics appeared to us to be appropriate for use as indicators of the "success" of the change over to work modules in the stock transfer department.

It will be recalled that five separate sets of questionnaire data on job charactertistics and attitudes were obtained: (1) employees in Module One, after the change (October); (2) employees in Module Two before the change (October); (3) employees in Module One, long-term follow-up (March); (4) employees in Module Two, after the change (March); and (5) employees who were still working under the old system, that is, whose jobs had not been changed at all (March).

Means for each of the five sets of data are presented in Table 8.2; three sets of planned comparisons were computed for each of the dependent measures listed. A liberal significance level (.10) was established for these comparisons to increase the chances of revealing any

Table 8.2. Dependent Variable Means for Each Experimental Group

	Means				
	October 1973		March 1974		
Measures	Module One (postchange)	Module Two (prechange)	Module One (long-term follow-up)	Module Two (postchange)	Employees Not Yet in a Module
Job Characteristics					
Skill variety	3.17	3.52	2.92	2.82	4.26
Task identity	3.79	4.29	3.32	2.88	3.92
Task significance	5.92	5.44	4.92	5.23	4.60
Autonomy	3.76	3.02	3.29	2.86	3.92
Feedback from the job	4.28	4.10	3.97	4.09	5.02
Feedback from agents	3.50	4.04	4.53	3.36	3.41
Dealing with others	4.43	4.57	4.50	4.40	5.58
Motivating Potential Score (MPS)	81.3	59.0	62.4	55.9	89.9
Affective Reactions					
General satisfaction	4.91	4.33	4.33	4.27	4.75
Internal work motivation	5.48	4.69	5.31	4.75	5.00
Specific satisfaction:					
working conditions	4.55	5.00	4.58	4.82	3.62
pay and benefits	2.36	2.89	3.50	2.45	2.50
coworkers and clients	4.70	4.93	4.69	5.15	4.96
supervision	5.55	5.26	5.36	4.58	4.88
opportunities for growth	4.57	3.86	3.90	3.66	3.84
N	11	9	12	11	8

Note. All measures are on 7-point scales; 1 is low and 7 is high.

trends in the data. The comparison, and results obtained, are the following:

1. Comparison of Module One employees after the change with Module Two employees before the change (both sets of data collected in October). No significant effects were obtained for any of the measures.

2. Comparison of Module Two employees before the change (October) with the same employees after the change (March). Only one comparison was statistically significant: Module Two employees experienced *less* task identity after the change to work modules than they had before.

3. Comparison of employees who were still working under the old system with Module One and Two employees (averaged). These data, collected in March, provided the most general test of employees in modules versus those who were not. Comparisons were statistically significant for three of the measures of job characteristics (skill variety, feedback from the job, and dealing with others). In each case the employees in modules scored *lower* than employees working under the former work system.

In sum, these results suggest that the change to work modules had almost no impact on the characteristics of the jobs on which stock transfer employees worked. Indeed, the few statistically significant results obtained were in the "wrong" direction, that is, jobs tended to get worse rather than better after the change to work modules. The means in Table 8.2 suggest a similar pattern for employee *reactions;* Module Two employees are lower on almost all measures in March, after the change, than they were before it. Moreover, the table shows that Module One employees tend to score lower on the dependent measures in March (seven months after the change) than they did in October (one month after the change), even though the October scores themselves were relatively low in comparison to those of employees who at that time were working under the old system.

WHAT HAPPENED

It is tempting to conclude from the findings reported above that job enrichment did not work in the stock transfer department. Indeed, exactly that conclusion was reached at the end of the project by several managers who had been involved in it. Such a conclusion is misleading, however, because the data show that the *jobs themselves* actually changed very little. To ask about the effects of enriched jobs in such circumstances is to ask an empty question. Instead, the critical issues in this project have to do with the reasons *why* the jobs were not substantially changed and why those organizational changes that were carried out had no positive impact on employee attitudes or work behavior.

The Process of Implementation

As already mentioned, Module One was implemented for the most part as planned. Operators were given additional tasks such as classifying and checking the types of stock they were working with and verifying the work of others. Legal and correction clerks were separated from colleagues who performed like functions and joined the module. Neither the computer-based feedback system nor cross training of employees, however, was installed when the module was begun. As the time to implement Module Two approached these innovations still had not been introduced; nevertheless, it was decided to proceed with Module Two on schedule.

The workload originally assigned to Module One turned out to be less than the capacity of module members. Therefore management assigned Module Two twice the amount of work that had been given to the first module to test the upper limit of module capacity. It was expected that after a few weeks of experience with Module Two the workload in both modules could be adjusted to a near-optimal level.

Shortly after the start of the second module the data processing system began to malfunction with a frequency that was clearly debilitating to the entire department. A new set of programs for handling stock transfers had recently been installed, and "bugs" in the system were both more frequent and more disruptive to the operation of the department than had been anticipated. As a result, operators often had to remain idle for several hours during the day and were then required to work overtime to compensate for the lost time. The computer difficulties continued, and by the third month of operation of Module Two employees were putting in eight times as many overtime hours as they had the month Module One was instituted. Moreover, the manager who was primarily responsible for overseeing the installation and operation of the modules found it necessary to spend a substantial portion of his own time trying to get the computer system to work. Soon members of the management team were embroiled in philosophical and logistical conflicts about department priorities.

The situation was further aggravated by the onset of the Christmas season, with its accompanying work holidays and increased workload. During the most difficult periods many part-time employees were brought in to help get the work done. Although this remedy provided needed manpower, it also tended to undermine the integrity of the modules as self-contained units.

Shortly after the holiday season the executive vice-president, who had been instrumental in the initiation and follow-through of the project, left the bank for a several-month executive development program at a distant university. His temporary replacement was skeptical about the basic philosophy of job enrichment and preferred an alternative behavioral science approach to organizational change. At about the same time the contract of the external consultant expired, although he continued to visit the bank to discuss the project with members of the management team.

After the departure of the vice-president the management team decided to delay the start of any additional modules until the problems with the first two were straightened out. Legal and correction clerks were returned to their original work groups where they could be supported by other people doing similar work. Neither cross training nor the computer-based feedback system had been installed and no initiatives were visible toward getting these activities underway. As we left the bank it was officially unclear whether the first two modules would be reconstituted or whether additional modules would eventually be created, but the informal word was "pessimistic" about such prospects.

Impact of the Change Process on the Jobs

The installation of the modules should have "boosted" the job ratings on at least four of the five job dimensions that contribute to the Motivating Potential Score. Given that such improvements did *not* occur, what went wrong?

Skill Variety. This aspect of the work should have been substantially affected by the cross training scheduled to take place among module members, but because crosstraining never took place, workers in modules wound up utilizing about the same range and level of skill in their work as before. Although operators were given additional tasks, the impact of these new duties on the job as a whole (and on their reactions to their work) was not great. Operators reported in interviews that their jobs had "felt different" shortly after the change to modules but that it seemed to be mostly "the same old thing, just more work" after the new tasks had been learned.

Task Identity. Because each module was to be assigned certain corporations for processing on a permanent basis, it was expected that module members would come to experience the entirety of the stock transfer task for those corporations as collectively "theirs." Thus, even though no individual module member would be performing the whole job at any given time, task identity at the *group* level would be expected to increase.

In fact, the data show a slight *decrease* in task identity as a result of the change, apparently because the boundaries of the modules were too open and too weak; for example, the following applied:

- When an overload of work for the corporations was assigned to a module (a frequent occurrence for Module Two), some of that work would be distributed by management to other employees on the floor.
- Conversely, if workers in a module finished their own tasks, they often were required to assist others outside the module who had unfinished work.
- Temporary workers were often rotated through the modules.
- Module workers typically left work with others in their functional specialty rather than with other members of the module.
- Work coordinators were not fully trained in all functional specialties in the modules; therefore employees frequently found it necessary to return to their original sections when they needed assistance on a work-related problem.

For all these reasons employees continued to regard themselves more as functional specialists than as members of an interdependent group with a whole and identifiable group task. In this retrospective context the failure to find an increase in task identity as a result of the change is not at all surprising.

Task Significance. Because the stock transfer jobs were high in task significance to begin with, there was no attempt on the part of management to increase the workers' experience in this respect as part of the plan for the work modules. It is not surprising, therefore, that there were no substantial changes in the task significance of jobs as a result of the creation of the modules.

Autonomy. It was planned that employees would experience more control in the modules than they had before because each module would be an autonomous "miniature stock transfer department" that made its *own* decisions about how and when to carry out its tasks. No structural alterations were provided, however, to require or encourage module members to take real responsibility for the corporations that had been assigned to them. Moreover, management continued to give some individuals specific work assignments and to intervene whenever there was a work crisis. In effect, management retained the "real" responsibility for getting the work out and employees wound up feeling about the way they had before joining the modules—namely, that they had little "say" or autonomy in planning and carrying out their work.

Feedback from the Job. The original plan for the modules specified that feedback would be increased by means of several different mechanisms (i.e., operator-verifier pairings, computer-based feedback, and increased interaction between correction clerks and other module members). Because of unanticipated pressures on management, the changes that would have been necessary to get such feedback mechanisms operative and functioning as intended were never made. The net effect was no increase in the feedback module members received about their individual or unit effectiveness.

Summary

The original plans for the modules included a number of changes in work structure and procedures which, if carried out, should have substantially increased the standing of module jobs on the core job dimensions. For a variety of reasons most of these plans were either not initiated or initiated and not carried through. In effect, the work redesign project was an intervention that affected many aspects of the organizational unit but *not the work* itself.

LEARNINGS FROM THE FAILURE

In this concluding section we attempt to summarize some general learnings that emerged from the stock transfer experiment. They are presented as four prescriptive guides for implementing job enrichment (as well as for other organizational change activities that involve redesigning work).*

* For other discussions of the conditions required for successful implementation of job enrichment see Beer (1975), Glaser (1974), Hackman (1975) and Sirota and Wolfson (1972a, 1972b).

Guide 1. Work redesign projects should be based on theory and such theory should be congruent with the kinds of change contemplated.

Most work redesign projects, if grounded in theory at all, tend to be based on the motivator-hygiene theory of Herzberg (1966) or, less frequently, on some version of sociotechnical systems theory (e.g., Emery, 1959). The reason is simply that until recently these two paradigms have been about the only ones available for guiding work redesign activities. Now, however, a number of alternative conceptual approaches to work redesign have begun to appear, some of which specify explicit "principles" for improving jobs (see Glaser, 1974, for a partial review). As a result the knowledgeable practitioner currently has considerable choice about the conceptual approach he will take in planning a work redesign project.

Although some theories may be objectively "better" than others, our observations suggest that the specific details of various theories may not be so important as the fact that *some* theory is used to guide the implementation of change and to keep change activities focused on the intended objectives. Moreover, a good theory can help to identify and specify the kinds of data needed in planning and evaluating the changes and can alert implementers to special problems and opportunities that may develop as the project unfolds.

The theory must, however, be *appropriate* to the kinds of change contemplated. Therein lies one of the major difficulties of the present change effort. Although the stock transfer project was originally developed on the basis of one theoretical approach (the Herzberg motivator-hygiene theory), that theory focuses exclusively on the enrichment of *individual* jobs. The stock transfer project, of course, had to do primarily with the creation of enriched *group* tasks (i.e., the work of semiautonomous modules), although it was anticipated that individual jobs in the modules would be substantially enriched as well.

At least two major difficulties developed because the theory used did not address the particular problems of designing work for interacting groups. First, because those responsible for implementation found the theory of limited use as a guide for planning and installing the changes, it gradually dropped from their attention, and without the benefit of theory-specified guidelines for change the project became increasingly diffuse in focus. It eventually emphasized matters that had little or nothing to do with the work itself.

Second, because there were no conceptual guidelines to point out the importance of group-level phenomena to the success of the project, many critical interpersonal issues were never recognized or seriously considered; for example, the plan for module members to cross train one another required significant interaction between older and younger employees for the first time and also that some individuals share their own "special" expertise with individuals they perceived as having little to offer in return. Because such interpersonal issues were not addressed, the degree to which some of the planned changes could actually be implemented was impaired and the impact of other changes (that were "officially" introduced) was seriously compromised.

It should be noted that the evaluation reported here was to some extent compromised on the same grounds. All structured data collection devices used in the evaluation were oriented toward *individual* attitudes and behavior. The importance of group-level phenomena in this project was forced to our attention as we conducted supplemental interviews and observations after the project was underway. Our data on group-level issues are therefore much less robust than they would have been if we had initially adopted a theoretical position that acknowledged the essentially interpersonal character of the change project.

Guide 2. An explicit diagnosis of the target jobs and the surrounding social and technical systems should be carried out before the changes are initiated.

The results of the stock transfer experiment suggest that at minimum the following questions might usefully be asked in prechange diagnoses. Can the jobs under consideration be meaningfully changed? More simply, can job enrichment make enough of a difference in the jobs to have a measurable impact on the people who do them? If the jobs are open to meaningful change, what specific aspects of the work are particularly problematic at present? Some jobs in the stock transfer department (e.g., legal clerks) were probably about as "good" as they could be at the start of the job-enrichment project; the change to create work modules, if it had been effective, probably would have stripped some of the richness from the present work of some of these individuals. Other jobs had enormous room for improvement, but the specific changes planned for them were developed more from managerial intuition than from a systematic diagnosis of the actual tasks.

Are the employees reasonably ready for change and capable of handling their new duties afterward? Are they generally satisfied with bread-and-butter issues of pay, supervision, and job security or would an attempt to improve jobs run into resistance because of high existing dissatisfaction with these issues? Unless employees' basic needs are satisfied, job enrichment, even if well designed, may not work. In the project reported here these matters had little chance of compromising the reactions of employees to their new jobs because the work itself did not change substantially. It is worth noting, however, that a preliminary assessment of employee attitudes, skills, and satisfactions carried out as an input to planning for the change might have altered the content of the changes that were attempted and increased the chances that they would "take."

Is management itself ready to handle the extra burdens and challenges that will be created by the changes? In the present case external problems encountered in attempting to institute the job changes appeared to raise significant conflicts and difficulties among members of the management team charged with implementation, problems that apparently had been just below the surface before the project was begun. Retrospective analysis suggests that if a diagnosis of the internal dynamics of the management team had been carried out before the project some of the intrateam issues could have been dealt with in a way that would have increased the team's readiness to face the significant external challenges it subsequently had to meet.

What is the nature and extent of the commitment of top management to the change project? As noted earlier in the stock transfer experiment only a single vice-president was strongly committed to it. When he left, albeit temporarily, support for the project at higher levels vanished and the very survival of the project was jeopardized. If prechange assessment of the commitment of upper management to the project had been made, educational activities might have been undertaken to develop a stronger and broader base of informed support for the experiment.

What other aspects of the surrounding work system are likely to be affected by the change (including both clients and holders of adjacent jobs)? Are these groups ready and able to handle the different demands that the change might bring or is developmental work required with them before (or as part of) the change project? Will the change require problematic alteration of equipment or technical procedures? In the present case some planned changes in the focal jobs were found to be impractical because they created "interface problems" with surrounding units (especially the computer system). An unfortunate side effect was that managerial energy was constantly being diverted from crisis to crisis; little of it remained for the crucial developmental work required to get the job-enrichment project off the ground and functioning.

Diagnoses that address such questions are not easy to make. They involve the raising of anxieties at a time when most participants in the project are instead seeking comfort and assurance that everything will turn out all right. Moreover, the tools and methodologies required for undertaking such diagnoses are only now becoming available (e.g., Hackman and Oldham, 1975; Jenkins, Nadler, Lawler, and Cammann, 1975; Sirota and Wolfson, 1972b). Our observations of the stock transfer experiment suggest that the diagnostic task itself may be one of the most crucial of all in a job-enrichment project.

Guide 3. Contingency plans should be prepared beforehand to deal with the inevitable "spin-off" problems and opportunities that emerge from work redesign activities.

By making explicit contingency plans for dealing with possible problems at least two advantages accrue. First, all employees, managers, and consultants will be well aware (and share the awareness) that certain types of problem (e.g., tension in superior-subordinate relationships, technical problems, and coordination difficulties at the interfaces of work systems) are likely to emerge as the change project develops. This simple understanding may help to keep surprise and dismay at manageable levels when the problems do, in fact, appear and thereby decrease the opportunity for people to conclude prematurely that "it failed."

Second, preplanning for possible problems can lead to an objective increase in the readiness of all parties to deal with those problems that do emerge. It is true that what can go wrong in an organizational change project often does, usually at the worst possible moment. Therefore having a few contingency plans filed away can lessen the chances that unexpected problems will get out of hand before they can be dealt with adequately—before draining needed energy from the change project itself in the process.

Clearly, the success of the stock transfer project was negatively affected by the lack of contingency plans for dealing with predictable problems. As noted earlier, insufficient diagnostic work was carried out to identify possible problem areas, which made contingency planning nearly impossible in any case. Little preparation was made beforehand even to deal with those that were anticipated; for example, it was known before the start of the changes that systematic cross training of employees in the modules would be needed so that they could switch from task to task and complete the work of the module efficiently as a whole. Yet even as they began to work in the modularized work system no training procedures had been developed. Similarly, although it was anticipated that there would be difficulty in identifying the appropriate workload for the modules, no workload measurement system for modularized work was ever developed.

Not all contingency plans can be worked out in detail beforehand. Indeed, they probably should not be, for until a project is underway it cannot be known for sure what the specific nature of the most pressing need and problems will be. One can, however, be *ready* to deal with common problems that may appear; for example, the training department can be informed that some training may be required if managers find it difficult to supervise employees after the work is redesigned; those responsible for the reward system can be asked to engage in some contingency planning on the chance that the new work system may require nontraditional compensation arrangements. To recapitulate, one does not *begin* with these matters, but one is well advised to anticipate some of them and to prepare to deal with them when and if they appear.

Guide 4. Those responsible for work redesign projects should anticipate setbacks and be prepared for continuous evaluation and revision of action plans.

Given the inevitability of problems and crises in work redesign projects, it is often tempting for employees, managers, and consultants to use a problem that seems especially serious as the basis for abandoning the project as a "failure." An often effective antidote to these tendencies is the adoption of a view of the project by the central figures that legitimizes *learning* as an important outcome. Such a stance permits interim disappointments to be used as an occasion for reconsideration and revision of the content and approach rather than as a time for disillusionment and abandonment. This may be especially important in projects involving work redesign because there is still no neat "package" available for installing job enrichment (and, indeed, there may never be one). As a consequence it seems essential that implementers will have to learn as they go how to design, implement, and manage enriched jobs most effectively in their own organizations.

To take a "learning" orientation to work redesign projects effectively however, requires that trustworthy data be collected and used to monitor and evaluate the project throughout its life. Without data that can be trusted, it is difficult for those responsible for the project to test and revise their own perceptions of how things are going.

In the stock transfer project, for example, we agreed to keep the research and evaluation data we were collecting confidential. As a consequence *those who were deciding "what to do next" did not know that the work itself had not been significantly changed,* even though we had data in hand relatively early in the project which suggested that alterations in the jobs had not been substantial. Similarly, our data provided early warnings of other problems that subsequently contributed to the failure of the project. In the end we found that in the interest of "clean" research we had kept from the responsible individuals precisely those data that they most needed to steer the project back on course.

This is not meant to suggest that "clean" research is of little value. If we had provided interim feedback to the change agents in the present case, the possibilities of obtaining a robust understanding of the dynamics and effects of the planned change would have been reduced. Indeed, provision of such feedback would have been an intervention, deserving of evaluation in its own right, but that would have been a different change strategy and would have required a different type of evaluation.

Conducting evaluations of work redesign projects is a costly and often stressful undertaking. In our view such costs must be accepted because they can lead to long-term gains in knowledge and expertise for the employees, managers, and change agents involved, because they can foster learnings useful to other people in other organizations as they plan and implement work redesign, and, perhaps most important, because accepting the work and the plan of an ongoing evaluation may be among the ingredients most crucial to the long-term success of the change project itself.

III
DIFFUSION

"Most of us would expect that an organizational pattern that is working better than the one it replaced will be recommended by superiors and emulated by peers," writes Richard Walton. This section describes why it isn't recommended, why it isn't emulated, and why a change effort isn't diffused through an organization or, in one case, why it isn't replicated when applied in a neighboring community.

The spread of new knowledge and innovative practices has been of central concern to educators, social planners, change proponents, and inventive individuals from all walks of life. We have asked why communities won't fluoridate their waters, why couples won't utilize modern birth control methods, and why organizations won't adopt organization development techniques. Just as we are investigating the spread of water fluoridation (McNeil, 1957) and the adoption of birth control practices (Rogers, 1973), the authors in this section are studying the diffusion of organization and community development techniques.

The formal study of the diffusion of innovations began early in this century, spurred by the influence of sociologist Gabriel Tarde (1903). "Our problem is to learn why, given one hundred different innovations conceived of at the same time . . . ten will spread abroad while ninety will be forgotten" (p. 140). Rogers (1962), in his compendium on the *Diffusion of Innovations*, traces the development of this line of inquiry thereafter, through anthropology, rural sociology, medicine, education, and industry. He introduces his review with Wellin's (1955) account of "Water Boiling in a Peruvian Town"—a diffusion effort that failed. The authors in this section continue in the same tradition.

Richard Walton's essay begins this section on diffusion by "explaining why success didn't take." He reviews eight diffusion efforts in industrial organizations in the United States, Canada, Great Britain, and the European continent. He also revisits the General Food's Topeka Plant, where, several years earlier, he participated in the design of an innovative organization but today finds that it has not been adopted by other facilities in the firm.

Walton's essay begins with a general model of work diffusion or, more precisely, "lack of diffusion," in the examples he reviews. He describes the problems of strategies and models of change, the absence of top management commitment to further innovation, the loss of key people critical to the spread of change, and, finally, the confusion surrounding exactly "what is to be diffused." He also considers the role of unions in the spread of change and the bureaucratic barriers that have risen to seal its fate. Walton concludes with a discussion of the factors that might increase the number and pace of successful diffusions; he adds: "But how many diffusions and how fast the pace, I can't even begin to guess."

Jay Nisberg's case is an insider's look at the spread of organization development through a division of an automotive manufacturer in which top management communicated "an interest in organization development at all levels" but line managers learned that all they had to do was "fake" it. Thus he urges practitioners: "Do not let a large financial investment convince you that there is an equally consistent and sincere commitment by management. . . ."

As an internal consultant for a time, Nisberg describes the rivalry between change agents in competing OD groups, each trying to "win" clients with "promises," "politics," and "pie-in-the-sky." He discusses the effects of this competition on the inconsistent diffusion of OD practices and techniques. His lessons, reported throughout the case, offer some seasoned prescriptions for large organizations and for the internal OD practitioners in them.

Roy Lewicki's case, which concludes this section, describes a change effort designed to "improve the working relations among small businessmen in two New England communities." Lewicki and his colleagues were interested in studying the application of team-building techniques in a community organization and in stimulating economic growth in a community development program. The case describes the success of their efforts in one community in which a group of businessmen, guided by an effective community leader, took some "collective action" toward solving some of their town's immediate problems. When Lewicki and his colleagues tried to replicate their success in another community, however, a series of unexpected troubles spoiled the change effort.

Lewicki analyzes the differences between the successful and unsuccessful change effort, contrasting the characteristics of the communities, the development efforts, and the effectiveness of the change agents in each case. He concludes with a candid and self-effacing look at the errors in the change and offers counsel for others contemplating future ventures among community groups.

Both the cases and the essay in this section provide insight into the diffusion of organization development and change techniques. The authors encourage researchers and practitioners alike to take a longer look at their change efforts and to consider not only the immediate success but its long-term durability. They encourage organizations to coordinate the delivery of OD services, not only planning change efforts but their continued evolution. Too often, they suggest, we have neglected to "follow up" our change efforts. Their articles detail the consequences and suggest some alternative directions.

9

The Diffusion of New Work Structures: Explaining Why Success Didn't Take

RICHARD E. WALTON

When organizations engage in experimental projects in work restructuring, an underlying assumption is that if the innovation is effective it will be adopted by other units in the organization. Most of us would expect that an organizational pattern that is working better than the one it replaced will be recommended by superiors and emulated by peers. Experience, however, shows this not to be necessarily true: the assumed tendencies are sometimes nullified and offset by competing organizational dynamics.

I have studied a sample of organizations that made early efforts at the comprehensive redesign of work, asking how much diffusion has occurred, particularly within the same firm? What are the vehicles for diffusion? What barriers are encountered? How does the character of the innovation affect the rate of its diffusion? Answers to these questions can help us formulate better diffusion strategies and tactics.

Adapted from "The Diffusion of New Work Structures: Explaining Why Success Didn't Take." *Organizational Dynamics,* Winter 1975, 3–21.

I wish to acknowledge the helpful comments of Chris Argyris on an earlier draft of this paper and the support for this research provided by the Ford Foundation and the Division of Research, Harvard Graduate School of Business Administration.

EIGHT EXPERIMENTS

The eight firms in the study had the following mutual characteristics: all started their research on work redesign in the 1960s, their early experiments involved relatively comprehensive work restructuring, these experiments were judged initially successful; these firms had a number of physically separate facilities, usually geographically dispersed, the change efforts of all received substantial publicity.

Of the eight firms, two are in the United States, two in Canada, one in Great Britain, two in Norway, and one in Sweden. The firms in the United States are Corning Glass, which initiated a study at its Medfield, Mass., assembly plant in 1965, and the General Foods Corporation, which initiated an experiment at its pet food plant in Topeka, Kansas, in January 1971, although it had begun planning for change in 1968. The Canadian organizations are the Sales and Fabrication Division of Alcan and the Advanced Devices Center, a division of Northern Electric Company, subsequently renamed Microsystems International, Ltd. In 1964 a group of Alcan managers launched a project in one plant of the works at Kingston, Ontario; over time the innovations developed in the first effort at Kingston were extended to other existing Sales and Fabrication Division plants and eventually to a new cold rolling mill. The Northern Electric unit designed a radically different organization for a new semiconductor facility occupied in January 1966.

The European companies form the remainder of the sample. Shell U.K. introduced change in several locations in the mid-1960s, including a new refinery at Teesport, which came on stream in 1968. Several Norwegian projects were carried out in different industries in the Industrial Democracy Project, an action research program sponsored jointly by the Norwegian Federation of Employers and the Trades Union Council of Norway and guided by social scientists associated with Oslo's Work Research Institute. The two projects included in this study were the fertilizer plants at Norsk Hydro in Porsgrunn and a department in the Hunsfos pulp and paper complex near Kristiansand, both initiated in the mid-1960s.

A Swedish experiment in Volvo's truck assembly plant in Lundby, begun in 1969, has been followed by similar changes in a neighboring auto assembly plant, the design of a revolutionary car plant at Kalmar that went on stream in 1974, and a commitment to an advanced form of work structuring in a new Volvo plant in the United States planned for 1975.

An important similarity existed in the change strategies employed by seven of these eight firms. An early experiment in one unit of each firm was regarded as a pilot project from which the larger organization could learn. The positive results, if any, could demonstrate the value of work restructuring. Lessons gained from the experiment could then be made available to other units. The eighth, Shell U.K., by contrast followed a change strategy in which the demonstration projects were not the point of departure.

The extent of diffusion that has occurred in these eight firms has varied widely. In four companies (Corning, Northern Electric, Hunsfos, and Norsk Hydro) it has been nonexistent or small; in three companies (General Foods, Shell U.K., and Alcan) somewhat more has occurred. However, the rate either has been slow or it has not been sustained. Only in one company in my sample, namely Volvo, was diffusion truly impressive, yet managers involved in all the changes, including those at Volvo, clearly had expected them to be more rapid and extensive.

GENERAL MODEL

Before exploring the diffusion of "work restructuring," or the lack of it, let us clarify what we mean by the term. The restructuring approach pursued in the eight cases studied embraces many aspects of work, including the content of the job, compensation schemes, scope of worker responsibility for supervision and decision making, social structure, and status hierarchy. The design of each element is intended to contribute to an internally consistent work culture, one that appropriately enlarges workers' scope for self-management, enhances their opportunities for acquiring new abilities, strengthens their sense of connectedness with coworkers, increases their identification with the product and manufacturing process, and promotes their sense of dignity and self-worth. The word "appropriately" is used in the preceding sentence to signify that the entent to which work structures can realistically depart from today's conventional work organization depends on many situational factors, especially the type of technology, composition of the work force (is it educated and skilled?), and economic forces (do they favor the expenditures of time and money involved in a comprehensive attempt at job restructuring?).

Each diffusion effort had its own unique characteristics but they all also shared many points:

Step 1. Initiation of the pilot experiment

Although perhaps similarly inspired, pilot experiments took a variety of forms. Some were in new plants, others were in established plants, and still others were initiated simultaneously in both old and new facilities.

Some experiments involved relatively radical and comprehensive work restructuring at the outset: GF's pet food plant, Norsk Hydro's fertilizer plants, Hunsfos' chemical pulp department, and Shell U.K.'s new Teesport refinery. Significantly, each of these four facilities is relatively small, employing fewer than 100 workers and involving a continuous processing technology. Also the way work was restructured in these continuous processing plants is remarkably similar. Self-managing teams were formed to take responsibility for large segments of the process. Job rotation among team members was encouraged to improve control of the technology and provide intrinsically satisfying learning experiences for workers. Support activities, such as maintenance, quality control, and cleaning were incorporated into operating team responsibilities. Because of the diverse abilities required to manage, operate, and maintain these technologies, team members received heavy doses of training. Pay was based on the relevant skills and knowledge a worker had acquired rather than on the particular job he was performing. New information and measurement systems were developed to enable teams to keep on top of their enlarged responsibilities.

Northern Electric's Advanced Devices Center, because it focused on professional and managerial personnel, featured a matrix organization, functional and business teams, elaborate communication schemes, open office layouts, and nontraditional titles and reporting relationships.

Other experiments in the new plants at Alcan and Corning and the existing facilities at Volvo and Shell U.K. involved more moderate changes. Significantly, two of them, Corning and Volvo, are assembly plants in which the nature of the tasks and technology provided relatively little opportunity for upgrading the abilities of the work teams. Thus in these plants emphasis was placed on freeing workers from the tedium of short repetitive work cycles and on steps that would improve communication. Bound by those constraints both were bold efforts at work restructuring. The changes that evolved over several years were rotation among and/or enlargement of assembly tasks, the formation of teams, and mechanisms for worker participation or consultation.

An incremental approach to work restructuring in the projects at the Alcan plants and Shell's refineries was necessary in part because of constraints related to collective bargaining.

The initial experiment in a majority of cases occurred at the urging of a middle-level line manager, typically a plant manager, or with his active participation. Staff people and outside consultants or researchers also played an active role in designing and implementing most of the early experiments. In the Norwegian projects the researchers actually sought out the companies and persuaded them to collaborate in undertaking the projects. Similarly, in the Corning experiment, a corporate consultant began by stimulating interest among supervisors to try their own mini-experiments, which, if successful, could lead to plantwide work restructuring. It is interesting to note that, although management and worker members of the Norwegian and the Corning experiments subsequently came to "own" the projects, dependency on outside experts long remained a factor and that in each case little intracompany diffusion resulted.

Step 2. Pilot experiment declared early success

This study included only those experiments that were judged successful after a year or two, when participants had gained significant experience with the new work structures and when operating results could be assessed.

Spokesmen for these projects claimed improved performance, increased worker knowledge and skills, and a generally more responsible and motivating work culture. In no case were there wholly independent performance audits or measurements that would persuade the most ardent skeptics of work restructuring. Although my own field visits led me to conclude that in most cases some discounting of claims seemed to be required, I accept the original judgments of early success.

Results claimed on both the hard and soft sides of the benefits ledger varied: only about 25 percent of the Northern Electric workers said they experienced a relatively large gain in the quality of their working life; among General Foods workers it was 80 percent. The balance, at least during the initial periods, would fall somewhere between. Six cases reported quality improvement and more efficient production due to decreased scrap, less down-time, or more efficient methods. Most companies also reported reduced turnover and absentee rates. A case in point: the petfood plant after 18 months reported an overhead rate 33 percent lower than in the old plant. The absentee rate was 9 percent below the industry norm and turnover was far below average.

Step 3. Recognition and resources provided for further work restructuring

After becoming acquainted with the results of the pilot experiment top management typically gave its blessing to the approach. In several cases it became company or division policy to diffuse work restructuring throughout the various facilities. In Hunsfos it became company policy to spread work restructuring to other departments in the mill complex. At Volvo the recognition of work restructuring became very strong. The new president took a special interest in the subject and made a dramatic commitment to the program in existing plants in the early 1970s. He personally pressed for and contributed to a revolutionary approach to the designing of a new auto assembly plant in Kalmar that involved a 10 percent higher capital investment to accommodate the desired work structure. This action gave work restructuring a high priority in other plants. Exceptions should be noted in the cases of Corning and Northern Electric, where apparently no strong encouragement of diffusion came from other than organization development groups.

In a few cases recognition eventually took the form of a management philosophy hammered out by a group of line managers with the assistance of staff consultants more familiar with work restructuring. A General Foods statement, for example, emerged shortly after other corporate measures had been taken to promote diffusion.

Another diffusion measure was the assignment of specific responsibility for promoting work restructuring; for example, at General Foods the line manager responsible for pet food operations at the divisional level was transferred to the corporate level and made an internal consultant to several dozen plants.

Step 4. More general interest in work restructuring aroused

In every case these experiments have been the subject of widely circulated written reports in the news media, oral presentations to other groups, and visits by interested parties to the experimental site. Dissemination activities often helped the project leaders to secure top-management recognition and approval, but they also had other objectives. They were intended to interest and inform managers and union officials of sister units in the same firm and those outside the firm. The visibility and favorable acclaim, of course, were gratifying to the participants who were proud of the work culture they had created and the performance results they had achieved.

Step 5. Change agents' interventions extend throughout the corporate system.

We have already noted the tendency to designate some individuals or committees to help initiate projects and monitor their development.

The change interventions led by the internal consultant at General Foods will help to illustrate this aspect of a diffusion effort, although, with the exception of Shell U.K., the activities are more elaborate than in other companies.

In late 1971 Lyman Ketchum, the newly appointed GF internal consultant, addressed a group of 150 top managers from operations, engineering, quality assurance, and personnel, as well as several corporation group vice-presidents. Forms of work restructuring and their rationale were discussed. The chairman of GF and a key vice-president sanctioned the role of the new change agent.

A steering committee comprised of the division operating managers was formed to guide the change activities. Change initiative occurred in new and recent plants because more progress could be made with less effort. The change agent began working with plant managers who manifested the most interest in change.

The change agent's work began with a three-day meeting with the plant manager and his staff who were encouraged to explore their own values and the connections between values and work structures. These initial meetings by themselves seldom produced much action. After a month or so had elapsed the change agent usually scheduled another meeting with a group drawn from the next level below the plant manager's staff. As a parallel activity the corporate change agent organized three-day seminars on the techniques of work analysis and design; these were attended largely by staff personnel such as engineers.

When a commitment to work restructuring developed, the change agent helped to form a plant steering committee made up of key line and staff managers and, when appropriate, union officials. Subordinate action committees were formed to explore and recommend specific projects within a limited area of the plant. The change agent himself and other consulting resources were made available to the plant committees to assist them in the actual work restructuring.

Step 6: Facilitative networks develop

This is a step taken in only a few of the change programs studied. An interunit network of personnel engaged in work restructuring is created to exchange ideas, to provide a supportive reference group for its members, and to build a constituency for change in corporate policies and procedures more favorable to the program. At GF networks of plant managers and their personnel managers are developing to a point at which many of their members can serve others as outside consultants.

Step 7. Personnel movement occurs

The transfer of experienced personnel from an innovative unit is a way of exporting the knowledge, values, and skills at the heart of work restructuring. The innovative unit can then educate the new managers who transfer into the unit.

A few favorable moves can be cited to illustrate the possibilities. In a strategic move at Norsk Hydro the person who had been personnel manager in the Porsgrunn area was promoted to corporate headquarters. He was intimately familiar with the fertilizer project and an articulate proponent of its underlying philosophy. He moved to a better position to advise top management on the diffusion of work restructuring. It is not surprising that the advantage of this move to headquarters was partly offset by the loss felt in the local area.

THE SHELL U. K. ALTERNATIVE

A major variation on the procedure in the other seven firms, that of starting small with a single experiment, is provided by Shell U.K. From the outset the approach was conceived as companywide, comprehensive in its effect on the work situation, and planned to last 5 to 10 years.

The first step was not a demonstration project. Work redesign was undertaken only after large amounts of organizational time had been spent in sessions developing and affirming a supportive managerial philosophy.

Attitudes, in short, were changed before structure. Tavistock social scientists worked closely with an internal staff resource group to design the activities in this and subsequent phases, beginning in 1965 with the development of a philosophy to which senior managers could commit themselves.

The second phase was intended to ensure that the operating philosophy was freely accepted by all 6000 members of the organization from senior managers to hourly workers.

The implementation phase was launched by a third top-management conference. Later it was altered and responsibility for change was placed on the department-manager level across the company, an approach made possible by the massive dissemination process. To enable department managers to initiate their own change projects short training courses were provided to teach them techniques of work analysis and principles of work restructuring.

Finally, a network of committees representing both management and unions helped to change work rules that otherwise would prevent many types of restructuring, such as flexible manning patterns and paying workers for multiple job skills.

Evaluation conferences were held in March 1967 and shortly thereafter a number of changes took place that served to arrest the diffusion process and tended to demoralize the innovative systems already introduced.

PROBLEM AREAS IN DIFFUSION

My investigation attempted to find out why diffusion was not more rapid and extensive. The reasons ranged from defects in the design of the original experiment to unanticipated consequences of the success of the initial pilot project.

Regression in the Pilot Project

Because diffusion typically occurs over a significant period of time, the sustained success of early experiments can help to build momentum for companywide change; conversely, emergent weaknesses in the pilot projects can erode initial support for change.

A clear correlation between the continued success of initial projects and the rate of diffusion is found in several extreme cases. Volvo's truck plant experiment has continued to be effective and has been followed by relatively high diffusion. The Northern Electric experiment was discontinued and also produced no significant diffusion within the company. A similar consistency is found in the demoralization of Corning's Medfield experiment after a period of effectiveness and a lack of diffusion throughout the firm.

Both Shell U.K. and Alcan experienced moderate effectiveness in their early experiments and have shown moderate amounts of diffusion, although causal connections are not indicated. Shell U.K. achieved its diffusion soon after its change program was undertaken; the initial projects subsequently became somewhat demoralized and no further diffusion has occurred. Alcan has recently diffused the ideas of the earlier experiments into a new mill, although there has been a decline in management and worker involvement in the plants in which the earlier innovations were established.

There is not always a correlation between initial success and diffusion. The strong success of GF's Topeka plant is not matched so far by a high amount of diffusion, and at Norsk Hydro and Hunsfos there is even less correlation. Continued success of initial change projects appears to be only one of the many influences on diffusion.

What can cause a successful early experiment to deteriorate later on? I have noted several factors: (a) internal inconsistencies in the original design; (b) loss of support from levels of management above the experimental unit; (c) premature turnover of leaders, operators, or consultants directly associated with a project; (d) stress and crises that lead to more authoritarian management, which in turn demoralizes the innovative unit; (e) tension in the innovative unit's relations with other parties—peer units, staff groups, superiors, and labor unions; (f) letdown in involvement of participants after initial success with its attendant publicity; (g) lack of diffusion to other parts of the organization, which isolates the original experiment and its leaders.

The last factor or principle, succinctly stated, is "diffuse or die"; it suggests that a circular relationship exists by which a lack of diffusion can *eventually* undermine the viability of the initial project, just as weaknesses that develop in the initial project can undermine the diffusion effort. The converse of this circular relationship is not strong; as I have noted above, continued success in the initial project does not necessarily lead to diffusion throughout the larger organization.

Poor Model for Change

Even if the pilot project remains viable over time, it may be an ineffective model for diffusion in the firm because it lacks either visibility or credibility. These deficiencies may reflect the behavior of leaders of the experiment or they may relate to the way policy is formulated by higher officials. Also, many characteristics inherent in the site of the initial experiment affect its ability to stimulate further change. Consider the many conditions of the GF pet food plant that enhanced the success of that project: the Topeka plant was new; it was located in a favorable labor market, required few workers, and was geographically separate from headquarters and other existing facilities of GF. Because it was a new plant with a new work force, no union agreement was required to establish the new work structure. Many of these conditions, of course, did not exist elsewhere in GF, and many managers asked, "is work restructuring possible in other situations; for example, in a large, established, unionized plant?"

The credibility of the Corning and Northern Electric projects suffered not only for similar reasons but also from an additional site characteristic: the technology involved in the experimental plant was significantly different from that employed in other plants in the system.

In terms of site characteristics, Volvo, Alcan, and Shell U.K. appear to have presented relatively good prospects for further diffusion of a successful experiment. They were initiated in large, established, unionized facilities and involved technologies typical of the larger systems of which they were a part.

The way in which the project leaders present the experiment to others in the firm will influence its visibility and credibility. One basic choice is whether to maintain a low profile or to seek a place in the corporate environment.

A low profile reduces the career risks associated with failure and less publicity also minimizes the risk of creating a "showcase" complex with long-run adverse effects on the work climate. In the cases studied, however, the incentive to publicize the experiments increased substanitially once they appeared to be successfully established. Visibility, it was felt, was essential if diffusion were to occur, and the natural pride in the innovation was accompanied by a desire for wider recognition inside the company and beyond. Favorable publicity often created an appetite for more. The project leaders sometimes lost control of publicity to other corporate officials and the media.

Except possibly for Corning's Medfield and Northern Electric's Advanced Devices Center, the initial experiments in my sample achieved sufficient visibility throughout their corporate organizations.

Confusion Over What to Diffuse

Even if the initial site is favorable for eventual diffusion and the project leaders manage the publicity effectively, higher management can botch up the process in the way they formulate and communicate the diffusion policy.

If the form of work structure indicated by company policy is stated too conceptually, the policy may be dismissed as abstract and platitudinous or action may be delayed because managers don't know how to translate the concepts.

On the other hand, if the ideas about the desired forms of work structure are stated too operationally, they may be rejected as inappropriate by managers whose units have different types of work force, different technologies, or different economic conditions.

Norsk Hydro presents an interesting case in point. Six years after the initiation of the fertilizer experiment and many years after it had become official company policy to diffuse this type of work innovation managers still complained about the lack of clarity. Was the policy to diffuse "job enrichment," "autonomous groups," "organizational development," "sociotechnical systems," or something more general that underlies them all?

There was general agreement that diffusion would have proceeded more rapidly if it had been clear that the policy was for managers to pursue certain *aims* (such as making better use of the talents of employees and allowing for more day-to-day influence by employees over their work) rather than to employ particular *techniques*.

Inappropriateness of Concepts Employed

The long-run diffusion of work restructuring is affected by another issue. Although the concepts should be inspiring, they must also be realistic.

"Autonomous groups" was the key concept employed in the Norwegian experiments to characterize the work restructuring innovations. The term, which many found inspiring, was later dropped because it was not feasible for many groups to become truly autonomous.

"Equal status" was a concept in the design of Shell U.K.'s Teesport work system. The term captured the imagination of the workers as well as the originators but overstated what higher management was prepared to do. Differences persisted between blue- and white-collar workers, although all employees were placed on salary. The differences remaining were especially resented because of the expectations aroused by the "equal status" concept.

Deficient Implementation

The initial project may be viable in itself but the follow-through may be inadequate in terms of locating accountability for the change and providing "how-to" knowledge.

The first point has already been illustrated. Norsk Hydro attempted unsuccessfully to place the responsibility for diffusion with joint consultation boards and then shifted it to middle management. Shell U.K. started implementation by selecting a few projects with heavy reliance on a few staff people but then shifted to a policy in which all department heads become accountable for changes in their units. Accountability for work restructuring in Volvo was clearest; it was an essential part of the plant managers' responsibility, period!

As in many types of change in organization, "how-to" knowledge must be provided by training, consulting, or both. Resources for this seemed to have been a limiting factor at one time or another in GF, Corning, and Alcan.

Lack of Top Management Commitment

A period of sustained priority for work restructuring is important in achieving diffusion. The continuing interest and commitment of Volvo's president is a prime case in point. By contrast, the shifting priority given work restructuring in the studies of several other firms hindered diffusion. An illustrative case is Norsk Hydro, at which the work restructuring objective received lower priority during 1970–1973 than it did in 1967–1969.

The priority declined for several reasons. First, when the initial experiment was launched there was a high sense of urgency about improving industrial relations and productivity, but with the general improvement in industrial relations and the competitiveness of the business the sense of urgency receded.

Second, according to their own testimony, middle-level managers have come under increasing pressure to meet demanding volume and cost objectives, making it risky in the short run to start any major projects. One manager said, "I have the freedom to innovate but not the time."

Third, the company has been transformed by rapid expansion and revolutionary changes in the raw materials and processes used in much of its business. The changes absorbed the attention of top management and the director-general became more formal and less accessible to members of the organization—at least to those who wanted to lobby for work restructuring.

In many cases inconsistencies in higher management's behavior weakened diffusion efforts. Even before they perceived that the program had been downgraded Shell U.K. managers were concerned that although they were asked to protect and develop their human resources they were being assessed mainly on their handling of the technical system alone.

Toward the end of the 1960s Alcan division management reportedly shifted toward a more directive, top-down type of leadership and away from a consultative, problem-oriented management pattern. This directly contradicted and undermined the innovative work structure that had been developed at the Kingston works and had an inhibiting effect on further diffusion of work restructuring in the division.

Union Opposition

Like sustained top-management commitment, union support or acceptance is a necessary condition for any significant diffusion of work restructuring. In some cases union support has been on balance, a positive factor. In others perceived opposition by the union has been a reason for not trying to diffuse work restructuring into unionized plants. As a rule, unions have had more complicated effects on the process of introducing change, the nature of the work structures introduced, and the work climate.

The Scandinavian union movement has been more positive toward work restructuring than trade unions in the United Kingdom and North America. Clearly, joint union-management sponsorship of the Norwegian experiments served to legitimize the program for workers. However, actual effects of union officials on diffusion at Norsk Hydro and Hunsfos were mixed, just as effects on the management side were mixed.

At Norsk Hydro the loss of support of a key union official who had moved from the area hurt the diffusion effort. At Hunsfos, whose chief shop steward and company president were strongly committed to the diffusion program, local effort received no backing from the trade union movement. Although the trade union movement as a whole was not averse to the changes pioneered at Hunsfos, the chief shop steward reported criticism from other quarters. He said that he took risks with his own constituency every time he "stuck his neck out" (e.g., on a change that resulted in a crew reduction). Also, radical sociologists accused him of selling out to management and increasing company efficiency at the expense of workers.

At Volvo, the unions have played an active and positive role in the work restructuring program. Both management and the union claim joint ownership of the total project.

In the case of the Shell U.K. program the union deliberately slowed down the rate of diffusion of work restructuring during 1965–1968 until productivity bargaining had progressed to the point at which they had been able to establish the economic quid pro quo for certain changes.

A factor at Shell is tension around manning. Top management continues to put pressure on refinery managers to reduce the work force. When we recall that guarantees against dismissal and provisions for extra pay were a quid pro quo in the initial change program, we can see how reviving the issue has led to poorer union-management relations and inhibited the further diffusion of work restructuring.

To summarize, unions' effect has taken many forms:

First, unions have influenced the basic climate for change. When they helped to legitimize work restructuring or entered into an informal problem-solving pattern consistent with the work culture sought by the work restructuring experiment the effect was positive. When they inhibited management's attempts to diffuse change or formalized and politicized relations contradictory to the spirit of the work culture being diffused the effect was negative.

Second, unions have complicated the change process by requiring additional consensus-seeking efforts.

Third, unions have affected the preconditions for change or limited the nature of the change itself. Sometimes they have obtained assurances on job security and earnings maintenance and have bargained for workers to share in the increased productivity that resulted from more flexibility and reduced work crews. Sometimes they have prevented certain changes; for example, modifications in job content that affect union jurisdictional boundaries or historical patterns.

Bureaucratic Barriers

The importance of this issue belies the simplicity with which it can be stated. Diffusion efforts are frustrated by vested interests and existing organizational routines that limit local autonomy.

Innovative plant managements have often felt harassed by staff groups, who for their part have often become irritated and impatient with many of the plants' demands for self-sufficiency and exemption from uniform company policies. These tensions may be present during the establishment of the initial experiment and are escalated when serious diffusion begins. "Experiments," by definition, minimize the scope and duration of the effects of the change involved. When the changes are declared enduring or an attempt is made to spread them, however, the stakes are raised for the groups affected.

Bureaucratic barriers can be illustrated by the experience of one company in which managers themselves introduced the term. One problem relates to the level at which decisions are made in the line organization. In 1973 workers were operating informally without supervisors on two of the four shifts, but formalization of this arrangement and extension to a third and fourth shift were not within the authority of the manager of the innovative plant.

The experience of General Foods, Shell U.K., and other firms in which an ambitious diffusion effort has been undertaken is rich with similar illustrations that involve such issues as whether quality assurance procedures at plant level must be uniform throughout the corporation, whether a common job evaluation scheme should be applied to plants with radically different work structures, what the respective roles of central engineering and local staffs in plant expansion programs should be, how much local autonomy should exist in creating and filling plant management positions, and whether reporting requirements must be applied uniformly throughout the system.

Threatened Obsolescence

A restructured work situation requires new roles and new skills and makes others obsolete. We have already mentioned the resistance of staff groups who may have to acquire new knowledge, develop new consultative patterns for imparting their expertise, and see some of their functions performed by nonspecialists.

The greatest threat, however, was to first-line supervision. The number of first-line supervisors was often decreased, and sometimes the position was eliminated. When it was retained, it was changed in ways that required new attitudes and greater interpersonal and group skills.

Supervisors individually and as a group are weak compared with other groups potentially affected by new work structures. They themselves have not mounted much effective opposition to the diffusion or tried to shape the form of work restructuring. The one exception is Volvo, at which, within the last year, the supervisors' union has taken an active role to protect its members' interests. In many other cases management's uncertainty about how to handle the potential obsolescence of existing foremen has been a factor that inhibited diffusion.

The resistance of supervisors and other salaried personnel has not always been due to a direct threat to their existing roles; instead, they felt neglected by comparison with blue-collar workers. They resented the fact that blue-collar workers' jobs were enriched and their status and influence upgraded, whereas their own lot had not improved.

Self-Limiting Dynamics

In companies that employed the most comprehensive diffusion strategy there was a tendency for pilot projects to be self-limiting or "self-sealing."

It was strongest in companies like Norsk Hydro, Hunsfos, and General Foods in which a single small unit was involved in the original experiment and serious attempts to introduce work restructuring into other units came only after widespread publicity of the success of the experiment.

One dynamic involved a "star-envy" phenomenon, which can be illustrated by Norsk Hydro. The original experiment in the fertilizer plants received an enormous amount of publicity in Norway and other countries. The fertilizer plants became the target of innumerable visits by managers, trade union officials, social scientists, and schoolchildren. Top management looked approvingly on the project and made it company policy for others to follow its lead. It was not surprising that the attention given the fertilizer groups engendered resentment and envy among other persons who were asked to adopt the innovation in their own operations. This resentment was accompanied by resistance to the work restructuring program. The experience at the Topeka plant of General Foods was strikingly similar.

A second dynamic involved a shift in the reward structure. Payoffs for pioneers and those who followed them in the same organization differed in important respects and thus provided a much less favorable benefit-risk picture for subsequent users of organizational innovations. Managers who adopted innovations and succeeded were given less credit than the pioneer had received. If they had failed, they probably would have lost more standing in management than the pioneer if he had failed. Managers who did not accept innovations may have figured that although they would be prodded and goaded for not taking organizational initiatives ultimately they would be judged on the basis of production and profit performance. In short, they felt that they could afford to resist pressure.

A third dynamic involved the tendency for participants to regard themselves as special and their experimental work system as superior. On the one hand, this point of view reinforced their commitment to the group and was a positive factor in helping to establish a new form of social organization. On the other, it tended to lead outsiders to conclude that the culture created was unique and to discount the general applicability of the experiment.

A fourth dynamic came into play at a later date. Rivalry sometimes developed among those engaged in work restructuring. Minor differences were stressed in their approaches but the similarity in underlying values and assumptions was ignored. One effect of this form of rivalry among change agents and innovative units was to weaken their ability to form the collegial networks described earlier as part of the general diffusion model.

A fifth dynamic also became apparent at a later stage in those cases in which diffusion did not make rapid progress. It was a secondary consequence of two factors related above: the bureaucratic barriers and the special self-image developed by experimental units. The leaders of some innovative units had engaged in so many skirmishes with superiors and staff groups over corporate practices and were so aggressive in asserting the correctness of their positions that they hurt their own careers. Observing this, some peers resolved not to get similarly burned.

CONCLUSIONS

One important reason for the unimpressive rate of diffusion in the eight companies studied is that these innovations, especially in their more comprehensive form, have many attributes that make their diffusion inherently slow. Even if they offer relative advantages over existing work structures, their character and results are not highly communicable, they are not congruent with existing norms and values, their potential effect in a given work situation is pervasive rather than fractional, they are not readily reversed without incurring social costs, and too many affected parties serve as gatekeepers for their effective implementation.

Another set of explanations for the actual diffusion observed in the eight companies relates to the barriers encountered by the diffusion efforts and the efficacy of the strategies and tactics of the companies.

Many key areas are readily identifiable. Does the experiment continue to show good results? Is the experiment sufficiently visible and convincing? Is organizational accountability for initiating change clear and is the know-how for implementation available? Is there sustained support for diffusion from powerful groups such as top management and union officials? Careful planning is required to ensure that the answers to these questions are positive.

Two problem areas deal with organizational dilemmas generated by the nature of the innovations. Work restructuring requires an increase in local autonomy, thereby threatening the power of central staff groups and some managers. It also threatens to make some roles obsolete or to eliminate the positions of some staff specialists and first-line supervisors. These problems, though not easily resolved, require imaginative solutions—solutions not yet obvious to me.

Last of all, perhaps the most interesting type of barrier to diffusion is the self-limiting dynamics of pilot projects. Ironically several are unexpected consequences of the success of the project. The greater the attention given to pilot units, the more likely that managers of peer units will be "turned off" by the example. The more successful the pioneer, the less favorable the payoffs and the greater the risks for those who follow. The more esprit de corps and sense of being special that develop in the unit, the less generalizable they will appear to others.

Some of the implications of our analysis of these and other self-limiting tendencies will become apparent once the dynamics are understood. There is an advantage to (a) introducing a number of projects at the same time in the same firm, (b) avoiding overexposure and glorification of particular change efforts, and (c) identifying the innovative program with top management at the initial project stage.

As the examples of work restructuring in the larger society become more numerous, however, the self-limiting tendencies should pose less of a problem.

In conclusion, I expect relatively little diffusion of potentially significant restructuring in the work place over the short run, yet the long run may tell a different story.

What more and more employees expect from their jobs is different from what organizations are prepared to offer them. Work restructuring is the preeminent answer to closing the gap. I expect the latent dissatisfactions of workers to be activated and pressure for work restructuring to increase as the issue receives more public attention and as more successful examples of comprehensive work restructuring raise the general level of worker expectations. I should also be surprised if future experiments did not profit from the pioneering efforts. Together these factors should generate an increase in the number of diffusions and a hastening of the pace of diffusion. But how many diffusions and how fast the pace, I can't even begin to guess.

10

The Light at the End of the Tunnel Is a Train Coming in the Opposite Direction

JAY N. NISBERG

During the last several years organizational development has become a new phrase in the jargon of management. In many organizations it has represented an important part of a new approach to the management of people. In others it has led to confusion and has become difficult to define in clear-cut terms. This chapter shows how this confusion can develop in a large corporation in which the definition and structure of this management philosophy differs for each department, work unit, and situation.

Certainly there are some commonalities in most organizational development (OD) programs. Rather than seeking improvements in individuals or isolated problem areas, organizational development is a long-range process planned to improve the effectiveness of the *total* organization, whether work group, department, plant, hospital unit, or top management staff. It can involve many types of activity such as greater participation in decision making by employees in their jobs and work areas, better communication, team building, and changes in job content, supervisory relationships, and organizational structure. In the final analysis organizational development involves the concerted efforts of the entire organization to stimulate a positive change in the attitudes, behavior, and performance of all employees so that its business goals can be more effectively achieved on a long-term basis.

This is only a general perspective; as OD spreads through large corporations it can take many forms. During a recent top management meeting of the Car and Truck, Body and Assembly Division of Continental Motors (CM), a leading automobile manufacturer, a panel sought to define OD and its basic principles and to determine whether it was being consistently applied throughout the division. To accomplish this a number of OD projects, some successful and others unsuccessful, were reviewed. The panel was composed of line managers, myself, and another internal OD specialist, all of whom had taken part in many of the major projects. The three-hour meeting also featured extensive discussion between the panel members and other participants from the division.

As a result of these exchanges and some mulling over my own experiences I believe I have gained some valuable insights into the success and failure of the varied organization development activities at CM. By recapping some of the more significant learnings it is my hope that they will help to prevent others from making similar mistakes when developing a more comprehensive and rational approach to OD in their own organizations.

The Problem at Continental Motors

My own experiences in many departments at CM have provided me with the opportunity, fortunately or unfortunately, to develop the following list of reasons why their OD projects were so different and why many were not so successful as they should have been:

- Inconsistent top and middle management commitment and involvement.
- Commitment built on promises, not probabilities.
- Poor coordination and planning of OD activities.
- The lack of a top-down approach to OD.
- Minimal ownership of the OD process by the client system.
- Handing OD to the client system as a (laid on) packaged program.
- Misunderstanding of the OD process and technology by the consultants.
- Little follow-up with the client system.

I believe that each of these factors contributed to the unsuccessful organizational development programs at CM. As I review them, I shall report the lessons that we learned.

Commitment

In recent years the climate at Continental Motors for organizational development can best be described as inconsistent. Although top management has expressed interest in and concern for organizational development at all levels, middle management and supervisors have taken varied approaches to the implementation of its concepts and techniques. Some CM units have been serious in their approach to OD. Others, however, have questioned the merits of this business philosophy and have tried merely to give the appearance of being interested. In fact, some managers have come to me as a consultant and requested ideas for "faking" it. Therefore, although the total climate of the corporation appeared to be positive toward OD, particular managers have expressed little commitment.

Lesson No. 1. Be as certain as possible that the climate is conducive to an OD effort. Test the readiness of your immediate client system and get an overt commitment from all parties.

A note of caution for internal consultants should be inserted here. One apparent indicator of CM's commitment to the OD process was the amount of money being spent on it. Although I have no access to information regarding the total expenditures of these activities, both inside and outside the corporation, I do know that CM divisions spent more than $1,000,000 in one year (1972–1973) for OD projects and that the amount has continued to increase. Furthermore, that figure does not account for salaries paid to managers who participated in these OD activities or the cost of replacement personnel while others were engaged in training functions.

Lesson No. 2. Do not let a large financial investment convince you that there is an equally consistent personal and sincere commitment by management to an OD effort. In many instances a large financial investment can be a political move to show top management that a department or unit is heavily involved in OD. Unfortunately this involvement can be more financial than anything else.

Verbal commitment to the notion of comprehensive OD activities has also been in greater evidence at CM, but it is increasing in some areas and decreasing in others. Although some managers are sensitive to the need for change in their units, others prefer to stay away from change projects. Their feelings are understandable, however, because they have been disappointed by experience; for example, a multitude of survey data gathered in recent years thoroughly documents management's uncertainty about the claims of OD practitioners. In informal interviews and sophisticated surveys evidence suggests that the internal OD consultants promised more than they could deliver. They "bought" their client systems commitment.

Lesson No. 3. Do not build expectations in your client system that are too pie-in-the-sky. Do not make promises and guarantees of positive changes in hard data that you may not be able to keep. Do not promise that an OD activity will solve their turnover or performance problems. Build the client's expectations on reasonable probabilities.

The panel agreed that strong managerial commitment was a major ingredient of successful OD, and although top management commitment was in evidence we felt that the climate had dampened in recent years. We found three reasons for the involvement of line managers in change projects:

1. Because they have been told to do so.
2. Because they believe they can help to produce results.
3. Because they feel that OD is morally and psychologically good for people.

In many cases OD projects were undertaken for the first reason. Department managers were translating top management's interest into "change by decree." As a result most of the OD activities hardly scratched the surface in developing significant skills and ongoing techniques to meet the operating goals of the corporation. Symptoms that indicated that the promises made to the departments had not been fulfilled were still observed. There was little reduction in the problems facing the corporation, problems that OD efforts were supposed to have relieved. There were signs of low trust in the various units, low morale, low-to-moderate commitment to the corporation's goals, and a wavering commitment to the OD efforts themselves. Thirty-five unionization attempts by salaried personnel in 1972 highlighted the ineffective programs and inauthentic commitment. Ministrikes at some locations reflected the lack of effective team-building programs for union and management employees. These disappointments illustrate the problems of OD based on inconsistent commitment and change by decree.

Commitment based on a combination of reasons two and three was needed for successful implementation of the OD processes and techniques. That commitment, tempered by realistic expectations, would lay the foundation for the successful spread of OD in the firm. In this case, however, available resources and top management commitment led to more show than substance. The reasons can be traced in part to the coordination and implementation of OD techniques.

Coordination and Implementation

At Continental Motors three OD groups, staffed by internal consultants, were actively seeking units, departments, and divisions to which they could deliver their services. One group, located at the CM corporate office building and referred to as the *CM Corporate Training Group* was understaffed and overfunded. The second group, also housed in the corporate offices and known as the *CM Organizational Research and Development Group (ORD)*, had similar OD responsibilities. The third group, located in various cities across the nation, was referred to as the *Management and Organizational Development Staff* (or more often as the "MOD Squad" which didn't help matters). Although the training group had the "ear" of many key decision makers, it was readily apparent that the second and third groups had the best resources. Still they had their downsides. The ORD group had "clout" at corporate headquarters but less trust in the potential client system. The MOD Squad had little clout at corporate headquarters but more trust in parts of the client system.

As might be suspected, these groups became highly competitive and their OD efforts were often redundant. On many occasions they would submit competing proposals to the same client system. They would try to win approval with promises and politics. They would often borrow one another's resources and constantly tried to find allies in their client systems who could be called on later to support their respective claims for additional human and financial resources. Each group, struggling for survival, adopted strategies that would ensure that survival—often at the expense of the other OD consulting groups.

Lesson No. 4. Be certain that the resources that provide OD services in your organization are supportive of one another, noncompetitive, and report into the same management structure.

Another problem that could be traced to this lack of integration was the absence of a systematic OD plan. In the heat of competition each consulting group sought as many clients as possible. As one division tried to develop team assembly procedures, another might be working on team development. Projects that differed in scope and intensity were underway at various levels of the hierarchy. Many of the problems of overlap and inconsistency were due to the lack of a coordinated OD strategy from division to division.

Another form of competition affected the operating divisions. It became obvious that they were competing among themselves by trying to impress top management with the fact that their division had the "best" OD effort going. This, of course, was counterproductive to the maintenance of the OD effort. In some cases the competition resulted in an overload of time and money spent on OD. Eventually these expenditures became the target of an anti-OD faction. In other cases, though, it brought about efforts to block the programs already begun in competing divisions. One of the panel members commented:

> The rest of the organization also has to be tied in so that they let that department or section get into a new "people program"—at least let them go in on an experimental basis. If the rest of the organization blocks that, there is a very grave risk that the new program—even if it's good—isn't going to last. You raise people's expectations and if they can't do anything with them you would have been better off not to have done it in the first place.

To integrate the delivery of OD services and prevent the competition and pressure among the client systems requires attention to the following:

Lesson No. 5. Control the economic resources and delivery capability for OD activities from one central point and be certain that all divisions fully understand the intent of an OD program before implementation.

Top-Down Change and Client System Ownership

Another major problem which stemmed in part from an inconsistent commitment and in part from the lack of an integrated strategy of change was the absence of a top-down approach. Because projects were being initiated at different levels and in different divisions, there was a concern that things were moving too quickly without the "ownership" of the immediate client system. This led to more confusion and resistance and often affected the success of the changes that occurred.

Comments by some of the panel members, both top and line managers, illustrate their feelings in regard to the need for a top-down approach:

You can't move it (OD) on to a more advanced step unless your organization is ready for it. In your enthusiasm to get it spread right down to the hourly people immediately, you've got to make sure that you've got your whole team working together on it before you do it. So you have to be a little patient—you've got to recognize the pitfalls, why people are not accepting the program, and get the ownership to *them*.

You've really got to work with your supervision for a long period of time before you actually get into the hourly involvement. They have to be convinced that this is the way to go. I really want to emphasize that point because one of the mistakes that we've made is to say: "Go do something to the hourly people and change their attitudes." If we think that they're the only people whose attitudes have to change, we're really missing the boat. . . . If we try to change the hourly people's attitudes first, we are in trouble.

Legislating change from the top is one tough job to do. It's got to be owned by the plant. It's got to be bought by the plant. It's got to be their project if it is going to go.

This top-down approach to change does not imply that change must begin at the top. One participant noted: "It's more difficult when there isn't total active involvement from the top—but not impossible." It does mean, however, that "We've got to have some support from the top." Nor does the top-down approach mean that every division will adopt the same strategy toward OD. Instead it means that the projects must be planned and coordinated in a manner that will ensure an integrated OD effort and permit an individual unit to define its specific program for change.

Lesson No. 6. Be sure that the various phases of your program, although generally consistent for all management in your corporation, are developed to provide the flexibility necessary to meet individual unit and situational needs. Provision should be made for the integration of local unit data or operating procedures. Those involved in the OD effort must also work to build the OD design. People are more committed to the technology if they have some ownership of it.

Lesson No. 7. A representative group of key line managers should form a "steering committee" to ensure the continuity and appropriateness of the OD process over time.

Although the action of a steering committee may provide some coordination, it will not guarantee the client's acceptance of the change. In one project, for example, change was mandated by top management and a committee was formed to guide it through. The committee had little hand, however, in diagnosing the problems and designing the change. Data on absenteeism, turnover, and staff composition were reviewed only by management and staff personnel. Alternative change projects were also evaluated by management. Finally, employees were given lectures on the upcoming plans but were not invited to design the implementation. It was an example of top-down change in form but not in spirit. It suggests the problem of mechanical and rigid change adopted by some of the internal practitioners.

Packaged Organizational Development

There was a tendency in many departments for internal consultants to conduct a thumbnail diagnosis and immediately prescribe a particular sort of change. One panel member commented:

> There is also a grave risk, I think, in looking for panaceas, looking for the right package—jumping to the conclusion that "it looks good, let's bottle it up and put it over."

Many of the internal consultants had "the little boy with the hammer syndrome" that says, "if you give a little boy a hammer, he finds everything needs pounding." They had their favorite change techniques and found that all their clients needed them. Effective change is based on comprehensive diagnosis and fitting the change technology to the client's needs.

Lesson No. 8. Be certain that what you deliver to your clients (with respect to content and technology) represents an OD strategy. Fit the technology to the need.

This lesson dictates that each element of the OD plan contain opportunities that will fit the problems of the level of management and the operating division. In addition, these OD elements should be integrated with the actual operating problems faced by managers in the organization. This defines their "felt needs" and makes the change program meaningful to them. Many of the OD activities at CM were seen as "attacking the symptoms" rather than the problems and needs. One of the panel members describes the situation:

> Some of the people in the organization will look to this "new package" to

solve their problem. A superintendent or general foreman will say, "Give me this program so I can get my absenteeism stopped." You've got to watch the pitfall that you're putting out something that they think will solve all their problems for them.

This was a recurring problem at CM. As a result the change programs alleviated some symptoms but seldom solved the problems.

Lesson No. 9. Avoid the expectation of a "cookbook" approach to OD. There is no step-by-step solution that will shake out all the answers for all the problems in the "human side of enterprise."

This expectation was encountered in many divisions of the corporation. Concern with the appearance of "doing OD" was so pronounced that ready solutions were immediately seized and rapidly implemented; but it was the consultants who helped to promote this approach by their misunderstanding of the processes and technologies of OD.

The Internal OD Practitioners and Follow-Through

Many of the OD change programs covered old material in a new format. Indeed the suspicions among managers at CM were based on their inability to distinguish the new OD technologies from those implemented under the label of management development. Often consultants were not offering a new management philosophy; instead they were rebuilding the wheel. Managers, however, were catching on to the "same old thing" and complaining "here we go again."

Many of the internal practitioners and managers were not aware of the current trends in organizational change and were unable to take full advantage of the advances in the behavioral sciences. Some consultants were relying on outmoded or, at least, incomplete theories. This was apparent in one work redesign project in which job changes were implemented under the Herzberg model but changes in the pay, information, and control systems, all part of the sociotechnical perspective, were not made. Thus reinforcement of the original change failed.

Lesson No. 10. To ensure the availability of appropriate OD resources an innovative training system must be created by qualified people. In addition, internal OD consultants must be encouraged to attend a recommended curriculum of off-site programs consistent with their management levels and/or individual needs to increase their awareness of behavioral science technology.

The panel also identified a need to improve the process skills of the internal consultants, skills that were required to create a climate for change and to implement the change itself. Furthermore, special systems must be established for in-house follow-up and coaching after participants have experienced all phases of the OD program. It will often be necessary to secure assistance from a local training group in the development of the proper climate to ensure the success of organizational development efforts.

Follow-up, refinement, and further dispersal of change technologies require not only process skills but data. The general manager of the Body and Assembly groups stressed this concern by calling for sound measurement of the effectiveness of these OD activities. He emphasized not only the need to measure the results of good management, such as profit, return on investment, and productivity, but also the processes that would produce them. These benchmarks in the areas of employee attitudes, employee motivation and utilization, organizational climate, supervisory leadership, and work-group effectiveness are essential to monitoring and measuring the progress of the OD function.

In many change projects underway at CM measurement has been at best vague and generally absent. Its absence has prevented the ongoing refinement of the programs and the evaluation of their end results. No one can say whether OD activities have provided a return on the time and money spent.

Lesson No. 11. Encourage the evaluation of OD activities launched in your organizations. Try to measure what you do and, if possible, implement your measurements as early as possible. Nothing "sells" better than hard data. If your organization can design a solid measurement process, let it do so.

This list accounts for some of the major reasons why OD efforts were fragmented at Continental Motors and why many were not so successful as they could have been. Strong management commitment and a well-integrated and coordinated OD strategy are the major ingredients of successful change in a large and diffuse corporation. A strong consultant and manager-training package is also needed. During the spring of 1974 an ad hoc committee on organizational development pointed out many weaknesses in the training package at CM. Their warnings, and the many other problems, led to the panel discussion reported here. That discussion produced some of the findings that I have presented.

Where to Start

OD can spread too quickly. Without sufficient commitment, realistic expectations, coordinated services, and effective training, many new programs will never succeed. As OD spreads through an organization it must be directed to units that are ready for a change. OD needs a "starting point," and the following criteria are recommended when selecting a client for the beginning of a change.

Lesson No. 12. Begin where the greatest impact on the management of most people in your organization can be made, where the most direct and rapid impact can be made on the most serious problems facing your organization, and among those who need and solicit your help. "Don't go where you're not wanted and don't go by decree."

When these criteria were applied at Continental Motors, the following target populations were identified for continued OD activities:

1. Individuals in high-exposure line departments.
2. Newly appointed first-line supervisors.
3. Interdependent support groups serving high priority projects.
4. Corporate and divisional executives.

The Benefits of Success

Although I have reviewed the problems in OD at CM, many projects were quite successful. Their results illustrate the promise of OD:

1. Financial benefits can be (but are not always) realized as a result of a consistent and comprehensive organizational development plan. This will enable a participating unit to plan more accurately for the utilization of its human resources. As the intergroup and interpersonal skill levels of all participants are increased, they will be able to operate interdependently and more efficiently, with better group process and more openness and trust, and thus a more effective operating climate.

2. The "crisis style of management" which is used by some managers can be replaced with a well-planned, logical approach to the job of managing people, technology, finances, and systems.

3. OD enables an organization to draw on a larger number of highly skilled individuals for placement wherever the greatest need exists at a given time.

4. The plan can minimize duplication of effort and reduce the fragmented approach to organization development.

5. The plan does *require* the utilization of a wide range of resources from inside as well as outside the company from such places as universities and consulting firms.

These results show that the OD concept of management can work and get results. In Continental Motors' case, as in the early days of any new approach to management in any large corporation, there were bound to be problems and pitfalls. I have tried to document them and describe what I have learned. Two panel discussants seemed to sum up the major lessons; their comments represent many of the CM managers' views:

One of the things we found when we surveyed the hourly people is that they said, "Well, how do you expect to do things for us when you can't even work together as managers?" And that's true. As I see it, the only way OD works in a plant is if it starts at the top and goes down. You can't make it just an hourly motivational program. It doesn't work that way. But if you start, as in my case, departmentally and work with your supervisors—get them involved—you'd be amazed at the enthusiasm that is in a group like that that's just been lying there dormant. They enjoy this. The supervisors work harder on their jobs. They do a lot better job. Once you've got supervisory support, then you go to the hourly people and start working with them and getting them involved. You have to start with your supervisory group. That is a definite must.

There is a high risk in getting a department or a section really turned on too fast to OD.

11

Team Building in the Small Business Community: The Success and Failure of OD

ROY J. LEWICKI

This chapter describes an effort to improve the working relations among small businessmen in two New England communities. Although designed as a study to yield research data on small businesses and their role in regional economic development, the output of the research was adapted to feed back useful information to the communities as well. After sharing data with each community, the change agents stimulated new structures and processes in order to help the business community coordinate more effectively. In one town they were successful; in the other they were not.

It is useful to examine this effort for two reasons. First, although similar strategies were used in the two communities, it must be asked why one "failed" and the other "succeeded." What can be learned about the differences in the change agent's actions, or in the communities, to help us understand these different outcomes? Second, what can be learned about the application of organization develop-

---

I would like to thank Wayne Broehl, Eugene Hornsby, Raymond Miles, and the editors of this volume for their helpful comments on an earlier draft of this manuscript, and the Associates Fund of the Amos Tuck School, Dartmouth College, for financial support during the preparation of this chapter.

ment techniques to community development problems? What special problems are unique to community development efforts and what action strategies should be used in the future?

This chapter is organized in several sections. The first part contains detailed case descriptions of the intervention in the two towns. In the second part comparisons are made of the interventions to determine the factors that contributed to success in one town and failure in the other. These factors are grouped according to the characteristics of the towns themselves, the leadership behavior of community members who assumed key roles in the intervention, and the strategy and tactics of the change agents as they contributed to failure or success. The chapter concludes with an analysis of the key problems that these cases raise for successful implementation of change.

THE ORIGINS OF THE INTERVENTION

The intervention originated from the needs of the client and the research interests of faculty members at the Amos Tuck School of Business Administration. As a faculty member I was interested in the application of team building and organization development techniques to a broader range of organizations and environments. Another faculty member, Wayne G. Broehl, was concerned with the problems of stimulating economic and community development. He had studied the behavior of rural Indian merchants in the fertilizer distribution business and sensed that the entrepreneurial characteristics of these men were strongly related to their business success. Broehl designed an interview study to identify the successful agricultural merchants and to determine their attitudinal and behavioral correlates (Broehl, 1977). The exciting results from this research generated many questions about similar behavior patterns among small businessmen in the United States, and the relation of these patterns to regional economic development in rural areas. The researchers searched for an appropriate environment to explore these questions, and Marysville, New Hampshire, was selected as the first site.

ENTRY INTO MARYSVILLE

Marysville (a pseudonym) is a community with a population of approximately 7000. It is about 10 miles from a major interstate highway, 40 miles from the state capital, and 100 miles from Boston. It is a major recreation and tourist center situated near major ski areas and a large lake that is crowded with resorts and summer cottages. A large woolen mill, a manufacturing company, and tourism are the leading local industries. The geography of the town is characteristic of many small American towns. Most of the central business district is distributed along a wide main street with gas stations at both ends and lined with diagonal parking spaces. A number of newer small businesses have located along a second street that runs out toward the lake. Although no shopping centers had yet appeared on the outskirts of town to draw commercial business from the downtown area, that threat aroused constant fear on the downtown business community; shopping centers 20 to 30 miles away were already having their effect.

The interventionists made their initial contact with Marysville through two individuals: Peter Flannagan, the editor of the weekly newspaper, and Walter Williams, president of the woolen mill. Both men had had occasional contact with the Amos Tuck School and both expressed interest in having the business school help work on community business problems. They had also provided field sites for Amos Tuck students who were working on independent course projects.

Discussions with Flannagan and Williams led to a meeting with the president of the Chamber of Commerce and the town manager. At these meetings the interventionists ("we") outlined a research project: to explore the similarities and differences between Indian and rural American small businessmen. We proposed to measure the attitudes and behavior of small businessmen in the town, to discover the entrepreneurs among them, and to explore their perceptions and attitudes toward the business climate of the town and its geographical region. Data would be collected by interviews and questionnaires.* Once the data were compiled, the results would be made available to the community participants with the hope that this information would help them to approach their problems collectively. All four men enthusiastically endorsed the proposed study.

A letter of introduction for the three students was prepared by the president of the Chamber of Commerce and appeared with their pictures on the front page of the weekly newspaper. The letter and

* Although the research design was faculty-originated, we explained that the actual research would be conducted by several MBA students who were enrolled in an independent study course. It was clear to the Marysville businessmen that the faculty were not only helping the students negotiate their entry but that they would also be involved as directors of any long-range effort.

article were used as credentials and an introduction to each businessman interviewed.

The interview schedule included sections on the attitudes and behavior correlates of entrepreneurship, a number of general questions on the businessmen's perception of the community, and specific questions on key community issues. The first questions were derived from the Indian research and a pilot project with two other local communities; the specific key issues were derived from preliminary interviews with Flannagan, Williams, the town manager, and the Chamber of Commerce president. The final instrument was then separated into an interview schedule and a self-administered questionnaire for the respondents, addressing the following topics:

Characteristics: age, education, background and history, memberships in organizations, travel, exposure to mass media, knowledge of sources of business assistance

History of the founding and development of the business

Risk-taking propensity measured by responses to several hypothetical decision situations

Attitudes toward their jobs—motivation, satisfaction, future planning

Economic performance of the business

Perceptions of the community: the townspeople, banks, local institutions; feelings about the town as a place in which to live and do business

Attitudes toward regionalization, regional development, the role of various groups in shaping development, and local issues such as zoning and future town expansion

The data were collected by the students over a five-week period: 147 oral interviews were scheduled and completed; the interviewers left the self-administered questionnaire and returned to pick it up several days later. Each interview took at least an hour and a half. Only nine businessmen refused to be interviewed or to complete the questionnaire. Interviews were also conducted with town officials and with several regional and state planning officials to determine their perspectives on the current state of the Marysville business community and on the problems for future growth and development.

DATA FEEDBACK

Following a statistical analysis of the questionnaire data and a summary of the interviews, a 25-page report was sent to all town officials and every participant in the study. The report included a review of the project as we had conducted it and summarized our perceptions of "the state of business in Marysville." This included the town's strengths (prosperous community, banking center for the area; geographical attractions and tourist business; county seat) and its weaknesses (deteriorating downtown area; low aggressiveness of businessmen; conditions of roads and attraction of shoppers to other areas). Ideas that would create opportunities for future development while minimizing threats, deduced from the interviews, were mentioned. Statements (supported by questionnaire data) were made on the current lack of town-wide and regional planning, the services that were then available, and potential targets for planning. A "challenge" posed by the interventionists for greater collaboration and cooperation among small business owners stated the need to transcend their own small operations and work cooperatively on common problems. Finally, selected data summarized from the questionnaire profiled the small businessman and his attitudes toward his business and Marysville.

Feedback Meeting No. 1

In the feedback report we asked all interested parties to attend an evening meeting in Marysville to review and discuss the findings. About 20 people attended. To put the Marysville study in context a brief presentation was made of the India research and findings, followed by a summarization of the report by the students. To quote from our own notes, "by the time we were finished, everyone was at a common level but many of the people seemed bored."

The most critical aspect of the meeting was our attempt to transfer the initiative for action planning from the research team back to the community. In the discussion that followed we stated that any changes that might occur would have to come from the Marysville people themselves. We neither suggested a mechanism nor offered to be any more than resources to them. We stated our "hunch" that some "project" was needed to symbolize a renewed spirit of collective pride and cooperation in the business community but we were not more specific than that.

People responded that they didn't know where to begin, that they still hadn't thoroughly read and understood the feedback report, that it would be desirable to get more people out to a meeting (particularly more Main Street merchants), and that another meeting with us was needed. Everyone was urged to invite someone else to the next meeting, set for two weeks away.

Preparation for the Second Meeting

We felt that it would be critical to orchestrate the second meeting to ensure progress in assuming community-based initiative. We conferred with newspaper editor Flannagan and decided to hold a dinner meeting with well-respected business community leaders before the second feedback meeting. We also considered various techniques for actively involving those attending the meeting, the selection of a person to conduct the meetings, and the desirability of some type of steering committee to oversee action planning.

A major issue in the background of these efforts was the Chamber of Commerce. Normally the organization that would take the initiative to strengthen the small business community, the Marysville Chamber had a reputation among businessmen for stagnation and inactivity. People were afraid that any steering committee effort directly linked to the current Chamber would not be perceived as innovative or likely to undertake new programs. We had wanted to include the current president of the Chamber in any action planning, but we discovered during the data collection that his leadership style actively contributed to the Chamber's reputation. His personal style also did not facilitate open discussion of these problems, and we felt that it might be unwise to allow a large open meeting to attack the Chamber or its leadership.

The dinner meeting was organized by Gene Hornsby, one of the students, and attended by the president of the Chamber, Flannagan, Williams, two others who were prominent members of the business community, and us. We felt that this group represented some of the best ideas about the future of the town and some of the power needed to realize them. We reviewed our goals for the feedback meeting and managed to review, candidly but carefully, the reputation of the Chamber and our concern for it. We suggested that the group begin to explore ways to alleviate the broad-based apathy, indifference, and pessimism among the townspeople. Our major issue however—to decide how to turn over the initiative for future development from the Tuck team to a Marysville businessman—was left unresolved.

Feedback Meeting No. 2

The Tuck researchers prepared a written agenda. We proposed to summarize the feedback report once again briefly and to answer questions. This would be followed by our suggestion that an organization be created "to promote business directly and vigorously," and to "do things that can be done cooperatively . . . at a reasonable cost to the benefit of all." Although we tried to elicit suggestions from the participants about the *kind* of organization that would be most successful, we personally believed that a temporary "task force" model should study and recommend action in various areas. We hoped that the remainder of the meeting would be spent in generating agendas for task forces and creating an organization to implement these agendas. Forty-one people attended, twice the number at the first meeting.

The task force idea was raised and readily accepted. Several areas were suggested for task forces to work in: business promotion (promoting Marysville as a place to shop among local full-time and seasonal residents), new business (exploring the current "gaps" in Marysville as a full-service town and ways to attract new business), business image (enhancing the townspeople's image of Marysville), and business education (attempting to improve the managerial skills and practices of small businessmen). We took business promotion among seasonal residents as a "demonstration topic," presented a lecturette on brainstorming, and then helped the participants to generate ideas on how Marysville could do a better job of attracting seasonal residents to shop in their community. The meeting broke down into ad hoc task forces to brainstorm on the other three issues.

When each task force had reported back to the meeting on its ideas, we stated that we felt that the community by itself bore the responsibility for devising some form or organization to coordinate these proposals. Much to our dismay, a lengthy discussion followed on the current reputation of the Chamber of Commerce as it represented past inactivity and indifference in the business community. Should the group attempt to revitalize the Chamber, rebuild membership (among 150 businesses many were Chamber members but few were active), and encourage the Chamber to undertake new tasks? Several speakers wanted a "vote" to favor a new organization versus redeveloping the current Chamber. This vote was temporarily stopped by the Chamber president (who argued that it was divisive of the spirit of the meeting), but a straw vote was finally taken. Approximately 80% favored a "new" organization as a group to be closely related to the Chamber but separate in function and meetings. There would be no membership dues (like the Chamber) and membership would be open to anyone interested in working on the action steps raised by the earlier brainstorming.

The group "drafted" Jim Post into being chairman of the task force. The owner of a store on Main Street, Post was reasonably new to the community and believed that action was both necessary and possible. He accepted the draft with considerable enthusiasm and immediately began appointing committees. Among them was a general steering committee on which he asked three people who had voted for the "new organization" and three people who had voted for "the Chamber" to serve. He also enlisted a secretary and a person to find a site for the next meeting.

The meeting broke up in a spirit of enthusiasm and optimism. Most people wanted to come back in two weeks and bring more people with them. Planning for this meeting was to be left to the new steering committee. We agreed to come but accepted no responsibility other than to provide typed summaries of the output of the brainstorming.

Feedback Meeting No. 3

At the third feedback meeting Jim Post and Gene Hornsby reviewed the first two sessions—the feedback report, the brainstorming, and the proposal for a new organization. Post described the proposed organization: a chairman, and the chairmen of four major subcommittees (retail merchants, public relations and business image, regional and community planning, and business assistance and education).

Post had barely finished his report when questions from the audience turned to the purpose of this "new organization" against the current Chamber. Many thought that a new organization was necessary to inspire those interested in change; the image of the old organization, both to its members and to the outside community, suggested the unsatisfactory status-quo. Yet others did not want to be brutal in abolishing or abandoning the Chamber, in particular because it would represent an affront to the current officers. Although current Chamber officers owned up to some of the problems, they also did not offer to redesign, abolish the organization, or encourage internal change. As a matter of record the Chamber president continued to argue that it made no difference what you called the organization—in his eyes, the same few people would always do the work. Finally, any task force would require funds to operate. Where would this money come from? If dues were required, would people pay them and would the Chamber suffer even more (because it was already having trouble collecting current dues at $50/year)?

The mood of the meeting sank into despair. There was aimlessness, self-flagellation for past inaction, a need for action, yet a fear for the wrong kind, in the face of which Post made a massive sales pitch for the new organization, refusing to let despair dominate the meeting. He asked for immediate volunteers for the retail committee. The Chamber president wanted to have the task force chairman chosen first, but his request went unheard. On a suggestion from Williams Post drafted the existing active core of the Chamber's retail committee and added a new member. He then moved on to the other three committees, held a short discussion on each of them, and appointed several individuals to work as their cores.

After a 10-minute break and a lot of caucusing Post suggested that the task force become an independently functioning committee of the Chamber of Commerce, that the president of the Chamber select its chairman, and that task force members not be required to become Chamber members for six months. Agreement was finally achieved on these points. Post would be the temporary chairman of the task force until a permanent one could be appointed.

In talking to Post after the meeting he felt that this concession to affiliate with the Chamber was an important one, necessary to preserve good relations with as many businessmen as possible. He said that he would be satisfied if half the groups constituted that evening really accomplished something.

Early Meetings of the Task Force

We (Lewicki, Broehl, and Hornsby) purposely waited to be invited to the first few task force meetings, although we were most anxious to observe the early efforts. We wanted to minimize the possibility that we would be depended on to structure the tasks and were often divided among ourselves about how much monitoring and probing was necessary (and desirable) on our part.

From their own reports the first few meetings of the task force were groping ones, in which they searched for ways to begin action and to manage relations with the Chamber. Our previous suggestions that they initiate activities to ensure a "short success cycle" (i.e., limited goals and short-range projects) eventually caught on. When we attended a meeting a month later, activities were well underway.

The group met weekly, early in the morning before each man opened his own business. Each committee undertook a few short-run study projects, and meetings were devoted to reporting on their current efforts. What the Committee lacked in the skills of conducting an effective meeting, they compensated for in enthusiasm and commitment to their newly found sense of purpose. Post was particularly nondirective at these meetings, in marked contrast to his control over the third feedback meeting. Our notes recall the following:

> . . . (Post) is relatively laissez-faire with respect to leadership—maybe that's necessary and he is trying to find out how far the group is willing to move and whether they will accept his leadership. . . . There's some time wasted at meetings, there's some devotion to detail that could be worked out in subcommittees, there's some tendency to come in with prepared reports. On the other hand, people are really on top of the issues . . . they value the Tuck report in retrospect, think it was the major focus that got them off the ground and out of their lethargy, feel very good about the quality job that the students did in gathering and presenting it to them . . . and are interested in maintaining a relationship with Tuck.

Several major activities were undertaken by the task force during their first few months of operation. The business education committee believed that one of the major mandates of the task force was to upgrade the quality of management among Marysville's small businesses. The committee recruited a locally known industrial consultant to teach several sessions on motivation and employee-employer and business-community relations. The speaker was not particularly effective and did not know enough about the Amos Tuck project to build bridges between his topics and the feedback report. His three lectures over a two-month period were viewed with mixed feelings. However, a six-session general management program for the business community, designed and staffed by the Amos Tuck School faculty, was judged extremely successful by the 30 businessmen who attended.

The retail committee, which ventured into occasional forays with the town government, succeeded in having the site of a razed hotel cleaned up in the center of town and in improving the physical appearance of a boarded-up movie theater. Initial steps were taken to build a coalition of businessmen against the parking meters on Main Street, but the Retail Committee showed considerably more success in promoting effective coordination among themselves. Collective efforts were mobilized to synchronize closing hours for holidays and to sponsor a sports equipment exposition and town-wide store sales to coincide with a fair on the town green. Bumper stickers promoting the town were printed and distributed. The newspaper sponsored a contest quiz on one of the town's most famous citizens.

A new town manager came to Marysville in August. He was invited to join the task force and regularly came to meetings. This was an important step that provided a strong link to long-run coordination with the town government.

One of the town's most influential businessmen who had never taken an active part in the task force asked them to join other citizens groups in sponsoring a fund-raising effort for a new athletic recreation complex near the town schools. The task force agreed and actively contributed to the success of the project.

In spite of all this, tension continued between the task force, brash and enthusiastic, and the Chamber of Commerce, lethargic and status-quo. In the eyes of one town observer, while the Chamber "sawed sawdust" they nevertheless expressed strong jealousy of the task force for activities that seemed to conflict with the aims of the Chamber. Moreover (as we recorded in our notes),

> . . . there is some negativism against the new group, manifested mostly in pessimism. People feel that (the Task Force) are a bunch of do-gooders running around town getting things changed. Observers believe that all of this really isn't going to work because it never worked before.

This negativism was often discussed at task force meetings, in whose eyes the problem was often cast as "newcomers," enthusiastic about progress and change, versus "oldtimers" satisfied with the past and present. On one hand the task force tried to remain enthusiastic and independent and avoided having its spirit contaminated by the sluggishness of the Chamber. On the other hand, it knew that it was not a viable organization on its own, hence spent much of its time trying to manage its relations with the Chamber. The two groups competed for the voluntary time of their members and had potentially the same goals but different styles of activity that were incompatible. The net consequence was that task force productivity was being eroded by the very thing it was trying to avoid: contagion with the Chamber. Fear of taking action and of incurring the undercurrent of resentment from Chamber members almost doomed the task force to be as ineffective as the Chamber had been.

Post's commitment to bridge the gap between the groups was a key issue that the Amos Tuck group confronted in a brief six-month follow-up questionnaire. Businessmen were asked about their perception of changes that had occurred since the Amos Tuck School survey, and interviews were conducted with 15 of the most active people in the change effort. Although no significant change was recorded in attitudes toward Marysville or toward doing business in the town, most people felt a positive change in the spirit and intent of the business community. Task force leaders remained enthusiastic but frustrated by attempts to work with the Chamber. Chamber people wanted to envelop the task force more completely, to make it the activist arm of the Chamber, controlled by the top Chamber leadership. The task force did not respond well to this initiative.

The frustration was best symbolized by Post's attempt to resign at a task force meeting following this study. He seemed tired and dejected and believed that he had been cast too long as a radical in the business community. The agenda, which he prepared and distributed to the meeting, listed under new business: "Plan of Action!!!! 1. Appoint new chairman." It was followed by "A Quote to Remember . . . 'The more we love our friends, the less we flatter them; it is by excusing nothing that pure love shows itself.' " The task force would hear nothing of his intended action and refused to accept his resignation.

The first major turning point in Chamber-task force relations came when the new board of directors of the Chamber was announced. Five of the most active task force members were nominated to the board, all of whom agreed to join 10 past directors at the annual Chamber meeting in late January. At the first directors meeting after installation six of the 15 directors attended, including four of the new task force members.

> The discussion then turned to how to give the Chamber a new direction and a new image. The first problem was how to get the Directors to attend meetings and when would be the best time to hold them. A morning meeting was suggested because of the success of the morning Task Force meetings. The idea of a breakfast meeting was proposed, but there was no restaurant open at that time. One member then agreed to cook pancakes if they could think of a place with kitchen facilities—the bank president readily offered his bank. . . . A Task Force member was appointed temporary Chairman, and every director was to be contacted personally and invited.

Not only was the breakfast meeting a huge success, but task force members were elected to the presidency of the Chamber and other major positions. New committees were formed. We quote from the Chamber newsletter, written by the executive secretary of the Chamber and well known for initial opposition to the Task Force:

> The new Directors . . . and the Tuck Task Force met a week ago at a new place and a new time. The bank building lower floor is now known as the

Elliot-Post Pancake Parlor. One would not think there could be much done at 7:00 A.M., especially after consuming unbuttered experimental flapjacks, but the results suggest that we may need more meetings of that type. Among other things, your officers are . . . .

New projects during the winter and spring included securing the town's permanent membership in the regional planning commission, changing the name of the Chamber of Commerce to reflect the larger Marysville region, several open meetings of the Chamber for the larger Marysville business community, and efforts to widen the interface with the town government, school district, and regional population. In late May the Chamber hosted a Salute Breakfast for 86 local businessmen and friends—a record turnout for any Chamber of Commerce function. The Amos Tuck School group was awarded a Salute of Achievement for its efforts in the Marysville business community.

RIVERSIDE, N.H.: A SECOND INTERVENTION

Early in April 1973, while we were beginning our feedback meetings in Marysville, Wayne Broehl was approached by Bill Fenton, a bank president in Riverside, and asked to come to a meeting of business leaders to discuss the possibility of conducting a similar study. The Riverside area is geographically identified with a large lake, surrounded by summer cottages (population 4500), motels, and tourist homes. Six or seven small communities are located around the lake. Riverside itself (population 1800) is located several miles south of the lake, and most regional residents depend on it for central services.

Broehl attended the first meeting at the bank with a number of Riverside community leaders: the owner of a major restaurant, the owner of a major construction business and chairman of the Board of Selectmen, the president of the Chamber of Commerce, a real estate broker, and several others. Broehl described the work that we had been doing in Marysville and the model that we had designed for survey construction, interview and questionnaire data collection, and feedback in the form of a report and public meetings.* In return, the men told Broehl about some of the major problems in the Riverside community. Relations between the central Riverside community and

* Hornsby, in reviewing this article, believes that we may have told them much more about our "success" in Marysville than described here. Hence we may have created impossible expectations in Riverside from the beginning, based on what we said about Marysville.

the "satellite" lake towns were often strained because resources and facilities were shared. The lake and its related tourist business was the central economic activity but also seasonal in nature. Thus, although the tourist industry was an important concern, many businessmen were seasonal occupants and not fully integrated into the town's informal business groups. Finally, there was one major employer: a large manufacturing plant. The labor market was particularly tight, for few new skilled applicants were available, a situation that projected poor prospects for new industrial development in the region.

As we thought about these problems, we decided that the most useful focus for our study was an understanding of the Riverside area in regional terms: a central town and with six or seven satellite communities, moderately interdependent, and with only moderate intrusion from neighboring regions. Its lake for summer tourism was its major economic resource. A few small ski areas provided some winter traffic but not so significant as the summer trade. Could the assets of the region be exploited more profitably and generate more year-round economic productivity? If so, what changes in business practices, regional cooperation, or economic development would be desirable and feasible to bring it about?

At meetings with the ad hoc group to develop the data instruments we presented this perspective and recommended that the study be framed in these terms. We suggested important areas that would need to be investigated: the economic base of the town and region, the growth and development of individual business firms, relations among businessmen in the town and region, and the impact of the tourist industry on Riverside. The ad hoc group reviewed our plans, modified only slightly many of the questions we had used in Marysville, and suggested new questions on key local issues such as planning, zoning, and public transportation.

By early July the data collection phase was well formulated. Hornsby, having graduated from the Amos Tuck School, assumed a position as research associate and took full responsibility for all interviews and questionnaires. The bank president and Chamber of Commerce president helped prepare the letter of introduction, the lists of people to interview, and appropriate announcements in the local newspaper; 166 business people were approached, questionnaired and interviewed. A shopper's market survey was conducted to find out why people shopped in Riverside, the kind of purchases they made there, and what changes they thought would make Riverside a better place to shop. Finally, we also interviewed selectmen, state representatives, school administrators, lawyers, doctors, a local judge, and representatives of the Regional Planning Commission and the State Office of Planning, Economic Security and Economic Development.

Soon after the data collection began, in early summer, New England—and the Riverside region in particular—was plagued with heavy rains and severe flooding. The publicity was significantly worse than the actual damage and the tourist business dropped abnormally for the peak of the summer season. Much of our data, we feel, reflects the depression of local businessmen who were being affected by this event at the time they were interviewed.

Data Feedback

Early in January 1974 we released our feedback report to the Riverside community. Copies were sent to all who had participated in the data collection and offered to the general public in a series of news releases. Similar to the Marysville report, the Riverside report reviewed the data collection procedures and presented our perceptions of "the state of business in Riverside." Natural resources such as the lake and ski areas, physical attractiveness, and a cautious but prosperous business community, very satisfied with their businesses and life style, were its strength. Weaknesses included the limitations of the natural environment, largely underdeveloped and characterized by a lack of public works facilities and zoning, deficiencies in business and public services, and the dependence of *most* Riverside residents on local business *only* for convenience (not selection of goods, favorable prices, or pleasing appearance of stores). The major weakness appeared to be poor integration among summer and year-round residents and among seasonal and year-round businessmen (downtown merchants versus resort managers). In addition, an energy crisis was being projected for the region as a result of the Arab oil boycott, and an interstate highway that potentially would draw tourists farther north, away from the region, had recently been completed. Thus there were many opportunities for cooperation among the business community: attracting tourists, developing more year-round accommodations, integrating loyal summer residents into the community, and strengthening business by cooperative management, development and cost-reduction training procedures.

The report suggested an "operation local," a major task force operating as an arm of the Chamber of Commerce (an organization somewhat more vibrant than Marysville's but nevertheless anaemic and lethargic). Subcommittees of the task force would be in charge of promoting the town and the region to tourists, primarily with an advertising brochure, enlisting the cooperation of summer tourists, retired persons, and new businessmen, planning the renovation of downtown businesses and working on problems of downtown merchants, upgrading the quality of small business management, and developing opportunities for new businesses.

Planning for the feedback Meeting

In planning the feedback meeting, we faced many of the problems that we had encountered in Marysville. First, we knew that we would need to review the report in some way. Second, we wanted to transfer control of implementation from ourselves to the community. Although we did not want to abandon the townspeople, we also did not want them to believe that we would control the implementation stage of the project. There was another problem that we had not faced in Marysville. Hornsby, having conducted all the interviews, was convinced that Fenton (the bank president), the Chamber of Commerce president, and several other local businessmen formed a de facto oligarchy for the region. The "power structure" in the Riverside business community was essentially monolithic; it controlled all financial, real estate, and town government activities. Although the report called for broad-based participation and change in developing the Riverside region, Hornsby felt that implementation would fail if members of the de facto power bloc drove out the broad-based active participation of all segments of the community. It was our responsibility as interventionists, he argued, to explain this to the current business leaders and to express our belief that if progress was to be made in Riverside these individuals would have to be willing to refrain from exerting any initial control or direction over emergent task forces at the feedback meetings.

These points were deliberated extensively by Broehl, Hornsby and Lewicki. We thoroughly debated the wisdom (no less the delicacy) of asking the most prominent business leaders to assume a "standby" position, particularly when the time arrived for selecting task force leadership. Hornsby's commitment to his belief prevailed, and we decided to ask these people to refrain from assuming any leadership should Task Force groups be initiated. Broehl and Hornsby went to Riverside to explain this decision to Fenton and the real estate agent weeks before the feedback meeting. These men understood the significance of our request and the possible consequences of becoming involved in early efforts at change; they agreed to remain in the background during the first feedback meetings.

This action, however, compounded the problem because we also wanted to be able to anticipate who might be likely to assume task force leadership. We had been reasonably certain in Marysville that any one of several people would emerge as a leader and that their leadership would be effective and respected by the community. After our interviews with the business population of Riverside we feared that the wrong people would seize control. This led Broehl and Hornsby to ask Fenton and the Chamber president to suggest who might have the time and interest to lead such an effort (unpaid) while not encumbered by past allegiance and reputations.

Fenton suggested two individuals: a retired corporate executive and Fritz Hamilton, a retired executive from a large New England public utility. Fenton recommended Hamilton as his first choice and offered to approach him informally. Hamilton responded enthusiastically and came to Tuck in mid-December to meet the researchers for the first time.

Our memories of the meeting are vague (and remarkably poorly documented in our notes) but what we do remember is ambivalence. Hamilton had clearly translated the tentative feeler into a firm commitment. He sold himself to us as the right person for the job, eager and ready to act. He already seemed to have a number of ideas for projects, but we felt that he didn't bear the stigma well of being "hand-picked" by the bank president. He also had a personal style that was more representative of big-city, big business management than small-town, small business management. Hence we were apprehensive, not wanting to commit ourselves firmly to Hamilton. Eventually we decided to take the risk, hoping that his interest and enthusiasm for the position would outweigh suspicions generated by his personal style and his friendship with the bank president.

Feedback Meeting No. 1

The first feedback meeting was held in the new town library. It drew 57 people, representative of many businesses and all the towns in the region. We began by explaining the background of the project and described the similar projects in India and Marysville. Rather than repeat the report in lecture form, we asked the people to generate ideas on the major questions we had identified: what are the major strengths and weaknesses, opportunities and threats of the Riverside region? This gave people a chance to emphasize their own ideas and to paraphrase the report in their own words. We then divided the group into "brainstorming" subgroups to work on ways to capitalize on opportunities and minimize threats. At the end of the meeting Hamilton was introduced by us as someone who had agreed to assume interim coordination of ideas and projects that might result from the brainstorming.

The feedback meeting was extremely well received. People reidentified the strengths and weaknesses, threats and opportunities that we had diagnosed in the report, amplified them, and provided anecdotal evidence of their validity. The meeting and the report received extensive praise from reportorial and editorial coverage in the local newspaper. We were buoyed by the indications that the spirit and content of the report would be successfully implemented.

Feedback Meeting No. 2

In collaboration with Hamilton and several of the original liaison group we developed an agenda. There were a number of goals for the second feedback meeting. The first was to build on the strengths and weaknesses, threats and opportunities that had been identified by the participants at the first meeting. The second was to move from identifying these factors toward some priorities for action. The third was to turn the full initiative for further progress over to the task force to confirm the decreasing role of the Tuck group and the increased responsibility placed on Riverside to manage their own planning process.

Fifty-three people attended the second meeting, most of whom had been at the first meeting. As chairman, Hamilton thanked the newspaper and others for favorable promotion of the meetings and introduced Broehl and Lewicki. We answered questions about the report briefly and amended, as people wished, the lists of strengths and weaknesses originated at the first meeting. Smaller groups of 10 to 12, jointly led by Tuck and Riverside people, then reviewed these lists and assigned priorities to the five most important short-range projects. It was emphasized that the project should be attainable in the near future in order to begin a "success cycle" of achievements and build the cooperation necessary to pursue more long-run goals. The most significant priority was assigned to "clean up/green up" activities such as roadside rest areas, trash service, and information booths. Zoning and planning were identified as second priority, regional advertising, promotion, and public relations, third, and better coordination among merchants, fourth.

Hamilton assumed responsibility for directing the remainder of the meeting. Once the priorities were identified, the "task force" model was suggested to commence work on action alternatives. Twenty-four volunteers, including some people who had been a part of the original liaison group, but not the most active leaders, agreed to serve. A meeting was set for 10 A.M. the next day (a remarkably short time). Broehl, Hornsby, and Lewicki, as they headed home that snowy night, thought that they had achieved a second major success in implementation, one that would be free of the frustration and intergroup rivalry that had plagued the early stages of implementation in Marysville.

Initial Meetings of the Task Force

Because of the one-hour driving distance, winter traveling conditions, and the desire to let the Riverside group operate under their own head of steam, we did not attend the 10 o'clock meeting. We had talked to Hamilton before the second feedback meeting, and he had described the hopes and plans he had for the task force. We felt that perhaps Hamilton was much too organized for the fledgling group. One of Hamilton's first acts was to send a letter to all participants in the study in which he summarized the two feedback meetings. He indicated that at the first task force meeting the group reflected strong concern for the energy crisis and its implications for gasoline availability and tourist traffic in the region. This was the first mention of gasoline scarcity as a critical regional problem, although it had been a national problem in the preceding months.

We attended the second task force meeting two weeks after the feedback meeting. Subcommittees had been organized and were already working: merchants committee on projected gasoline availability, beautification committee on town clean up and improvement of individual businesses, promotion committee on attracting tourism to the region and publishing a business directory, and other projects. After the meeting Fenton nevertheless expressed a concern for "getting things moving." "Fritz is great orator," he said, "but I'm not sure how he will be at getting action out of the task force." Fenton also agreed to recruit better representation of downtown merchants at the next meeting.

We thought we saw some task force progress in the next month. The energy crisis had seized the attention of the group and most of their efforts. A commuter bus service was being planned for the summer to provide local transportation for residents and tourists and to ease the pressure on gasoline, and a system for regular posting of gasoline supplies in town was proposed. Finally, events to attract people to the region—craft fairs, sports car rallies, and autumn foliage tours—were explored. Limited financial backing for publicity and mailing provided by the bank, Chamber of Commerce, and the manufacturing company precluded the immediate need for fund raising. When the question was raised, Hamilton said flatly that fund raising should be left to him. Finally, contact was made with the Town Planning Board.

By early April, however, people were talking about a "revitalization" of the task force. Although our evidence is incomplete and anecdotal, the following problems were present:

First, it often appeared that the only planning being done was on projects Hamilton considered important. Moreover, Hamilton heavily controlled the process of task force meetings: the amount of discussion time allowed, the delegation of "assignments," and the assumption of responsibility for taking action between meetings, enlisting volunteers, and so on.

Second, in spite of Hamilton's directive style at meetings, he was, in fact, a weak leader. Further, like those in the Chamber, some of the leaders of the task force were semiretired executives who drew their incomes from pensions and annuities. They seemed to assume their positions of leadership more for the prestige and status they would gain in the community than because their own businesses depended on them.

Third, each task force meeting was concerned with the report of only one committee; members of other committees did not attend or did not participate in discussion. Attendance dwindled rapidly from 20 plus at the first meeting to five or six at later meetings.

Fourth, acting as an arm of the Chamber of Commerce, the task force diluted its own goals and the activities of the Chamber. Hamilton often talked pejoratively in private about the elected officials of the Chamber and there was some indication that the feelings were mutual. Hamilton seemed to want to compete with the Chamber and to implement plans independent of them rather than in conjunction with them. As a result, community membership seemed to "line up" informally in groups. The downtown merchants, perceived as a monolithic power structure by other businessmen, did not attend task force meetings. Problems were compounded by the 10 A.M. meeting time, when most full-time businessmen were deeply involved in their own affairs. The meetings did attract a number of seasonal and "marginal" businessmen from the community, but these people were not in a position to implement action plans or to exert pressure on key people. An event that may have inflamed some of this competitiveness was the task force's attempt to suggest clean up and modernization of certain downtown businesses. In contrast, downtown merchants saw themselves as "holding back," waiting for the task force to catch fire before taking part. This action was attributable in a way to the Tuck intervention, but because these merchants were the principal change agents in the community, the act of holding back undermined task force effectiveness. Merchants came to see the task force as "all talk, no action." And it was true—the task force had no tangible achievements to claim as victories. It had undertaken extensive planning efforts, but little joint, public, visible, team-building action.

Even given the gasoline crisis and other "threats" identified in the feedback report, each merchant seemed to have an excuse for disengaging himself from the task force (or even the Chamber). Occasional requests came to the Tuck group to help "revitalize," "kick," or "rejuvenate" the task force and we discussed these pressures, but because they had come from neither the leadership of the task force nor the Chamber and because of our own waning commitment no intervention was made.

In mid-May Hamilton announced that most of the short-range programs—beautification, merchants committee, public relations, advertising, and promotion—were well under way in coordination with the Chamber of Commerce or other service organizations in the region. (In reality, most of these projects had died in transition, been coopted by the Chamber, or been opposed as impractical or unfeasible—e.g., the bus service and the directory of merchants) "So now we are turning our attention to the long-range objectives," Hamilton announced. "The four major ones are (1) planning and zoning, (2) schools, (3) housing, and (4) industry."

Clearly, not only were these problems long-range but most of them were the responsibility of town and state governmens, not a volunteer group of businessmen. Hamilton went on to say that each of these committees was preparing reports and surveys, that he was about to take a month's vacation in Europe, and that the president of the Chamber of Commerce would chair the task force in his absence.

A telephone call from Hamilton in early July indicated that he was "now ready to get back to work" after his European trip. The Chamber president had done little with the task force in Hamilton's absence. A number of new projects and ideas were discussed on his return, but there was no evidence of action that could be credited to the task force. One of the local ski areas had been sold at a foreclosure auction, the gas crisis eased a little without any noticeable influence from the Riverside community, and no significant action was taken on appearance, traffic flow, parking, or cooperation among downtown merchants and public officials. Hamilton's reputation as a "talker, not a doer" continued. Although many of the influential people felt that the community somehow needed a "revitalization" from the Tuck School group, no one was sure what our point of entry should be nor whom we should work with. Hornsby left Tuck School to begin his career in business. Broehl and Lewicki, discouraged and exhausted by their two years of effort, believed that there was no clear mandate from the Chamber or the task force to take any specific action. Hence we decided not to intervene formally in Riverside in any way to "restimulate" the planning effort that had begun so optimistically six months before. No further contact was made with members of the Riverside community.

ANALYSIS OF THE EFFORTS—"SUCCESS" VERSUS "FAILURE"

Marysville and Riverside can be compared in a variety of ways. The intent is to discover the reasons for a generally successful intervention in Marysville and an unsuccessful one in Riverside. Before we analyze these two cases in detail a few introductory qualifications are needed. First, the interventionists want to clarify that the terms "success" and "failure" apply to the *implementation* stage of the efforts in Riverside and Marysville. All of our analysis and reflection suggests that the Riverside intervention broke down during the "transfer of control" from the Tuck people to the Riverside community. Although some factors may be traceable to our earlier decisions, our analysis focuses on the critical aspects of the "transfer of control" period. Moreover, we wish to note that the terms "success" and "failure" are applied to Marysville and Riverside in *relative* terms. Not everything about Riverside was a failure and not everything about Marysville was a success, but the weight of the evidence makes the terms success and failure generally useful. Finally, before we begin to explore the multifaceted dimensions of the Riverside breakdown, it is important to note that in both communities the survey feedback style of intervention proved to be a successful and viable model. Although we believe that we could refine some elements of this process in future community interventions, the critical events were similar to the application of survey feedback to traditional organizations (Hornstein, Bunker, Burke, Gindes, and Lewicki, 1971).

Entry

The primary function of this process was to begin the sensing of town problems for questionnaire design, to gain legitimacy and rapport with the client, to negotiate expectations and services with the client, and to serve as the initial point of contact for discussion of strategy and tactics.

Instrument Design and Data Collection

The key to success in this phase was the understanding of the most significant local issues and techniques for assessing them in interviews and questionnaires. We also collected a significant amount of other information in our study. Because one of us had a research interest in the entrepreneurial development of small businessmen, large amounts of data were collected on individual businesses that were never fed back to the community. Although much of this information was unrelated to the community change project, we found that small businessmen enjoyed talking about the history and development of their businesses and that these personal discussions produced candid opinions of the community and its problems. Had we not been interested in this information, we probably would have sampled attitudes on the business community rather than depending on questionnaire/interview contacts of the entire population. On the other hand, we also believe that the concern and interest we showed in individual businessmen enabled us to obtain much more information than expected from these normally taciturn and tight-lipped New Englanders.

Data Feedback

This process required a cooperative liaison committee to plan meetings that would draw people out where they could ask questions and encourage the belief that their ideas had potential for influential changes in the community. In both towns we believe that we successfully overcame initial community apathy and resistance by securing large turnouts at the meetings, by getting good editorial coverage in the local press, and by inviting large numbers of previously "uninvolved" businessmen and residents to the early meetings of the task force. In addition, community reactions indicated that we had successfully identified the community's most critical problems. Moreover, although we had suggested strategies for change that were not totally supported, our recommendations provided an excellent focus for discussion on ways to meet the short- and long-run challenges.

Given the generally smooth success in the entry, diagnosis, data collection, and feedback processes, what contributed to the initial uncertainty about progress in both communities and resulted in success in Marysville and failure in Riverside? In this analysis we try to identify the major differences in the communities, in the strategy and tactics of the interventionists, and in the effectiveness of the implementation processes as they contributed to the different outcomes.

Differences Between Riverside and Marysville

Some differences were apparent between the areas that we studied. First, Marysville was a larger community. It had two banks (rather than one), a much more cosmopolitan weekly newspaper, a large main street that offered more comprehensive services, and more full-time businessmen. It also had two large manufacturing employers (rather than one) and a broader employment base, for residents commuted to nearby towns for employment in manufacturing and tourist or other related industries.

These differences between Marysville and Riverside reflect Shapero's (1975) distinction between the "dynamic community" and the "in-migrant trap," two patterns of business ownership that relate to economic growth. The dynamic community is an environment in which a number of systems of reasonably equal power interact with one another—banks, small industries, and the diversified small businesses of Marysville. The in-migrant trap, on the other hand, is an environment in which one large employer or firm develops a number of satellite support systems, hence minimizes diversity and maximizes dependence on the single dominant figure. Because recent research seems to favor the dynamic community model as more favorable to stimulating entrepreneurship and economic growth, it is possible to understand how the single manufacturer, single bank, and centralized undiversified services of downtown Riverside could stifle growth and change by virtue of these characteristics alone (c.f. Broehl, 1977, for a fuller treatment of these issues).

Moreover, it must be remembered that the Riverside intervention was "regional": our efforts were continually directed at the town of Riverside *and* the six or seven small towns around the lake. These towns often had no more than a general store, a gas station, and a few tourist cabins, too small for a "critical mass" as a community. Because some of the small towns at the farthest end of the lake were closer to other business centers, Riverside itself was not the geographical center of the region, and only the economic or "psychological" center in the way people defined the area (e.g., the region was more commonly known by the name of the lake, not the town).

Most of the business around the lake was seasonal—tourist accommodations, restaurants, and marinas. This seasonality implied that their proprietors were also seasonal businessmen. They were sometimes family businesses, closed for the winter. Because the owners often moved to a warmer climate, they were only peripheral members of the central business community. These men lacked the "hard" business skills necessary to run a dynamic enterprise. These characteristics have several important implications. First, the Riverside intervention attempted to coalesce a group of businessmen whose collective sense of geographical identity, interdependence, and mutual fate was probably lower than in Marysville—we say probably because we have no quantitative measure of these factors in either community. Given the well-known relationship between environmental characteristics such as physical location and buildings and its relation to organizational identity and growth (Steele 1969), we can understand that collective identity and mutual fate would be harder to perceive in Riverside than in Marysville.

Second, because most of Riverside's businesses were smaller in volume and number of employees, business owners were also proprietors and needed to devote full time to their own. Seasonal business owners had somewhat more available time, particularly in the winter months (when our program implementation began). As a result, the more peripheral businessmen were the most active in the early stages of the task force. The "establishment" remained in the background during that time, but this group controlled the informal power structure of the community and the largest businesses, the bank, and the Chamber of Commerce. More importantly, they were the people who knew how to organize and run things in town; as a result of their managerial knowledge, they were officials in the town government and most active in civic and public school affairs. Hence the task force group not only represented the marginal commitment of part-time businessmen but was generally devoid of expertise on "how to get things done in Riverside." They lacked cohesiveness because of the diverse representation of the whole lake region and had no direct ties to the central informal power structure of the business community.

It should not be implied that the downtown merchants ever intentionally blocked the efforts of the task force. In fact, the major downtown merchants, the most significant group in the Chamber of Commerce, were the central core of the liaison committee during the design and data collection phases. They also agreed with us that during the implementation of any action steps the working group should include seasonal businessmen who were not Chamber members. Hamilton, speaking at a meeting of the Chamber of Commerce the morning after the first feedback meeting, stressed the importance of the Chamber's support and enthusiastically received it from the group. But the nature of the task force's membership, influenced by the interventionist's request to the insiders to hold back active involvement, and ultimately epitomized by Hamilton's leadership, created a "toothless" system from the beginning. Differences of opinion, lack of discretion, a feeling of powerlessness, and significant overlap in future projects between the two groups led the Chamber in a quiet way to absorb the task force that spring.

Factors Related to Community Implementation of the Task Force

The geographic factors, the regional emphasis, the involvement of many peripheral businessmen, and the failure to include the downtown business leaders in the task force set the stage for the events that followed. In this section we try to assess the factor that contributed to an initially successful call for volunteers for the task force (more so in Riverside than Marysville) but to a reverse in the trends as the implementation proceeded. Two factors stand out: Hamilton's style of leadership in Riverside as opposed to Post's in Marysville and the types of problem that were selected by the task forces in their early meetings in both communities.

Leadership Styles of Hamilton and Post. Hamilton and Post clearly demonstrated leadership styles that contributed to the differential effectiveness of the task forces. Post was an important businessman in the central business district. As a proprietor of a store on Main Street, he was a full-time resident, but had moved to Marysville only a few years before. He was central to the business district in location but not so long a resident that he had built up an informal reputation or become entrenched in the problems of the town. His own business stood to profit in an almost direct relation to the efforts of the task force. He was well known, well liked, and a peer of most of the other community leaders.

Hamilton, on the other hand, was a retired executive whose age, relation to the business community, and orientation to problems clearly made him a "marginal" member. Although he had lived in Riverside for a number of years—first as a summer visitor, then full time—his experience had been in the management of large public utilities. He had no experience as a small businessman but thought he understood their problems. In an environment in which experience was important to acceptance by the other businessmen, Hamilton could not pass the test. Moreover, he was not well known in the community, had no financial stake in the success of task force efforts, and was probably motivated most by the public service opportunity the job would offer, the increased prestige it might gain him among full-time residents, and his own need to feel productive in his retired years.

These differences in the background and "centrality" to the informal community organization were magnified by the styles of exerting leadership of these men. Post was ambivalent about his leadership of the task force, and at least once (that we know of), in a dramatic gesture, tried to resign because of feelings of frustration. His style at meetings was clearly participative; he encouraged others to take responsibility for subcommittees, run meetings, and share in influencing the direction of the task force. Meetings were "collective efforts," and everyone participated in suggesting direction, proposing strategies, and testing alternatives. Post and the group were always at the same point, trying to work as a team, coaxing and helping one another over the rough spots. Although this often became a "group grope," it nonetheless built a collective solidarity and a commitment to maintain the spirit of optimism generated at the feedback meeting.

There was no question that the Riverside task force reflected a style of organization different from Marysville's. Hamilton interpreted his role as initiator, coordinator, and delegator, as well as orchestrator. Perhaps it was the management approach he thought was necessary for this type of group or one he had used successfully in managing a public utility. Perhaps it was his free time, which allowed him the leisure to consider what he thought the town and region needed, hence to try to implement his reflections. We often talked to Hamilton by telephone, and he would muse about his ideas of Riverside's needs; several weeks later we would discover that he had assigned a committee to investigate the idea. After the first few meetings the organizational structure did not allow people who were not on a particular committee to attend and offer their opinions. When problems were encountered—whom to get to fill a chairmanship, how to approach a problem, what action was most needed—Hamilton always had strong ideas. He developed the agenda for the meeting himself, marched the group through it fairly rigorously, and actively contributed his own ideas as each item was discussed. It is not surprising, therefore, that his autocratic control over the task force meetings made them a one-man show.

If Hamilton's more autocratic leadership was not sufficient to minimize the sense of teamwork and cohesiveness in early task force meetings, other factors contributed. Hamilton's own role as a peripheral member of the community made it more difficult for him to know the internal politics of the Riverside community or the people who run them. He often stepped on people's toes in studying a problem because he didn't know whom to go to, how to get the information, or how to test an idea informally with key people before he announced it publicly as a goal of the task force. He often identified important problems, but their solutions were under the control and jurisdiction of other community groups. This created resentment and defensiveness that could not be publicly expressed. Moreover, Hamilton seemed to be more of a "talker" than a "doer"—skilled in knowing how to study the dimensions of a problem but weak when it actually came to implementing solutions. Although it is possible that his lack of skill in implementation could be related to his peripheral role in the community, it is also interesting to speculate on this aspect of his style as it reflected his public utility management experience. Public utilities are often known for their lethargic response to change, often due to ambiguous performance objectives for efficiency or effectiveness. Thus, although Hamilton's early actions appeared productive as committees were organized, all efforts seemed to die when the committees were ready to implement plans.

The Types of Problems Selected. The projects considered by the Riverside task force were in areas in which other groups had already initiated action, had low public visibility, were long-range, or required influence on businessmen who were not centrally involved in the task force. Beautification programs were coordinated with other clean-up groups, which was efficient but gained the task force little recognition. Planning for town fairs in the fall was too far in the future. Attempted leverage on the newspaper (to publish a weekly events calendar and continue active news coverage of the task force) was semicoercive and met with resistance. Concern for the physical appearance of the downtown Riverside area could not be translated into action because few downtown businessmen were on the task force. All in all, few projects were identified which had immediate, visible effects and would create the sense of pride and cohesiveness that apparently was critical to Marysville's success. Most of the projects envisioned benefited only a few people in the region and/or yielded results that were too intangible to establish that time was worthily invested. As a result, the "every man for himself" mentality never changed.

The final factor was that prevailing economic conditions in the spring of 1974—the energy crisis, economic downturn, and the national sense of despair contributed by the death throes of the Nixon presidency—created a mood that was hard to counter. Riverside residents were afraid that the economic conditions would severely hurt the summer outlook for the tourist business. Their fears worsened as gasoline became scarce in the region and all attempts to influence the regional allocation of gasoline failed. The largest manufacturer laid off one-third of his work force as a result of the severe economic downturn, and the final blow was the foreclosure auction of one of the ski areas.

Faced with a pattern of national and regional events that had severe local implications, the task force needed more than ever to work on collective survival. Activities that they chose, however, were coopted by other groups, were too ambiguous or long range to define, or threatened influential businesses and established groups in the community. Moreover, the efforts were designed and pushed by one man who was an "outsider" to the community, who lacked the expertise and credentials in small business management, and whose style was antithetical to the fledgling volunteer organization he was trying to build. There was no teamwork in the task force—it was Hamilton and several other "outsiders"—and when Hamilton took his vacation in Europe in the late spring the task force died a quiet death. Attempts to revive it, under the guise of the Chamber of Commerce, failed in midsummer of 1974.

Failures in the Role of the Interventionists

In our attempts to learn from our comparative success in Marysville and our failure in Riverside several action steps on the part of the intervention team must be defined as less than optimal. We say "less than optimal" because we were aware that the decision was important at the time; we considered alternatives that on hindsight would have been preferable and chose strategies or tactics that, also on hindsight, actively contributed to the failure process. We believe that others can learn from these failures, although in many cases we also believe that the issues will always remain fuzzy and imprecise, given the community environment in which we are operating.

Failure to Confront the Power Structure in Riverside. The decision to set up a task force, outside the organizational structure of the Chamber of Commerce, was dictated by our success with this model in Marysville. In that town steps were taken to circumvent the ineffective leadership and reputation of the Chamber, and the action took place in a tense but reasonably open discussion at the feedback meetings. The reputation of the Chamber was discussed, the consequences of locating the task force under the Chamber umbrella was openly explored, and the task force developed as a rival group with energetic new leadership.

The process of creating the task force and its leadership in Riverside can best be described as a collusive political subterfuge by the intervention team in the style of old-time back-room politics. Hornsby argued, on the basis of his extensive interviews (and as the closest to feeling the pulse of the Riverside community), that any change effort would die if the "establishment" became actively engaged. People would assume it was the same old group with the same old ideas and few new people would volunteer. Broehl and Lewicki argued that it was presumptuous on the part of the intervention team to exclude systematically some of the central figures or to determine who would serve on the task force and in what capacity. As a team we had been approached by the top leaders of the Riverside community and had asked them to serve on the liaison committee for data collection. How were we going to ask them to refrain from helping to reap the fruits of our labors?

Our decision on this problem set the stage for the unfortunate chain of events that followed. Hornsby's arguments prevailed, particularly because of credibility generated by his closeness to the community during the data collection. We suggested to members of the "establishment" that data from the interviews required new patterns of involvement in a wider area of the business community. This created concern about leadership for the new group and initiated the procedures by which Fenton "handpicked" Hamilton. When we met Hamilton and watched him at the feedback meetings, we knew that his style was going to be a problem, but he had been handpicked by a person we trusted and his enthusiasm made it next to impossible to deem him unacceptable for the job.

We felt that we had to act to avert implementation failure because the "same old group" would take control. What we did not consider was that we probably needed to involve this same old group if any successful implementation was to be had. Moreover, we failed to remember a lot of the actions Post had taken in Marysville. Not only had his emergence as leader been determined by the community but his leadership style also turned out to be critical. He had constituted most of the committees as amalgamations of Chamber people and new volunteers. He had constantly worked to build a team rather than to be highly structured and initiating in his own leadership. He and the task force had come to us constantly for advice and counsel; we probably had some continuing influence on his management style and tactics.

In contrast, once we had colluded with the community establishment in the process of picking Hamilton, we did little to influence his leadership style. Although we felt that this influence was unnecessary and undesirable, given our commitment to decreased involvement, a clash of other motivations was certainly attributable. Perhaps we felt guilty about having chosen him; perhaps we wanted to disassociate ourselves from him in case he flopped; perhaps, once we had decided to handpick leadership, we should have done a more thorough search, or our fatigue after two years of OD work allowed more slippage than was desirable. Perhaps we should have worried less about where the leadership would come from and more about what personnel were represented on the task force. Perhaps we should have directed the client toward a joint committee of insiders and outsiders. All of these alternatives make extremely good sense in hindsight not only because they might have contributed to success but because they would have solved the most important problem in the business community: intragroup relations between the insider-outsider subgroups.

Two important bridges to social psychological theory are useful here because action implications from existing OD theory are not available. The first issue relates to the team-building functions of conflict. On the one hand, recent authors (Deutsch, 1969; Janis, 1972; Harvey, 1974) have argued that intragroup conflict is integral to effective decision making; conflict minimization leads to lower quality decisions. Can teams be built without conflict? Can high quality performance be obtained by a group that organizes in harmony rather than in tension? If we had built a "representative" task force from various constituencies, would we be more likely to have a political body, compromising and qualifying ideas in shifting coalitions that might emasculate their effectiveness, or would we generate productive conflict and better decisions? In Riverside we tried to achieve task-force effectiveness by averting conflict over power relations and Chamber ineffectiveness. In Marysville we were relieved that the task force seemed to be effective in spite of the continued tension between it and the Chamber. In hindsight, however, assets may have been liabilities and liabilities, assets. The role of the substance, type, and mode of resolution of conflict as it contributes to team building and effectiveness rather than to team fractionalization and ineffectiveness is not sufficiently clarified for us or for most organization development practitioners.

The second theoretical issue relates to the first: can the differences in leadership style between Post and Hamilton be related to more general theories about the appropriate leadership style for this type of group? Hersey and Blanchard (1972) propose that individual leadership styles (degrees of task orientation and people orientation) can be related to leadership effectiveness by knowing something about the goals of the group and the maturity of the followers. (Maturity is defined by the level of achievement motivation, willingness and ability to take responsibility, and task-relevant education of the followers.) In both towns the short-run goals of the task force were to build a cohesive and optimistic organization, primarily by the experience of working together on short-run action projects. The long-range goal, obviously, was to have a strong impact on the overall cooperative development of the business community. The followership was of "average" maturity—moderately motivated for success, moderately willing to take responsibility, and moderately experienced in working on business problems. By the Hersey and Blanchard model, therefore, a high task and high relationship leadership style is necessary to build team relations and cohesiveness as well as to begin the short-range goal setting accomplishment cycle.

This style clearly describes Post's behavior in Marysville. Hamilton, on the other hand, seemed to be much less concerned with team building and relationship issues. His more autocratic control of the agenda and direction of the task force underestimated and minimized the sophistication of his task force members and probably turned some of them off; moreover, because he did not have the personal clout to implement any of his own plans, he could not count on others to help him; hence the resources of the task force members were totally underutilized.

From this description of leadership style one might conclude that a high task-high relationship leadership style is most appropriate for this kind of community leadership. We, like Hersey and Blanchard, would caution against this overgeneralization without serious consideration of the maturity and expectations of followers and the short- and long-range goals of the group. It is quite clear that the type of leadership style is absolutely essential to the efforts of new change implementation groups. Much more precise derivations of theory are necessary to help the practitioner specify the particular contingencies in any situation and the style of leadership desirable given those contingencies.

Who is the Client? As most OD consultants know who have worked with voluntary organizations, the participation and commitment of the members are often at the root of major problems. The willingness of members to invest energy and time is directly traceable to the involvement and feelings of satisfaction that they derive from organizational activities. In many communities the most committed and effective volunteers are often in demand to serve in many organizations. Dropping one organization for another, or dropping out of volunteer work altogether, is a common way in which individuals decide not to confront conflict, stress, or ineffectiveness in a particular voluntary system.

When attempting to build community organizations, the problems of voluntary membership in systems are magnified by the ambiguity of defining "who is the client." Is the consultant working for the group who helped him to come to the community? Is he working for the individual or group who may be paying for the research or consulting services? What happens if payment is being derived from outside grant support? Is the consultant working for that group who will probably be most capable or responsible for the implementation? If the contact, financing, and implementation groups are different, if they do not represent a formal system or community power hierarchy and disagree among themselves, to whom is the consultant to listen and how does he determine what is "best" for the community?

Defining the client is an extremely important problem in this kind of intervention. When the client is ambiguous because he changes from entry to implementation or because he may represent (at any stage) only part of the totality of people to be affected by the intervention, the interventionist is often left to his own intuitions to guide him through the roughest stages of implementation.

As interventionists we believe on the one hand that a stance of "planned ambiguity" was a valid one to take. We would resist attempts to be more specific about defining the client in the future before gaining a thorough knowledge of the community and its problems. We cannot spell out in advance the areas in which the interventionist should make decisions on his own, collaborate with certain community members, or let the community survive or fail on the basis of their own ability to seize the initiative. The client may have to be changed during the term of the intervention, and interventionists may have to renegotiate their relationship as the constituency changes. We may also have to learn that we can do too much for a client, particularly to "protect him from himself"; we probably should have let the Riverside task force emerge on the political floor of the feedback meetings, as it did in Marysville, rather than making back-room deals to create an image of an open and seeemingly united group.

It has become clear to us that the typical model of an OD interventionist (e.g., Argyris, 1970; Hornstein et al., 1971) has to be liberally spiced with the philosophy and tactics of the community organizer (Alinsky, 1971; Huenefeld, 1970). As interventionists we were the experts on the data and also on how to mobilize collective efforts. The weaknesses and threats to the communities were long-range and diffuse (as were the strengths and opportunities), and action could not be trusted to existing agencies. In many ways we *did* know what was best for the community and we had to be active and assertive in providing the energy and direction for change. This created the most ambivalence for us during the action phase.

Withdrawal from the Intervention. We felt most comfortable as interventionists during the diagnostic, data collection, and feedback phases; the methodology was known to us; we felt secure in our roles and we were clearly the experts. Contracting for these services, and carrying them out, proved to be no problem in either community.

When we moved to the transfer of initiative to the community and the long-term responsibility for carrying it out, the ambivalence of both interventionists and clients was apparent. We wanted to have positive things happen, as they did. We knew what kinds of action steps would probably lead to productive and satisfying outcomes and they agreed to our model. We wanted them to be successful, but we knew it had to come from their own initiative and control over the process, not ours. Like a parent teaching a child to talk, we constantly faced the tension between letting go and hanging on.

We had experienced much of this tension in Marysville in the early stages, as the task force grappled with projects, leadership, and relations with the Chamber and learning to develop its own identity. The task force developed its own integrity by having successfully survived that difficult maturation period, and to continue the parental analogy we constantly debated whether we should refrain or reenter during the more difficult periods (or be invited by the task force) in order to provide guidance and direction.

In Riverside our protectiveness got the better of us. We thought we knew how to create successful implementation without the stress and conflict. So we passed the control of the intervention from ourselves to a person much like ourselves in outlook: benevolent, parentally protective, and believing he knew what was best for the community; but his style of leadership repressed the development of initiative and teamwork by the task force and it never developed the self-esteem or cohesiveness to survive on its own.

What We Learned from These Interventions

As in any single case (or even the comparison between two cases), specifying "what was learned" has to be a somewhat tentative process. Nevertheless we feel that we can draw several conclusions.

First, following the research by Shapero and others, we learned that a community or region like Riverside may not have the environmental qualities that lend themselves to stimulating community development and eventually economic growth. The characteristics of "in-migrant trap" environments—a single large employer, monolithic community power structure, lack of diversity in goods and services—may simply require significantly different types of strategy to bring about change. Moreover, Riverside may have lacked the "critical mass" of people necessary to build a base for this type of change; we have already mentioned the lack of skilled labor force and the relative size of the town compared with Marysville. Finally, we might have learned whether the residents of the various satellite towns around the lake considered *themselves* as a region. Several of the towns at the far end of the lake tended to go to other larger communities for services. Hence we may have defined a region of towns as interdependent and usefully united but all of the towns may not necessarily have agreed.

We learned that our efforts to select the leadership of the Riverside task force actively contributed to the failure. What is unclear to us is how much of the failure is accountable to the *way* in which we picked Hamilton and how much to his *style of leadership*. We are not prepared to say that we would never again attempt to influence leadership selection, particularly in community-based interventions. We have no indication that the process of selection itself actually turned people off. Most seemed to be willing to give Hamilton a try, the "establishment" was willing to back off, and there appeared to be no feelings strong enough to inhibit people from volunteering for the early task force efforts.

In our view the more significant problems in Hamilton's leadership did relate to his style. We have just argued that our actions to appoint him leader may even have helped his initial credibility, but he was also an "outsider" to the business community and, more significantly, he adopted a leadership style that was inappropriate to the needs of the task force. One conclusion we can draw is that if we decide to become involved in the process of selecting leadership we ought to be unconflicted about doing the job thoroughly. We felt guilty and ambivalent enough about our actions to back off once Hamilton had been selected, even though we strongly suspected his style would be a problem. This abandonment probably contributed more to the eventual failure of the implementation than if we had considered what the characteristics of an effective task force leader should be and systematically interviewed people for the position.

I am not sure that we can draw a specific conclusion about the desirability of allowing a "floor fight," similar to the discussions in Marysville, on the intergroup relations problem in Riverside. Perhaps our own doubts are related to personal tendencies of conflict avoidance or to our ambiguity about which client system we should be serving. Perhaps we should have used a more public forum to ask the "establishment" to remain in the background. Perhaps we should have been more explicit about our previous discussions with them when we had the feedback meeting. In this way they could have discussed the terms of their involvement more fully with the new task force than we allowed by our backstage manipulations.

A number of scenarios were possible, each of which would have surfaced the perceived tension between the groups and allowed more discussion of it. What we are saying, however, is that it was not totally clear to us that this action by itself would have accounted for the significant differences in the impact of the Tuck task force.

CONCLUSION

Changing, Erring, and Learning

DONALD N. MICHAEL
PHILIP H. MIRVIS

We are in increasing danger of acting as if we know what we were doing when we don't—and then not being able to bear the consequences of having erred.

Robert Biller
Converting Knowledge into Action

This book, in which its many contributors have acknowledged the errors of unsuccessful change efforts and have proposed to learn from such errors openly and experimentally, is itself a response to the changes occurring in our traditional belief system. Of particular relevance to our concerns herein are the changes in that part of the belief system, and in its criteria for competence, that are encouraging us to embrace our errors and to learn their lessons. Central to our interests are the emerging beliefs about predictability and control in social endeavors and their relation to new standards of personal and organizational competence.

Nevertheless, the examination of unsuccessful change efforts and changes in the prevailing belief system remains a threatening and dis-

We would like to thank Dennis Perkins and Clayton Alderfer for their helpful comments.

tressing activity. This examination repudiates the old beliefs, and because we are only beginning to learn to accept our errors and to conduct ourselves as learners a future without the comfort of the old belief system provokes anxiety.* But its dissolution also carries the excitement of new potentials and new ways of self- and organization development. In order to appreciate the need for and the possibilities of the emerging belief system it is necessary to consider how our conventional beliefs have limited learning in the field of organization development and change.

OUR BELIEFS ABOUT SCIENCE, TECHNOLOGY, AND THE CONTROL OF CHANGE

Conventional organizational behavior and organization development activities both derive from and subscribe to the Western belief that knowledge is power; that is, knowledge makes possible *prediction* and technique (skill based on knowledge), in turn, leads to *control*. Therefore a *competent* person or organization is able to use knowledge to predict and control.

Sustaining this belief and sustained by it are certain other premises about the nature of reality. Central is the belief that reality is comprised of discrete objects and events, interacting in sequences that can be understood as chains of *causes* and *effects*. Expressed otherwise, these are means and ends or problems and solutions. As such the world can be sorted into parts and, one by one or in aggregates, the parts can be studied and their actions, predicted and ultimately controlled. Therefore one can alter effects by controlling the causes; one can solve problems by applying the "right" solution. This is a linear view of reality, a view optimistically transposed from the scientist's laboratory, in which the object of attention is disconnected from the rest of reality into the real world, where instead everything connects to everything else (Whitehead, 1947). Tacitly or explicitly, this positivist view of reality implies that it is feasible to make unilateral interven-

* We are using "belief system" in the same way others have used the word "myth"; that is, "the set of stories, images, and symbols by which human perceptions, attitudes, values and actions are given shape and significance. . . . In order to identify the myths of one's own culture . . . it is sufficient to ask: 'What constitutes my culture's sense of reality' " (Novak, 1970, pp. 16–17). For a more complete discussion of the social psychological aspects of "error embracing" and "living with uncertainty," see Michael (1973) on long-range social planning and future-responsive societal learning.

tions that will have specific and, therefore, circumscribed outcomes.*

Our most frequent experience, which until recently has seemed to many to verify this belief, has been the application of *physical technology,* itself presumably the product of, and a prerequisite for, prediction and control. DDT, for example, was developed from knowledge of the impact of certain chemical compounds on insect metabolism. It was designed to control particular insect populations. And it worked —except that it resulted in a host of equally if not more serious problems, including larger human populations, DDT-resistant insect mutations, and "silent springs." These results were unintended or ignored on the presumption that later technological "fixes" would solve them. This presumption remains unfulfilled because the positivist idea that things can be altered one at a time simply is not adequate in the real world of living things, much less of human beings.

Nonetheless, this belief system has also been evident in our expectations for *social technology* which are premised on the assumption that human behavior is just a subset of natural behavior; that is, a part of the natural (physical) universe. Thus it, too, is encompassable and comprehendable by scientific epistomology and methodology. Consequently human behavior is, in principle, expected to be predictable and controllable.

It follows, then, that knowledge-based interventions in the human situation should be able to produce predictable changes in behavior. From this same perspective evaluations should be able to clarify and verify how the changes came about; that is, what causes produced which effects. (It is ironic that these expectations have faced so little challenge, in important part because so few evaluations have in fact been undertaken. Consequently, there has been little disconfirming evidence: the assumption has simply persisted, buttressed by the power of the prevailing belief system.)

As a result of these beliefs, failure to produce the desired change in behavior is interpreted as a failure of knowledge, either in its substance or in its skilled application. Error, the failure to bring about the

* The subject-predicate syntax of our language makes it difficult and awkward to write in a way that avoids imparting linear, cause-effect, time-bound relationships. In reflecting on what follows, it is necessary to keep in mind that the circumstances we review play into one another and transform one another, as plucking one strand of a net alters the relationship of all the others, and these alterations, in turn, alter the plucked strand. Such is the human condition: contrary to the hopes of social scientists subscribing to the Newtonian-Aristotelian view of reality, cause and effect are not linear, nor are human beings the sum of discrete and independent "variables." One can start anywhere with these circumstances and find the others ineluctably implicated.

desired change, implies the threat of loss of control of the environment, of other people, and of one's self. This last threat is usually implicit: it arises from applying the positivist's view of the world described above to one's view of one's self. Consequently, errors are evidence of incompetence: they demonstrate an inability to apply knowledge and exercise control.

Although the benefits of this belief system have long been recognized, the costs for our complex world are becoming evident to growing numbers of people, including some concerned with the practice and results of OD—as the fact of this book demonstrates. Recognition of the costs of this belief system are both a consequence of its disintegration and a contributor to its transformation. Let us look, then, at the increasingly acknowledged costs of the conventional beliefs that are of particular relevance for the reconstruction of OD.

Costs of the Conventional Beliefs

In the first place there is growing recognition that the secondary and tertiary consequences of the interactions of technology with the rest of our turbulent society make prediction of the impact of all externalities impossible. We lack concepts for predicting the outcomes of emergent situations; that is, those situations whose outcomes are more than the sum of the "parts" that generated them.* Specifically, this means that in societal situations like ours, which are emerging into new but unspecifiable structures, we are unable to control the processes of change, and we are unable to predict the consequences of our efforts to control them. This is amply evident when we consider the history of our efforts to desegregate schooling; it is also evident when we attempt to foresee the social consequences of an energy control policy. To borrow a term from medicine, our efforts to control society tend to be iatrogenic: the solution to one problem produces new problems. Awareness of this situation is further heightened by the growing empirical evidence of our inability to control fundamental aspects of our society such as poverty, crime, and birth rate. That the benefits of "hard" and "soft" technology bring their unanticipated

* The same situation pertains in the physical sciences, but in that situation turbulent systems tend to self-destruct or go to equilibrium. So, even though the transition processes cannot be modeled, the outcomes are predictable. In human situations today it is precisely the transition processes that are important because we live in and by them (Polanyi, 1966).

costs both exacerbates the task of social control and mitigates the persuasiveness of the belief system in which the promise of technological progress plays so central a role.

In the second place there is, among thoughtful people and, in particular, among social scientists, an increasing appreciation of the limits of the conventional positivist epistemology for describing the human condition and the imperative need for a new perspective that goes beyond the one that emphasizes prediction and control (Maslow, 1969). There is a growing acceptance that values and subjectivity are inextricably embedded in the definitions we give to our situations—the social reality we attend to—as well as in the research we do regarding that reality, the data we interpret, the interpretations we make, and the interventions we undertake (Vickers, 1965). There is increasing recognition that the specification of a social problem depends in its very formulation on our views of what constitutes a solution (Rittle and Webber, 1972). All these "social realities" are infinitely far away from the "scientific reality" of the laboratory in which the encapsulation of time, human choices, variables, and options frequently engenders replicable quantitative data at the cost of applicability to the real and murky world.

What is more, there is an appreciation that because the real world context is not completely specifiable, hence is unpredictable to an unknown degree, humans always have options, always have the potential for becoming other than what they seem.* Their efforts to realize their potential, however, are only partly dependent on conscious choices; they depend in part on unconscious processes that profoundly influence what they choose to become. An acceptance of the importance of these unconscious processes compliments the growing recognition of what most other cultures have always known but ours has mostly suppressed for some 300 years: production, consumption, and rational reason are not enough to sustain a humane world nor are the models emphasizing such characteristics sufficient for understanding human behavior, much less for controlling it. Other human attributes and needs—the extrarational and the irrational—are enormously powerful. They show themselves sooner or later constructively or destructively and in ways beyond the predictable and independent of the

* The influence of unconscious processes on what we call conscious behavior is a major barrier to predicting and controlling human behavior on the basis of the knowledge derived exclusively from the positivist scientific mode of thinking. This barrier is neatly exemplified by our inability to predict or control creativity. This human activity, which by definition breaks through prediction and control, takes place in what is called the unconscious.

forces of control. In other words, no accumulation of aggregated or probabilistic statements can subsume all crucial aspects of human conduct: our times are replete with examples of humans dealing with their existential situations in ways that transcend past or average descriptions and that go beyond what can be predicted or controlled.

In the third place there is growing recognition of the personal and social costs of emulating the macho myth model of maleness—self-disciplined master of one's fate by tough-minded, rational action, accomplished by high-control aspirations and abilities. This model has been especially valued in the managerial and executive worlds and in corporate and governmental bureaucracies. Indeed, the history of complex organizations is a history of males questing for and in some cases attaining control of the natural and human environments. (It is more than symbolic that in the United States the first major stimulus to organizational complexity was the advent of a railroad system that sprawled across a continent. What more "masculine" enterprise could there be than controlling all that hardware and those hard men? And what better symbol of predictability than a railroad timetable—at least in those days?)

Overall, the conditions for organizational growth have been closely associated with the Western view of reality, whose success has been repeatedly demonstrated by proliferating technology, itself almost exclusively a "male form of play" (Henderson, 1976). Such macho-type maleness has been especially appealing and rewarding in organizations.

With the overall decline in the credibility of the Western world view has come a decline in allegiance to the macho model. Although many processes are contributing to this decline, it is sufficient for our purposes to emphasize that a culture that suppresses important parts of the male psyche must provide substantial rewards and strong punishments to maintain that suppression (e.g., status and affluence for compliance; ridicule and ostracism if other characteristics are displayed). And in our society the very success of the Protestant work ethic and its associated ethic of Promethian exploitation of the environment through science and technology is producing a level of affluence, education, and cultural heterogeneity in which the *social costs* of deviating from the macho model are growing smaller and the *personal benefits* of acting it out are growing smaller, as well.

As a result increasing numbers of males are appreciating the unmatched satisfactions of drawing on both sets of characteristics that each of us posseses but that have been conventionally assigned to *either* men or women. For men this means behaving in ways that are more receptive, intuitive, nurturing, and self-permissive and engaging the world more holistically and tentatively. This results in a greater feeling of authenticity and a deeper appreciation of one's limited ability or need to control, along with a greater potential to be open, aware, hence to learn.

In light of all these movements away from the conventional Western belief system, there is a growing recognition that the capacity to control is an insufficient, and often inappropriate, measure of competence. Acknowledgment that the social world is not "given" the way the inanimate world may be is altering our sense of what we must do and can do to guide our lives. It is also altering our sense of what constitutes competent behavior and performance. We are beginning to recognize that errors in *nonroutine* situations are neither shameful nor best responded to by punishment. We are beginning to see that that there is no need to fool ourselves, especially for males to fool themselves, into believing that we ought to be able to control causes to produce predictable and desirable effects. *There is no need to expect that with the application of knowledge and skill things should always turn out right.*

Instead, there is growing recognition that it is necessary and responsible to arrange all our human and organizational resources so they are future-responsive, so that they act in the present out of a concern for the future; that is, the task is to enlarge *awareness* of what is happening and what might happen. This means becoming *learners* as persons and organizations. It means *learning how* to become learners, and to be learners we must become embracers of error. Then, freed from the constraints on imagination, innovation, and commitment engendered by the fear of making mistakes, we can learn from errors—not to be right next time because "next time" in complex human situations will be different, but so that we can accommodate ourselves and our environment by enlarging our understanding and adjusting our behavior as we go along.

Thus the *competent* person is one who designs his or her activities to provide the *maximum amount of feedback* about what is happening in order to detect and respond to errors. Competence, then, is measured not by skill in avoiding errors but by skill in detecting them and in acting on that information openly so that all can continue to learn about where they are and where they might go—about what kind of world we have created for ourselves and what we might do toward recreating it.

It follows that an equally central criterion of competence is *the ability to facilitate learning, error embracing, and awareness in one's self and others.* Such ability, depending as it does on inter- and intrapersonal sensitivity, is incompatible with the macho model of competence.

Now, all this may make sense to the reader from his or her own experiences or in the abstract, but questions arise: "Even if I accept these emerging beliefs, will my clients? Don't most organizations resist learning and not tolerate errors much less error embracing?" To respond to these questions we must review the reasons that organizations have used OD. In doing so we shall also observe the influence of the conventional belief system.

Conventional Incentives for Using OD

Some organizations use OD because others use it—just as many organizations bought computers because it was what others respected or competitive organizations were doing. Some use OD hoping to glean good public relations from it by appearing to be in the vanguard of organizations employing advanced methods to improve productivity or to attain more humane working conditions. Some seek a competitive advantage, anticipating from OD improvements in efficiency and control which, in turn, increase profits, productivity, share of the market, and so on. Some use OD because of the charisma or power of some person or group in the organization who, for whatever reasons, wants to use it and possesses the leverage to do so.

All of these reasons merely sustain the conventional belief system's expectations for and definitions of status, control, and success. They are unsympathetic contexts for experimentation or for the creation of an organizational norm of continual learning. If OD is undertaken for these reasons, it is likely that there is an expected payoff; hence there is a premium on success—on not making errors. Then, if there is no such payoff, if errors occur in prediction or control, the chances are they will be suppressed or ignored rather than learned from—except the lesson: do not hire the same OD agent again.

An organizationally slack situation and its antithesis, crisis, are two other conventional reasons for undertaking OD. Slack means that resources are available for nonroutine activities. For any of the above reasons, then, or for the creative ones discussed below, if there is slack, OD may be undertaken. But slack can breed a sleepy contentment with the present rather than an active engaging of unpredictable futures. Moreover, in this kind of world slack is unlikely to persist, and the OD activities themselves may well remove this condition.

In a crisis, when organizational circumstances are desperate, OD may be turned to in the hope of transforming the situation. The costs of failure are such, however, that those sponsoring the OD will be looking for certain payoffs, not experiments or learning. Survival must come first. There are exceptions, of course, but the strong tendency in a crisis is to revert to previously learned successful behavior and that means also reverting to its associated belief system.

All of the above motives may transcend themselves and lead the organization to error-embracing, learning behavior, but as a rule they are not accompanied by conditions that provide the persistance needed for learning from error. In the situations described an organization can settle for whatever gains are produced by the OD effort without examining closely what was learned and how it might be further applied. If the effort does not produce the expected payoff, the organization usually cuts its losses because it is deemed too costly, financially and psychologically, to learn from the "failure."

New Incentives for Using OD

The decline of the conventional belief system, however; is stimulating some organizations—or, more precisely, some people in them—to look to OD in a spirit compatible with a learning mode. Clients, as members of this society, are more or less subject to the same currents of change as those discussed above (Yankelovitch, 1975). Indeed, given their range of exposures, change may be occurring faster among clients than among change agents! The process is dialectical: not all clients are changing but the overall interorganizational and interpersonal setting is changed by the fact that some are altering their norms and behavior.*

What seems to be required is charismatic leadership, based on the belief that, "I think I know how we should be organized but we're going to have to learn how to get there" or "I don't know how we should be organized but I do know that the way we're organized now is not fulfilling my expectations." (Such leadership can come from individuals or groups at whatever level in the organization; it need not be located "at the top".) Both of these beliefs recommend OD, but they also reflect the tentativeness that supports error embracing and fosters learning. From these perspectives organizations can assume the risks of changing and erring while learning new approaches to deter-

* It is for this reason that it would seem to be sound strategy to work with those organizations that are "on the way" rather than trying to convert those that will be unaccepting of errors and error embracing. One can then hope that the dialectic, and the experiences of those that have responded to the new belief system, will encourage and support change in the unconverted.

mining whether the change has fulfilled their expectations. Since the experience of participating in this evaluation will inevitably alter their expectations, charismatic leaders will value the learning for its affect on their perceptions and visions.

This posture contributes to and is in part a product of the dissolution of the conventional belief system. Associated with it are other changes in society and in organizations that should move organizational development toward a learning mode.

Changes are underway, for example, in the behavior, norms, and values of the nonexecutive members of organizations. They, too, are living in and often contributing to the changes in society's belief system. We are, of course, well aware of the growing demand for meaningful work on the job and of the growing impact of those who enter the work place through the doors of affirmative action. Women and minorities, just by those facts of life, bring different perspectives to the work place. One can reasonably speculate, too, that the conventional socialization forces in the work place are growing weaker because the belief system supporting them is weakening.

In addition, more people are more intensely linked to a greater variety of social change roles *outside* their work organizations. More of them are active or vicarious members of affirmative action and consumer groups, whether they be pro- or antifirearms, nuclear reactors, high consumption, or marijuana. They are also more dependent on supposedly competent others—those with the expertise and the authority—and at the same time are increasingly wary of them. (Consider, for example, the change in attitudes toward "helpers" like doctors and hospitals, evidenced in part by the growth in malpractice suits. Consider, too, the change in attitudes toward organizations that provide for the commonweal like teachers and schools, on which we place ever greater demands but from which we withdraw evermore support.) One way or another, these more expressive and assertive views of life and of one's place in it are carried into the work place, where they provide both incentives and a freeing-up of options for innovative organizational development directed toward learning what humanly effective organization might become in such a changing world (Vickers, 1973).

Corresponding changes are underway in the self-images held by those in management positions and in their visions of what might be and ought to be. Some younger members, destined for executive roles or already in them, have been educated in ways that emphasize interpersonal competence in a world more problematic than dreamed of in the positivist belief system. Young people from the sixties are moving in and up in the bureaucracies, and evidence from the research of the Harris surveys (1975) and Miller and Levitan (1976) strongly indicates that the values so vividly forwarded by a few in the sixties are increasingly subscribed to by many more in the seventies. Nor is it any longer strange to learn that, among others, government and corporate managers and administrators—some of them in their later years—meditate or experientially learn at Esalen or in encounter groups or in a variety of other activities aimed at "opening people up." It is characteristic of this kind of experience that it often results in changes of purpose and in growth in social concern, laments about the "new narcissism" notwithstanding. The need for meaningfulness, which carries with it a need for authenticity, also expresses itself in a need to work in organizations intent on respecting and responding to those needs in its members. Likewise, these needs are expressed as a willingness, even eagerness, to experiment, to learn, and in the process, to embrace error. For some members of some client systems this, then, is the new rationality—what it is reasonable to do.

One expression of this new mood, pressed on organizations by the emerging consumer movement and facilitated within organizations by those forwarding the changing values described here, is the move toward environmental and social impact assessments, toward incorporating externalities, toward work enrichment, and toward the open self-examining stance represented by the contributors to this book.

Thus the question may not be so much, "are clients ready for a new error-embracing, learning mode of operations?" Rather it may be, "are OD proponents ready to take the risks of error embracing and to take the trouble to seek out the potential clients for this odyssey of mutual discovery?" For those OD change agents and researchers who so choose, what then become their ethical and operational responsibilities? In our view they are to help the organization *learn* how to conduct itself as a learning system and to help it to *learn how to learn* to conduct itself this way.

THE IMPLICATIONS FOR PRACTICE

The first step in advancing these concerns is to acknowledge to ourselves and to our clients that we do not know how to fulfill these responsibilities, that we do not know how to develop the organizational structures and processes needed for embracing our errors and learning from them. Then, as we conduct new change efforts, make errors, and seek to learn from them, the development of a learning system represents a new and challenging undertaking.

The changes in our self-perceptions and in our visions of organization development discussed earlier prepare us for this challenge. They open us to the possibility of error in our endeavors and, with that, the potential to adopt an error embracing, learning mode of behavior. Yet they also leave us vulnerable for the prevailing belief system grips us even as we seek to transcend it. It is difficult to express new expectations for our change efforts when we are uncertain of the limits of our knowledge. It is also difficult to develop new norms in our change efforts when we are fearful of erring and discovering that events are not under our control. These accommodations themselves call for organization development—developing new expectations for change efforts and creating new norms that reinforce them. The task is to move toward an R&D mode of organizing in which we make the most of what succeeds and learn the most from what does not. This is not an easy task, but the contributors to this book, by their lessons and examples, join others of kindred spirit in undertaking it. Let us examine their recommendations for organization change and the implications for error embracing and learning.

Past Lessons and Future Directions

In past change efforts many practitioners have emphasized their knowledge and skill in changing organizations to convince otherwise apprehensive clients of the "payoff" of planned change. Indeed, they have considered this necessary for "getting a foot in the door" of client systems, where scientific knowledge is admired and professional skills are emulated. But the contributors to this book describe the consequences of this consulting arrangement. They show that admiration can inhibit open collaboration and that emulation can breed bland imitation. Moreover, by their open admission of errors and miscalculations they acknowledge that practitioners' claims to unfailing "know-how" and "expertise" lack credibility, not only for clients, but for themselves. So they urge them to reject this traditional consulting relationship and to free themselves and their clients of expectations that knowledge and skill guarantee successful change results.

At the same time they urge practitioners to become more knowledgeable and more skilled, not only in applying change technologies, but also in *learning* to apply them. They counsel practitioners to work with their clients as change participants, cultivating the mutual personal and work relationships needed for enduring intervention and fruitful learning. The contributor's lessons, in concert with those of others, signal the emergence of a new form of OD consultation in which change is explicitly intended to improve the organization's capacity for learning.

This represents a shift in the emphasis and intent of OD. In past change efforts, the importance of succeeding has often superceded any concerns for learning. This has been particularly true of unsuccessful efforts in which clients and practitioners have been unprepared for their errors, unwilling to evaluate them, and, thus, unable to learn from them. As a result, they have learned only to repeat what succeeds (hoping for the best), but not how to reverse what has not succeeded or how to apply the lessons to future ventures. Their change efforts have often been "hit or miss" propositions guided only by "trial and error" learning.

Certainly this has been an unreflective learning, like that of pigeons in a laboratory rather than participants in an organizational experiment. As an alternative, the organization change process envisioned and the kind of evaluation proposed here seek to make the relation between change and learning more reflective, more an integral part of the OD effort. They are premised on the emerging expectations for OD which hold that *the goals of a change effort are not only its immediate benefits but equally its opportunities for learning.* With this in mind, let us explore how a change effort might be designed, and its norms developed, for the purpose of learning from both successful and unsuccessful results.

In what follows we chart this exploration, but since it is only the beginnings of such a journey, and since the routes are influenced by our own values and predilections, some of the paths may prove misdirections. Nevertheless, we risk proposing them in hopes the readers will travel them and then, in the spirit of error embracing, learn from them and guide us further.

Change and Learning

Human learning is an ongoing process of forming a view of the world (i.e., awareness of reality) and undertaking actions in response to what is perceived (i.e., responsiveness to reality). It continues as humans adjust their views based on what they experience and alter their responses in light of what they foresee. As the change efforts of the past become the learning efforts of the future, practitioners and their clients will change and learn in analogous fashion. They will strive to become more *aware* of the personal and environmental forces that shape their behavior. They will be asking, why are we organized in this way? How does our organization contribute to our goals? In answering, they will be sifting past experiences, reliving past dilemmas, and diagnosing their present circumstances.

At the same time they will try to become more *responsive* to their personal visions and environmental opportunities. They will also be asking, is this the way we want to be organized? How might our organization be changed to meet our future expectations? In answering, they will be weighing current perspectives, anticipating future needs, and experimenting with new actions. Indeed, the overriding rationale for experimenting with new organizational structures and new behavioral styles will be that it can enlarge their *awareness* and speed their *responsiveness*, helping clients and practitioners learn to change and change to learn.

All of this is compatible with the emerging model of OD consultation, in some cases with the way it is being practiced today. It means that OD practitioners and their clients will examine the organization's policies and practices, considering their effect on individuals' behavior and the organization's mission and societal obligations. Such an examination led the R. G. Barry Corporation to adopt "human resource management," the TRW Systems Group to form a "technical democracy," and other organizations to embrace the "quality of work life" movement. Further, it means that OD practitioners and their clients will analyze the values reflected in the organization's policies and practices, assessing their compatibility with individual intentions and the organization's ethical responsibilities. This analysis led the members of the Graphic Controls Corporation to express shared assumptions about human nature and to air their philosophy publicly to the business community. Finally, it means that OD practitioners and their clients will continue to experiment with new organizational policies and practices to learn to guide their behavior and their organization in appropriate ways.

Toward this end, OD change agents and researchers will shoulder new responsibilities. Instead of teaching their clients McGregor's theory of organizational behavior,* or Herzberg's, or their own, they will be obliged to guide their clients through the difficult but enrich-

* It is ironic that McGregor (1960) never intended organizations to "choose sides over Theory X and Y"; instead, he wanted to "encourage the realization that theory is important (and) to urge management to examine its assumptions and make them explicit" (p. 246).

ing exercise of articulating their own theories and examining their own views of the world. In this way OD will become an effort to merge the practitioner's knowledge and skills with the client's insights and experience; it will synthesize their theories and subject them to joint inquiry. The "teacher" and "student" roles that have dominated consulting relationships in the past will become obsolete. In their place a new relationship will be formed which will link the client and practitioner together as learners.

The Practice of Change and Learning

There is little to guide the practice of change and learning, but the efforts of those who have begun this practice suggest that it will take as many forms and reflect as many disciplinary distinctions as OD does today. We can speculate, for example, that some practitioners will concentrate on individuals, helping their clients to understand how their own theories and values influence their actions and behavior. They might conduct learning laboratories in which clients can examine their theories away from the old role pressures that keep old theories steadfastly in place. The norms of these sessions would parallel those of the training group change laboratories of today. As such, they would invite the scrutiny of past perspectives and the experiential testing of new ones.

Argyris and Schon (1974) have recommended this approach for examining and evaluating personal "theories of action." Moreover, they advance it as well as an approach to organizational change, and Argyris (1976) has used this method to train individuals to analyze their theories in an organizational context. (His research also addresses the familiar problems of transferring laboratory training to the "real" world.)

Other practitioners will favor the examination of theories within the setting of an ongoing change effort. Alderfer and Brown (1975) describe an effort in which the change participants were able to generate and test their hypotheses of organizational actions and their consequences. (Their change effort was guided by unconfirmed hypotheses and unanticipated consequences, both discovered by their client's and their own attention to learning; see also Bolman, 1974.)

We can speculate, too, that there will be differences in regard to the conduct of organizational learning. Some practitioners, for example, will want to formalize the process and will propose that their clients maintain "theory logs" or "theory journals" much as change logs and journals are kept today. Others will contend that this learning should develop from a more intuitive state of mind that stays attuned to its values and assumptions and strives to incorporate them while experimenting with new actions and practices.

The merits of these new approaches to organization development are scarcely documented; practitioners are only beginning to experiment with them, but the experiments that are needed go beyond the cloistered world of the laboratory and beyond its mirror image in traditional field research. They welcome the clients into the experiment, not as naïve subjects but as informed participants. They recognize that if clients are to assume the risks and responsibilities associated with learning they must see themselves as both subjects and experimenters. Thus in future OD efforts practitioners and clients will be adopting a new experimental philosophy and method in which both will be *part* of a new experiment, indeed *in* a new experiment—an experiment in change and learning.

Erring and Learning

Of course, these new arrangements will lead to errors, but they will also provide a relationship conducive to error embracing in which clients will be experimenting with their own theories, participating in their own experiments, and conducting their change efforts in complementary relationships with the OD practitioner. In these relationships errors will be seen not so much as "failures" but as special guides to learning. They will not provide recrimination; instead they will stimulate reflection and responsiveness. They will provide the change participants with direct feedback and give them the opportunity to refine their theories and improve their technique by experiencing the limitation of past ideas and participating in the search for new ones.

By embracing their errors individuals will also enlarge their understanding of themselves and their endeavors. These new change efforts are unlikely to show that a particular theory of change is sufficient because new situations will demand refined theories and further changes beyond those used in their creation. Instead they will show that erring and learning are a rewarding approach to changing, for the examination of assumptions and the experiential testing of theories gives meaning and purpose to otherwise unconscious or unthinking personal and organizational actions. So, as errors show the change participants the limits of their knowledge, they will also make them more aware of themselves, what they do, and what they might do to change themselves and their organizations.

This approach to change and learning substitutes *awareness* and *re-*

sponsiveness for a naïve faith in knowledge and control. Indeed, by increasing their awareness of what is happening clients and practitioners will more fully appreciate the limits of their control. With that appreciation they may be better able to guide, if not control, their social and work activities in directions they would like to see them unfold. This approach to change and learning can be likened to white-water canoeing. One does not control the water; one guides oneself and the canoe, both in response to the water and to the canoe and oneself responding to the water. And by being aware of what is happening and by staying "loose," one increases the likelihood of having the "self" and the canoe go where one would like them to go.

Errors in change, then, can both increase awareness and guide responsiveness. But to serve this purpose they must be anticipated, reported, and reviewed. Let us consider how these new OD efforts can be designed so that practitioners and their clients can better prepare to err and learn.

The Practice of Erring and Learning

Again there is little experience to direct the practice of error embracing and learning, but we can speculate that, as practitioners and clients undertake these activities they will begin with theories that enlarge their awareness of the systemic properties of organizations and enable them to respond to the systemic implications of organizational change. Theories in a learning system will encourage a state of mind in which it is understood that although *A* might sometimes lead to *B*, other *A*'s might also produce it, and other *B*'s are invariably created. Such a state of mind is sympathetic to error embracing, for it reflects what Bennis calls "the hypothetical spirit" which includes "the feeling for tentativeness . . . the respect for probable error." Moreover, there are special advantages to embracing errors in this spirit, for their discovery heightens awareness of the other antecedents of *B* and stimulates responsiveness to the other consequences of *A*.*

To enlarge a learning system's capacity for embracing its errors,

* The systemic properties of organizations emphasize that everything that happens is dependent on everything else. Newcomb (1959) perceptively applied this notion to his analysis of social networks: "I have chosen to emphasize 'system properties' rather than single variables which contribute to them, and consequently none of the variables has an enduring status as independent or as dependent . . . a change in one system variable is likely (under certain conditions) to be followed by a specific change in another system variable, but according to others a change in the second is a precondition for a change in the first" (p. 388).

then, it will be necessary to enlarge the set of theories it uses for learning from change. For every theory there will be alternatives; for every outcome others will be foreseen. Yet as practitioners and their clients strive to learn from their errors they will be attentive to new alternatives and alert to unanticipated results. In the past change participants have considered primarily what is "supposed" to happen; in the future they will also ponder what "else" might occur.

With this foresight practitioners and clients will expect problems and will consider more options and review more strategies before embarking on a change. In addition, they will expect errors and will improve their error-detecting capabilities to direct their attention to the first indications of mistakes. Together, these expectations will promote the strategic and contingency planning necessary for anticipating and reacting to errors. Finally, clients will also lower their expectations in regard to their control of the change process. This will soften the dismay of disappointing findings and lessen the anxiety induced by evidence that the change did not go as planned. When hospital patients are forewarned about the pain and complications associated with their illnesses, they are more attentive to their symptomatology and more likely to recuperate without undo stress (Janis, 1958). Analogously, if members of a learning system are forewarned that errors are likely, they will also be prepared to discover them more quickly, review them with less anxiety, and respond to them more effectively.

In order to embrace their errors openly, however, the change participants will have to unlearn the personal dispositions that have discouraged this conduct in the past. Change practitioners have helped their clients to learn from early successes; they must help them learn from early failures as well. They might, for example, prepare their clients for the personal disappointments of erring by some form of "emotional role playing" (c.f. Janis and Mann, 1965). This will enable clients to rehearse the experience of erring and go through the "work of worrying" while supported by a social system that helps them both cope and learn. Practitioners might also prepare their clients for the organizational consequences of erring by an exercise in "reality testing" in which their fears can be previewed and disconfirmed (c.f. Harvey and Albertson, 1972). But when preparation ends and errors occur practitioners will have the responsibility to embrace their own errors, share them openly with their clients, and model the personal self-examination needed for learning from them. Practitioners will have to model and promote acceptance, support, and personal liberation—all in sharp contrast to the macho model that is unaccepting of such behavior. Just as practitioners have sought to create the open problem solving necessary for change in the past, so they will seek to create the open error-embracing norms necessary for learning in the future.

Evaluating and Learning

To assess errors, respond to them, and, at the same time, learn from them, practitioners and their clients will also have to devise new approaches to evaluation. In the past some change efforts have been evaluated on the basis of a post-experimental accounting of the "end results." This is the classical approach to evaluation, limited to the controlled conditions of the laboratory, not the uncontrolled context of change in the "real" world. In the future members of a learning system will be alert to the problems inherent in transposing this laboratory evaluation model to the field. They will recognize that during a change effort there are always more "causes" than can be controlled, more "effects" than can be observed, and interactions among these "causes" and "effects" during the experimental period and beyond. Thus they will strive to design evaluation studies that enlarge their awareness of these many alternatives while directing their responsiveness to both favorable and unfavorable results.

The Practice of Evaluating and Learning

There are advances underway in the evaluation of change efforts which are compatible with the new forms of OD. In the area of measurement, for example, both quantitative and qualitative measures that assess the impact of a change effort on the organization's structure and technology and its member's attitudes and performance are being devised (c.f. Survey Research Center, 1975). Moreover, many of these measures are suited to the ongoing assessment of change activities and can be applied throughout the "life" of an organization—an important consideration for experiments in a learning system will have indistinct beginnings and ends. New research designs are also being developed (such as the one used by Frank and Hackman) which can highlight changes in the ongoing flux of the experimental environment and changes in the meaning of the experimental measures themselves (c.f., Staw, 1976).

Each of these advances in scientific evaluation, however, can result in a greater separation between practitioners and their clients. To avoid this practitioners will have to educate their clients in these new methods of evaluation and invite their participation in the formulation of the research design, the development of the evaluation measures, and the conduct of the evaluation itself (c.f. Argyris, 1970; Guskin and Chesler, 1973). They will treat evaluation as an open and ongoing activity in which clients learn to evaluate and learn from their evaluations. This will affirm that, just as change efforts cannot be separated from the life of the organization neither can evaluation be separated from the change effort.

To this end, practitioners will acknowledge that measurement, however concealed, affects experimental activities—both their clients' and their own. Instead of searching for covert measures so that their clients will not know they are being evaluated, practitioners will work with their clients in devising overt measures that can be employed throughout the change effort and utilized by both parties in guiding and directing their activities. They will understand that people learn about themselves and their organizations and about their efforts to change themselves and their organizations chiefly by communicating with one another rather than by observing. In this way practitioners will bring evaluation into the experiment; indeed, they will make it part of the experiment.

Robust and rigorous as these evaluation methods may become, they will nonetheless confirm that much in social situations cannot be quantitatively explained. (The amount of "explained" variance in past organizational studies has generally hovered below 50 percent. Even if the "unexplained" and "error" variance were to become much smaller in the future, it would not vitiate the possibility of that tiny portion—the unlikely or idiosyncratic—"wagging the dog.") Thus these future evaluation studies will likely demonstrate that a great deal of human and organizational behavior is neither predictable nor under control.

Although some clients and practitioners might find this a disappointing conclusion, others will view it as an opportunity to explore other evaluation approaches. It will not be uncommon to find change participants emphasizing experiential understanding as much as quantitative analysis. They will share their feelings and reactions to the change effort, all the time considering how those feelings and reactions shape and color their impressions and influence the unfolding situation (as Berg has done). They will not only strive to interpret their quantitative findings but will search for meaning "behind the numbers" and even "beyond the numbers" by means of free-flowing brainstorming sessions or, perhaps, "guided meditations" (Torbert, 1972).

Past evaluation studies have informed change participants of what *has* happened and how it differed from what they might have preferred. These new evaluation studies will inform them of what *is* happening and how it might be guided in the directions they prefer. Client involvement in this process will enhance their appreciation of the reciprocity between causes and effects. Thus they will recognize the need for continuing evaluations of their efforts and for error embracing as part of them. Together these will facilitate the modification of actions, plans, and theories while increasing the change participants' appreciation of the ways in which they can interpret and guide their efforts.

Just as past evaluation studies have reflected the science of organizational change, these new evaluation studies will be equally concerned with its art. The artist's sense of purpose is continuously modified as actions produce changes in the material with which he/she is working. These changes alter the evolving sense of the goal and future actions toward realizing it. There is both looseness and control in this process, and the looseness, the artist's responsiveness to the uncontrolled in both artist and material is critical to the felicitous unfolding of the creation.

OD practitioners have not conducted such evaluations nor have they established the organizational relationships and norms that would endorse these evaluations as they learn to do them. As they help their clients change toward an error-embracing learning mode of behavior, they will also be learning how to conduct these evaluations and how to create the relationships and norms that will guide the organization toward learning. In these undertakings they, too, will be learning how to learn and how to become error embracers themselves.

All of this emphasizes that if organizations are to become learning systems the "kudos" should go to those who have the technical and interpersonal skills to arrange change and evaluation efforts so that errors can be quickly and decisively uncovered and the lessons incorporated into future actions. All of this recommends a new perspective on error accountability.

A New Norm of Error Accountability

For the most part past OD efforts have been treated as investments: continued when they have been successful but discontinued when they have not achieved the desired returns. Moreover, practitioners and project directors have been held accountable for the project's results. Accountability has been stressed to ensure sound investments and recognition of sound personnel. Yet oftentimes accountability has tried to ensure success at the expense of learning from failure.

In its current forms project accountability can leave clients and practitioners anxious over their errors and fearful of the consequences. This anxiety can restrict their perceptions of options and the fear can inhibit their ability to learn (c.f. Janis, 1958). Moreover, as the introduction reports, they may strive to protect their reputations by emphasizing the pleasant findings while repressing the unpleasant news or by blaming others for the problems while concealing evidence of their own responsibility. All this reduces and restricts the flow of valid information about the change effort and leaves the participants unable to evaluate what has occurred.

Clearly, a new type of accountability is needed for the emerging forms of OD. This accountability will foster different expectations for technology, different criteria for competence, and different norms for error embracing. Instead of holding people accountable for their errors, the new norm will hold them accountable for discovering their errors, sharing them with others, and continuing their change efforts mindful of the lessons they have learned from them. It will mean that the skills and motives of the *competent* person and organization should be devoted to this purpose.*

Some proposals for operationalizing this type of accountability have been advanced by the contributors to this book; for example, change agents might be guaranteed the employment security needed to experiment and to err as long as they are conscientious about learning from their mistakes. And organization members might be relieved of the threat of a postexperimental performance review as long as they continue in their efforts to experiment and learn. The feasibility and practicality of these and related norms of accountability are unknown and we will have to experiment with them as well. In this regard it is worth noting that our larger society, in which organizations are included, now finds it desirable to move in this direction. Like no-fault divorce, no-fault change could become another step along the way.

* It was once thought that learning without rewards represented only "incidental learning." More recent research has distinguished between the "motivational" and "informational" aspects of reinforcement. It challenges the supposition that learning is based solely on rewards and punishments and concludes "rather, what we have learned is that learning is *more complex* than we earlier believed" (McKeachie, 1976, p. 822).

Successful Failure

Practitioners, clients, funding agencies, and most of us interested in OD have been primarily concerned with recognizing, assessing, and rewarding successful change, presuming it to be the result of correct knowledge aptly applied for prediction and control. But we have seen that this promotes caution when risk is needed, short-run achievement when long-term persistance is needed, and the disavowal of errors when error-embracing is needed. Just as we are changing our presumptions about knowledge, prediction, and control, we must also change our criteria for recognizing, assessing, and rewarding change efforts.

We must learn how to recognize the presence of greater awareness evidenced by the way change participants review past decisions and enlarge current options, analyze past errors and elaborate contingency plans, and learn from past lessons and arrange evaluations for still more learning. Similarly, we must learn how to assess the presence of greater responsiveness evidenced by the way change participants monitor current decisions and consider their future implications, examine current errors and support their open disclosure, and undertake new actions and prepare themselves to learn from the errors that will occur. Finally, we must learn how to reward the personal vision and organizational commitment that fully recognize the problems in creating change, that fully accept that errors are inevitable in these undertakings, yet still choose to risk, to persist, and to learn from the errors in OD.

This vision need not dampen our motivation or hope for success. Instead, it will add the enriching motivation and fulfillment accompanying the satisfactions and accomplishments from learning—learning to be evermore aware and responsive in a turbulent world that will frustrate many of our efforts to use knowledge to predict and control. *This is successful failure in organization development and change.* This is the satisfaction and sense of accomplishment that the contributors to this book affirm.

References

INTRODUCTION

Argyris, C. *Intervention theory and method: A behavioral science view.* Reading, Mass.: Addison-Wesley, 1970.

Barnes, L. B. Organizational change and field experiment methods. In J. D. Thompson (Ed.), *Organizational design and research.* Pittsburgh: University of Pittsburgh Press, 1966.

Bennis, W. G. *Changing organizations.* New York: McGraw-Hill, 1966.

Bennis, W. G. *Organization development: Its nature, origins, and prospects.* Reading, Mass.: Addison-Wesley, 1969.

Birney, R. C., Burdick, H., and Teevan, R. C. *Fear of failure.* New York: Van Nostrand-Reinhold, 1969.

Crafts, K. and Hauther, B. *Surviving the undergraduate jungle: The student's guide to good grades.* New York: Grove, 1976.

Davis, L. E. and Cherns, A. B. (Eds.) *The quality of work life,* Vol. 1. New York: Free Press, 1975.

Fiedler, F. E. *Leadership.* New York: General Learning Press, 1971.

Fleishman, E. A. Leadership climate, human relations training, and supervisory behavior. *Personnel Psychology,* 1953, **6**, 205–222.

Galbraith, J. *Designing complex organizations.* Reading, Mass.: Addison-Wesley, 1973.

Goodstein, L. D. Case studies: Failures and successes, introduction. *Journal of Applied Behavioral Science,* 1975, **11**, 411–412.

Gordon, G. and Morse, E. V. Evaluation research: A critical review. *Annual Review of Sociology,* 1975, **1**.

Holt, J. *How children fail.* New York: Pitman, 1964.

Janis, I. L. Stages in the decision-making process. In R. P. Abelson, E. Aronson, W. J. McGuire, T. M. Newcomb, M. J. Rosenberg, and P. H. Tannenbaum (Eds.), *Theories of cognitive consistency.* Chicago: Rand-McNally, 1968, pp. 810–818.

Kahn, R. L. Organizational development: Some problems and proposals. *Journal of Applied Behavioral Science,* 1974, **10**, 485–502.

Katz, D. and Kahn, R. *The social psychology of organizations.* New York: Wiley, 1966.

Lawler, E. E., Hackman, J. R., and Kaufman, S. Effects of job redesign: A field experiment. *Journal of Applied Psychology,* 1973, **3**, 49–62.

Lawrence, P. R. and Lorsch, J. W. *Organization and environment.* Boston: Harvard Business School, Division of Research, 1967.

Marrow, A. J. *The practical theorist.* New York: Basic Books, 1969.

Maslow, A. H. *The psychology of science.* Chicago: Regnert, 1969.

Michael, D. *On learning to plan—and planning to learn.* San Francisco: Jossey-Bass, 1973.

Milner, E. *The failure of success.* St. Louis, Mo.: Warren H. Green, 1968.

Rosenthal, R. and Jacobsen, L. *Pygmalion in the classroom.* New York: Holt, Rinehart & Winston, 1968.

Tavris, C. The experimenting society—to find programs that work, government must measure its failures. *Psychology Today,* September 1975, 47–55.

United States Department of Health, Education, and Welfare: Report of a Special Task Force to the Secretary, *Work in America,* Washington, D.C.: U.S. Government Printing Office, 1972.

Vickers, G. *Freedom in a rocking boat.* Middlesex, England: Penguin, 1970.

Vroom, V. H. and Yetton, P. W. *Leadership and decision-making.* Pittsburgh: University of Pittsburgh Press, 1973.

Weiner, B., Frieze, I., Kukla, A., Reed, L., Rest, S., and Rosenbaum, R. *Perceiving the causes of success and failure.* New York: General Learning Press, 1971.

Weiss, C. H. *Evaluation research.* Englewood Cliffs, N.J.: Prentice-Hall, 1972.

Williams, R. M. *American society.* New York: Knopf, 1960.

Winterbottom, M. R. The relation of need for achievement to learning experiences in independence and mastery. In J. W. Atkinson (Ed.), *Motives in fantasy, action, and society.* Princeton, N.J.: Van Nostrand, 1958.

SECTION I: ENTRY

Argyris, C. *Intervention theory and method: a behavioral science view.* Reading, Mass.: Addison-Wesley, 1970.

Chapter 2

Alderfer, C. Boundary relations and organizational diagnosis. In H. Meltzer and F. R. Wicker (Eds.), *Humanizing organizational behavior.* Springfield, Ill.: Thomas, 1976.

Alderfer, C. Improving organizational communication through long-term intergroup intervention. *Journal of Applied Behavioral Science,* 1977, **13**, 193–210.

Blake, R. R. and Mouton, J. S. The intergroup dynamics of a win-lose conflict and problem solving collaboration in union-management relations. In M. Sherif (Ed.), *Intergroup relations and leadership.* New York: Wiley, 1962.

Kahn, R. L. and Mann, E. C. Developing research partnerships. *Social Issues,* 1952, **8**, 4–10.

LeVine, R. A. and Campbell, D. T. *Ethnocentrism.* New York: Wiley, 1972.

Levinson, H. *Organizational diagnosis*. Cambridge, Mass.: Harvard University Press, 1972.

Sherif, M. and Sherif, C. *Social psychology*. New York: Harper and Row, 1969.

Chapter 3

Argyris, C. *Intervention theory and method*. Reading, Mass.: Addison-Wesley, 1970.

Bennis, W. *Changing organizations*. New York: McGraw-Hill, 1966.

Blake, R. R., Mouton, J. S., and Sloma, R. L. The union-management intergroup laboratory: Strategy for resolving intergroup conflict. *Journal of Applied Behavioral Science*, 1965, **1**, 25–57.

Blake, R. R., Shepard, H., and Mouton, J. S. *Managing intergroup conflict in industry*. Austin, Texas: Gulf Publishing Company, 1964.

Doob, L. *Resolving conflict in Africa*. New Haven: Yale University Press, 1970.

Klein, E. B., Thomas, C. S., and Bellis, E. C. When warring groups meet. *Social Psychiatry*, 1971, **6**, 93–99.

Sherif, M. *In common predicament*. Boston: Houghton Mifflin, 1966.

Solomon, L. *Personal communication*. Boston University, 1971.

Walton, R. *Interpersonal peacemaking*. Reading, Mass.: Addison-Wesley, 1969.

Walton, R. A problem-solving workshop on border conflicts in East Africa. *Journal of Applied Behavioral Science*, 1970, **6**, 453–489.

SECTION II: CHANGE

Benne, K. D., Bennis, W. G., and Chin, R. Planned change in America. In W. G. Bennis, K. D. Benne, and R. Chin (Eds.), *The planning of change*. New York: Holt, Rinehart, & Winston, 1961.

Coch, L. and French, J. R. P. Overcoming resistance to change. *Human Relations*, 1948, **1**, 512–532.

French, J. R. P., Israel, J., and Ås, D. An experiment on participation in a Norwegian factory. *Human Relations*, 1960, **13**, 3–19.

Lewin, K. The Research Center for Group Dynamics at the Massachusetts Institute of Technology. *Sociometry*, 1945, **2**, 126–136.

Chapter 4

Alderfer, C. Boundary relations and organizational diagnosis. In H. Meltzer and F. R. Wicker (Eds.), *Humanizing organizational behavior*. Springfield, Ill.: Thomas, 1976.

Alderfer, C. Organizational development. *Annual Review of Psychology*, 1977, **28**.

Argyris, C. and Schon, D. *Theory in Practice*. San Francisco: Jossey-Bass, 1974.

Bloomfield, M. *American Lawyers in a Changing Society*. Cambridge, Mass.: Harvard University Press, 1976.

Cogan, M. L. Toward a definition of profession. *Harvard Educational Review*, 1953, **23**, 33–49.

Friedlander, F. and Brown, L. D. Organizational development. *Annual Review of Psychology*, 1974, **25**, 313–341.

Friedson, E. *Profession of medicine: A Study of the sociology of applied knowledge*. New York: Basic Books, 1970.

Goode, W. J. Encroachment, charlatanism and the emerging professions: Psychology, medicine and sociology. *American Sociological Review*, 1960, **25**, 902–914.

Gordon, G. and Morse, E. V. Evaluation research: A critical review. *Annual Review of Sociology*, 1975, **1**, 339–361.

Henry, W. E., Sims, J. H., and Spray, S. L. *The fifth profession*. San Francisco: Jossey-Bass, 1971.

Rice, A. K. *The enterprise and its environment*. London: Tavistock, 1963.

Steele, F. *Consulting for organizational change*. Amherst, Mass.: University of Massachusetts Press, 1975.

Chapter 5

Argyris, C. *Some causes of organizational ineffectiveness within the Department of State*. Washington, D.C.: U.S. Department of State, 1967.

Marrow, A. J. *Making waves in foggy bottom*. Washington, D.C.: NTL Institute, 1974.

Mosher, F. A. and Harr, J. E. *Programming systems and foreign affairs leadership: An attempted innovation*. Oxford: Oxford University Press, 1970.

Warwick, D. P. *A theory of public bureaucracy: Politics, personality, and organization in the State Department*. Cambridge, Mass.: Harvard University Press, 1975.

Chapter 6

Argyris, C. *Intervention theory and method: A behavioral science view*. Reading, Mass.: Addison-Wesley, 1970.

Argyris, C., and Schon, D. A. *Theory in practice: Increasing professional effectiveness*. San Francisco: Jossey-Bass, 1975.

Ashby, W. R. *Design for a brain*. London: Chapman & Hall, 1952.

Bridges, E. M. A model for shared decision making in the school principalship. *Educational Administration Quarterly*, 1967, **3**, 49–61.

Coughlan, R. J. and Cooke, R. A. The structural development of educational organizations. Ann Arbor, Mich.: Institute for Social Research, 1974 (mimeo).

Coughlan, R. J., Cooke, R. A., and Safer, L. A., Jr. An assessment of a survey feedback-problem solving-collective decision intervention in schools. Final report to the Office of Education, U. S. Department of Health, Education, and Welfare. Evanston, Ill.: Northwestern University, 1972.

Dreeben, R. *The nature of teaching: Schools and the work of teachers*. Glenview, Ill.: Scott, Foresman 1970.

Hawley, W. D. Dealing with organizational rigidity in public schools: A theoretical perspective. New Haven: Yale University, undated (mimeo).

Huse, E. F. *Organization development and change*. St. Paul, Minn.: West, 1975.

Maier, N. R. F. *Problem solving and creativity in individuals and groups*. Belmont, Calif.: Brooks/Cole, 1970.

Mann, F. C. and Likert, R. The need for research on the communication of research results. *Human Organization*, 1952, **11**, 15–19.

Mohrman, A. M., Jr., Cooke, R. A., and Duncan, R. B. A survey feedback organization development program for educational systems. In Data based change: Survey feedback and beyond. Symposium presented at the meeting of the American Psychological Association, Chicago, August 1975.

Mohrman, S. A., Mohrman, A. M., Jr., and Duncan, R. B. Data feedback in intensive technology contexts. In Data based change in organizations: Theory and practice issues. Symposium presented at the meeting of the Academy of Management, Kansas City, Mo., August 1976.

Nadler, D. A. The use of survey feedback for organizational change: Promises and pitfalls. *Group and Organizational Studies, 1976,* **1**, 177–186.

Seashore, S. E. Field experiments with formal organizations. *Human Organization*, 1964, **23**, 164–170.

Vroom, V. *Work and motivation*. New York: Wiley, 1964.

Zaltman, G., Florio, D. and Sikorski, L. *Dynamic Educational Change: Models, Strategies, Tactics, and Management*. New York: Free Press, 1977.

Chapter 7

Argyris, C. *Personality and organization*. New York: Harper & Row, 1957.

Asch, S. E. Effects of group pressure upon the modification and distortion of judgments. In H. Guetzkow (Ed.), *Groups, leadership, and men*. Pittsburgh: Carnegie, 1951.

Bavelas, A. Communication patterns in task-oriented groups. *Journal of the Acoustical Society of America*, 1950, **22**, 725–730.

Blau, P. The dynamics of bureaucracy. In A. Etzioni (Ed.), *Complex organizations*. New York: Holt, Rinehart, & Winston, 1961.

Bradford, L. P., Gibb, J. R., and Benne, K. D. *T-group theory and laboratory method*. New York: Wiley, 1964.

Festinger, L. A. A theory of social comparison processes. *Human Relations*, 1954, **7**, 117–140.

Fiedler, E. E. A contingency model of leadership effectiveness. In L. Berkowitz (Ed.), *Advances in experimental social psychology*, Vol. 1. New York: Academic, 1964.

Gouldner, A. W. Metaphysical pathos and the theory of bureaucracy. *American Political Science Review*, 1955, **49**, 496–507.

Kelman, H. C. Processes of opinion change. *Public Opinion Quarterly*, 1961, **25**, 57–78.

Leavitt, H. J. Some effects of certain communication patterns on group performance. *Journal of Abnormal and Social Psychology*, 1951, **41**, 38–50.

Lippitt, R. and White, R. K. An experimental study of leadership and group life. In E. E. Maccoby, T. M. Newcomb, and E. E. Hartley (Eds.), *Readings in social psychology*. New York: Holt, Rinehart, and Winston, 1958.

Likert, R. *New patterns of management*. New York: McGraw-Hill, 1961.

McMurry, R. N. The case for benevolent autocracy. *Harvard Business Review*, January-February, 1950, p. 82.

Schein, E. H. The mechanisms of change. In W. G. Bennis, E. H. Schein, F. Steele, and D. Berlew (Eds.), *Interpersonal dynamics*. Homewood, Ill.: Dorsey, 1964.

Schein, E. H. and Bennis, W. G. *Personal and organizational change through group methods*. New York: Wiley, 1965.

Chapter 8

Beer, M. The technology of organizational development. In M. D. Dunnette (Ed.), *Handbook of industrial and organizational psychology*. Chicago: Rand McNally, 1975.

Davis, L. E. and Taylor, R. N. *Design of jobs*. London: Penguin, 1972.

Emery, F. E. Characteristics of socio-technical systems. Document No. 527, Tavistock Institute of Human Relations, 1959. Excerpted in L. E. Davis and J. C. Taylor (Eds.), *Design of jobs*. London: Penguin, 1972.

Ford, R. N. *Motivation through the work itself*. New York: American Management Association, 1969.

Frank, L. L. and Hackman, J. R. A failure of job enrichment: The case of the change that wasn't. *Journal of Applied Behavioral Science*, 1975, **11**, 413–436.

Glaser, E. M. *Improving the quality of worklife . . . and in the process, improving productivity*. Los Angeles, Human Interaction Research Institute, 1974.

Gomberg, W. *Job satisfaction: Sorting out the nonsense*. AFL-CIO American Federationist, June 1973.

Gulowsen, J. A measure of work-group autonomy. In L. E. Davis and J. C. Taylor (Eds.), *Design of jobs*. London: Penguin, 1972.

Hackman, J. R. On the coming demise of job enrichment. In E. L. Cass and F. G. Simmer (Eds.), *Man and work in society*. New York: Van Nostrand-Reinhold, 1975.

Hackman, J. R. and Oldham, G. R. Development of the job diagnostic survey. *Journal of Applied Psychology*, 1975, **60**, 159–170.

Herbst, P. G. *Autonomous group functioning*. London: Tavistock, 1962.

Herzberg, F. *Work and the nature of man*. Cleveland: World, 1966.

Herzberg, F. One more time. How do you motivate employees? *Harvard Business Review*, January-February 1968, 53–62.

Herzberg, F., Mausner, B., and Snyderman, B. *The motivation to work*. New York: Wiley, 1959.

Hulin, C. L. and Blood, M. Job enlargement, individual differences, and worker responses. *Psychological Bulletin*, 1968, **69**, 41–55.

Jenkins, G. D., Jr., Nadler, D. A., Lawler, E. E., and Cammann, C. Standardized observations: An approach to measuring the nature of jobs. *Journal of Applied Psychology*, 1975, **60**, 171–181.

Maher, J. R. (Ed.) *New perspectives in job enrichment*. New York: Van Nostrand-Reinhold, 1971.

Rice, A. K. *Productivity and social organization*. London: Tavistock, 1958.

Sirota, D. and Wolfson, A. D. Job enrichment: What are the obstacles? *Personnel*, May-June 1972, 8–17. (a)

Sirota, D. and Wolfson, A. D. Job enrichment: Surmounting the obstacles. *Personnel,* July-August 1972, 8–19. (b)

SECTION 3: DIFFUSION

McNeil, D. R. *The fight for fluoridation.* New York: Oxford University Press, 1957.

Rogers, E. M. *Diffusion of innovations.* New York: Free Press, 1962.

Rogers, E. M. *Communication strategies for family planning.* New York: Free Press, 1973.

Tarde, G. *The laws of imitation* (translated by Elsie Clews Parsons). New York: Holt, Rinehart, & Winston, 1903.

Wellin, E. Water boiling in a Peruvian town. In B. D. Paul (Ed.), *Health, culture and community.* New York: Russell Sage, 1955.

Chapter 11

Argyris, C. *Intervention theory and method.* Reading, Mass.: Addison-Wesley, 1970.

Alinsky, S. *Rules for radicals.* New York: Random House, 1971.

Broehl, W. *The village entrepreneur.* Cambridge, Mass.: Harvard University Press, 1977.

Deutsch, M. Conflicts: Productive and destructive. *Journal of Social Issues,* 1969, **25**, 7–41.

Harvey, J. The Abilene paradox: The management of agreement. *Organizational Dynamics,* 1974, **3**, 63–80.

Hersey, P. and Blanchard, K. H. The management of change. Change and the use of power. *Training Development Journal,* 1972, **26**, 6–10.

Hornstein, H. A., Benedict, B., Burke, W., Gindes, M., and Lewicki, R. J. *Social intervention: A behavioral science approach.* New York: Free Press, 1971.

Heunefeld, J. *The community activist's handbook.* Boston: Beacon, 1970.

Janis, I. *Victims of groupthink.* Boston: Houghton Mifflin, 1972.

Shapero, A. Entrepreneurship and regional development. Proceedings of the International Symposium on Entrepreneurship and Enterprise Development, Cincinnati, Ohio, June 16, 1975.

Steele, F. I. *Physical settings and organization development.* Reading, Mass.: Addison-Wesley, 1969.

Conclusion

Alderfer, C. P. and Brown, L. D. *Learning from changing: Organizational diagnosis and development.* Beverly Hills: Sage, 1975.

Argyris, C. *Intervention theory and method.* Reading, Mass.: Addison-Wesley, 1970.

Argyris, C. *Increasing leadership effectiveness.* New York: Wiley, 1976.

Argyris, C. and Schon, D. A. *Theory in practice: Increasing professional effectiveness.* San Francisco: Jossey-Bass, 1974.

Biller, R. Converting knowledge into action: The dilemma and opportunity of post industrial society. In J. Jun and W. Strom (Eds.), *Tomorrow's Organizations: Challenges and strategies*. Glenview, Ill.: Scott, Foresman, 1973.

Bolman, L. The client as theorist: An approach to individual and organizational development. In J. D. Adams (Ed.), *New technologies in organizational development: 2*. La Jolla, Calif.: University Associates, 1974.

Guskin, A. E. and Chesler, M. A. Partisan diagnosis of social problems. In G. Zaltman (Ed.), *Processes and phenomena of social change*. New York: Wiley, 1973.

Harris Survey. Americans willing to change lifestyles. *Chicago Tribune*, December 4, 1975.

Harvey, J. B. and Albertson, D. R. Neurotic organizations: Symptoms, causes, and treatment. In W. W. Burke (Ed.), *New technologies in organizational development: 1*. La Jolla, Calif.: University Associates, 1972.

Henderson, H. Speech delivered at the University of Michigan. Ann Arbor, Michigan, 1976.

Janis, I. L. *Psychological stress*. New York: Wiley, 1958.

Janis, I. L. and Mann, L. Effectiveness of emotional role playing in modifying smoking habits and attitudes. *Journal of Experimental Research in Personality*, 1965, **1**, 84–90.

Maslow, A. H. *The psychology of science*. Chicago: Regnery, 1969.

McGregor, D. *The human side of enterprise*. New York: McGraw-Hill, 1960.

McKeachie, W. J. Psychology in America's bicentennial year. *American Psychologist*, 1976, **31**, 819–833.

Michael, D. N. *On learning to plan—and planning to learn*. San Francisco: Jossey-Bass, 1973.

Miller, W. and Levitan, T. *Leadership and change: The new politics and the American electorate*. Cambridge, Mass.: Winthrop, 1976.

Newcomb, T. M. Individual systems of orientation. In S. Koch (Ed.), *Psychology: A study of science*. New York: McGraw-Hill, 1959.

Novak, M. *The experience of nothingness*. New York: Harper & Row, 1970.

Polanyi, M. *The tacit dimension*. New York: Doubleday, 1966.

Rittle, H. and Webber, M. Dilemmas in a general theory of planning. Working paper #194, Institute of Urban and Regional Planning, University of California, Berkeley, 1972.

Straw, B. M. The experimenting organization: Problems and prospects. In the experimental organization, symposium presented at the meeting of the American Institute of Decision Sciences: San Francisco, August 1976.

Survey Research Center. *Michigan organizational assessment package: Progress report II*. Ann Arbor, Mich.: Institute for Social Research, 1975.

Torbert, W. R. *Learning from experience: toward consciousness*. New York: Columbia University Press, 1972.

Vickers, G. *The art of judgement*. New York: Basic Books, 1965.

Vickers, G. The management of conflict. In G. Vickers (Ed.), *Making Institutions Work*. New York: Wiley, 1973.

Whitehead, A. N. *Science and the modern world*. New York: Macmillan, 1947.

Yankelovitch, D. *Yankelovitch monitor*. New York: Yankelovitch, 1975.

INDEX